ELFQUEST
The Discovery

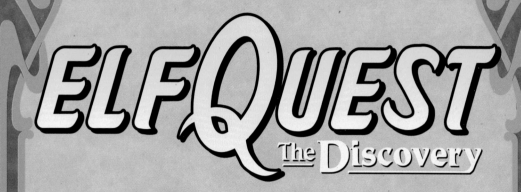

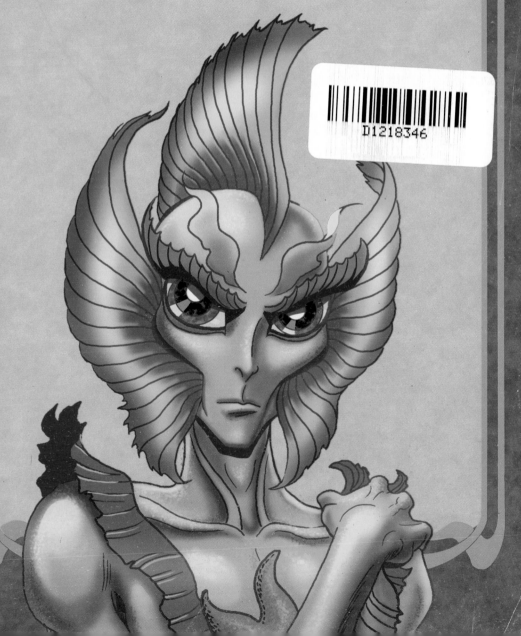

ELFQUEST: THE DISCOVERY

Published by DC Comics. Copyright © 2006 Warp Graphics, Inc. All Rights Reserved.
Originally published in single magazine form in ELFQUEST: THE DISCOVERY 1-4.
Copyright © 2006 Warp Graphics, Inc. All Rights Reserved.
All characters, their distinctive likenesses and related elements
featured in this publication are trademarks of Warp Graphics, Inc.
The stories, characters and incidents featured in this publication are entirely fictional.
DC Comics does not read or accept unsolicited submissions of ideas, stories or artwork.

DC Comics, 1700 Broadway, New York, NY 10019
A Warner Bros. Entertainment Company

Printed in Canada. First Printing.
Cover illustration by Wendy Pini.
ISBN: 1-4012-0958-0
ISBN 13: 978-1-4012-0958-2

ELFQUEST
The Discovery

STORY BY
WENDY & RICHARD PINI

SCRIPT, ART, LETTERS
AND COLORS BY
WENDY PINI

ELFQUEST CREATED BY
WENDY AND RICHARD PINI

CHAPTER ONE

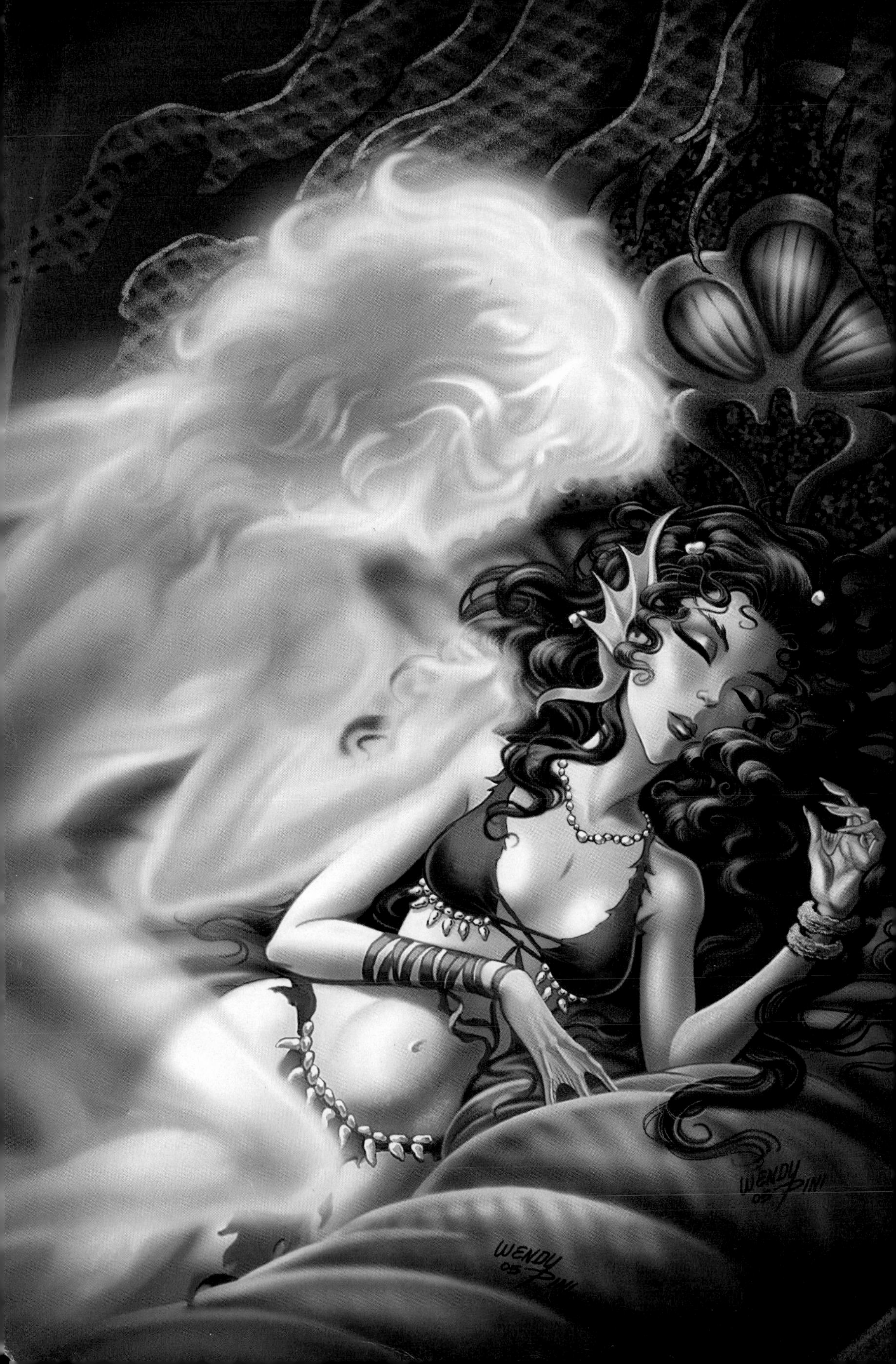

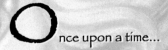

O nce upon a time...

The forest-born elves called Wolfriders fought a brutal human warlord to regain their most precious possession: the crystal Palace of the High Ones, the star-faring vessel that had brought the elves' ancestors to the World of Two Moons.

The battle was a bloody one, and the Wolfriders' chief Cutter suffered wrenching losses -- of more than one kind. But new alliances were made as well. The sweetest of these saw Cutter and his lifemate Leetah adopt the human girl Shuna (who had fought alongside the elves) into their tribe. Strange and wonderful were the new ways she learned under their guidance.

The Palace once again theirs, the Wolfriders turned to recreating a home in the forest of their birth -- a new Holt, a place of safety and peace. But even as they went about their nightly hunts and howls, the elves could sense that something was amiss.

Unsettling tendrils of ancient magical energy gone bad slithered from the deep woods. Cutter's son Suntop, a young mystic, took it upon himself to battle the stagnant pool of foul magic alone. Calling upon all the elfin spirits dwelling in the crystal Palace, Suntop used his own body as a conduit to hurl their Living Light against the festering darkness.

Exhausted but triumphant, Suntop was given the new tribe-name of Sunstream. The last living High One, Timmain, took Cutter's son into the Palace as her student, shrouding him in magical Preserver "wrapstuff" so that his body might sleep and heal even as his mind absorbed wisdom.

Since then, the Wolfriders have gone about their lives, following the seasons. Shuna and Treestump embarked on quests of their own, and came out much the wiser for their experiences.

Cutter still keeps alive his dream of reuniting the scattered children of the High Ones.

And Sunstream, his body yet slumbering but his powerful spirit active, is almost ready to emerge and fulfill that dream -- in a way that no one on the world of two moons could begin to imagine!

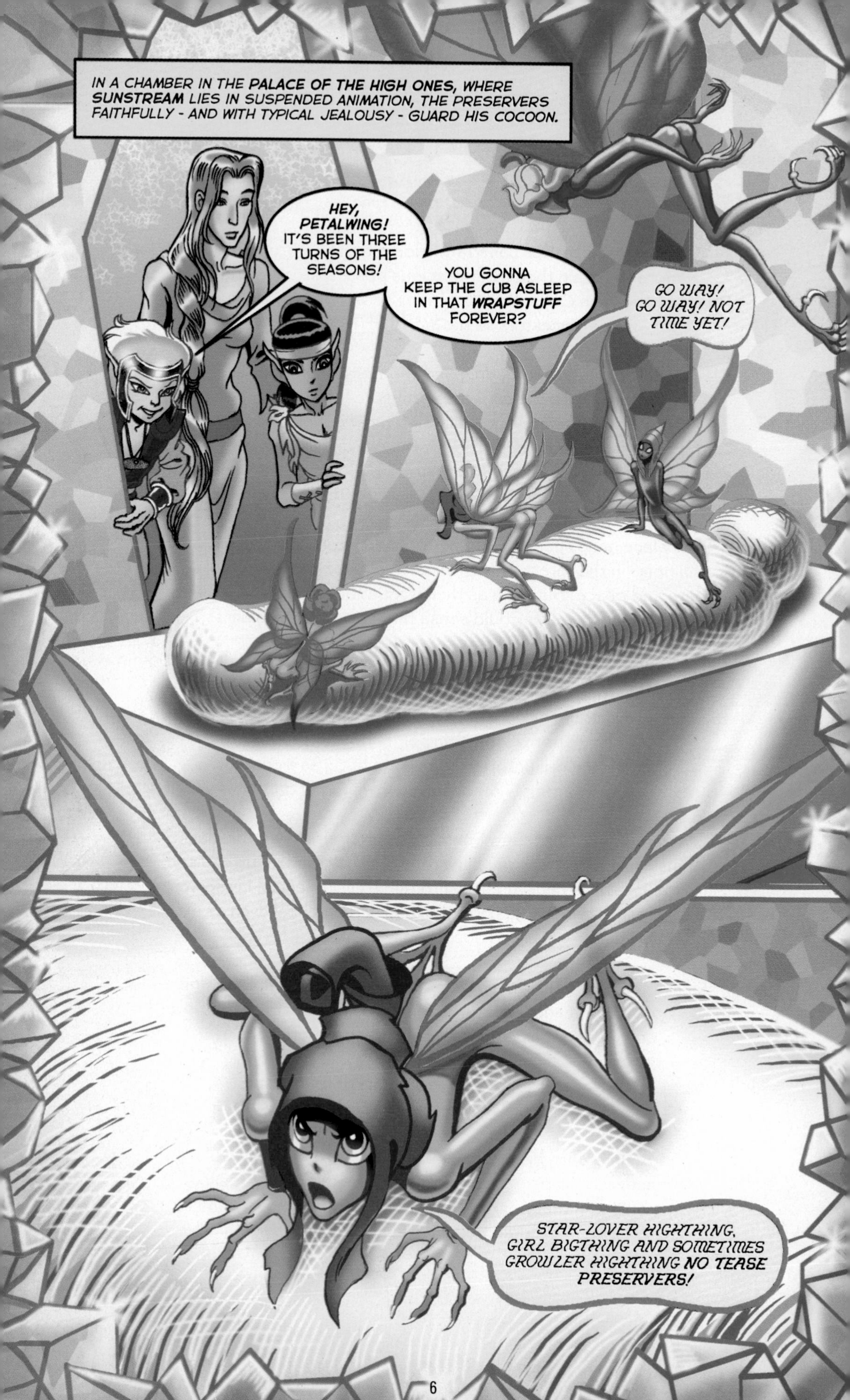

IN A CHAMBER IN THE **PALACE OF THE HIGH ONES,** WHERE **SUNSTREAM** LIES IN SUSPENDED ANIMATION, THE PRESERVERS FAITHFULLY - AND WITH TYPICAL JEALOUSY - GUARD HIS COCOON.
HEY, PETALWING! IT'S BEEN THREE TURNS OF THE SEASONS!
YOU GONNA KEEP THE CUB ASLEEP IN THAT ***WRAPSTUFF*** FOREVER?
GO WAY! GO WAY! NOT TIME YET!
STAR-LOVER HIGHTHING, GIRL BIGTHING AND SOMETIMES GROWLER HIGHTHING ***NO TEASE PRESERVERS!***

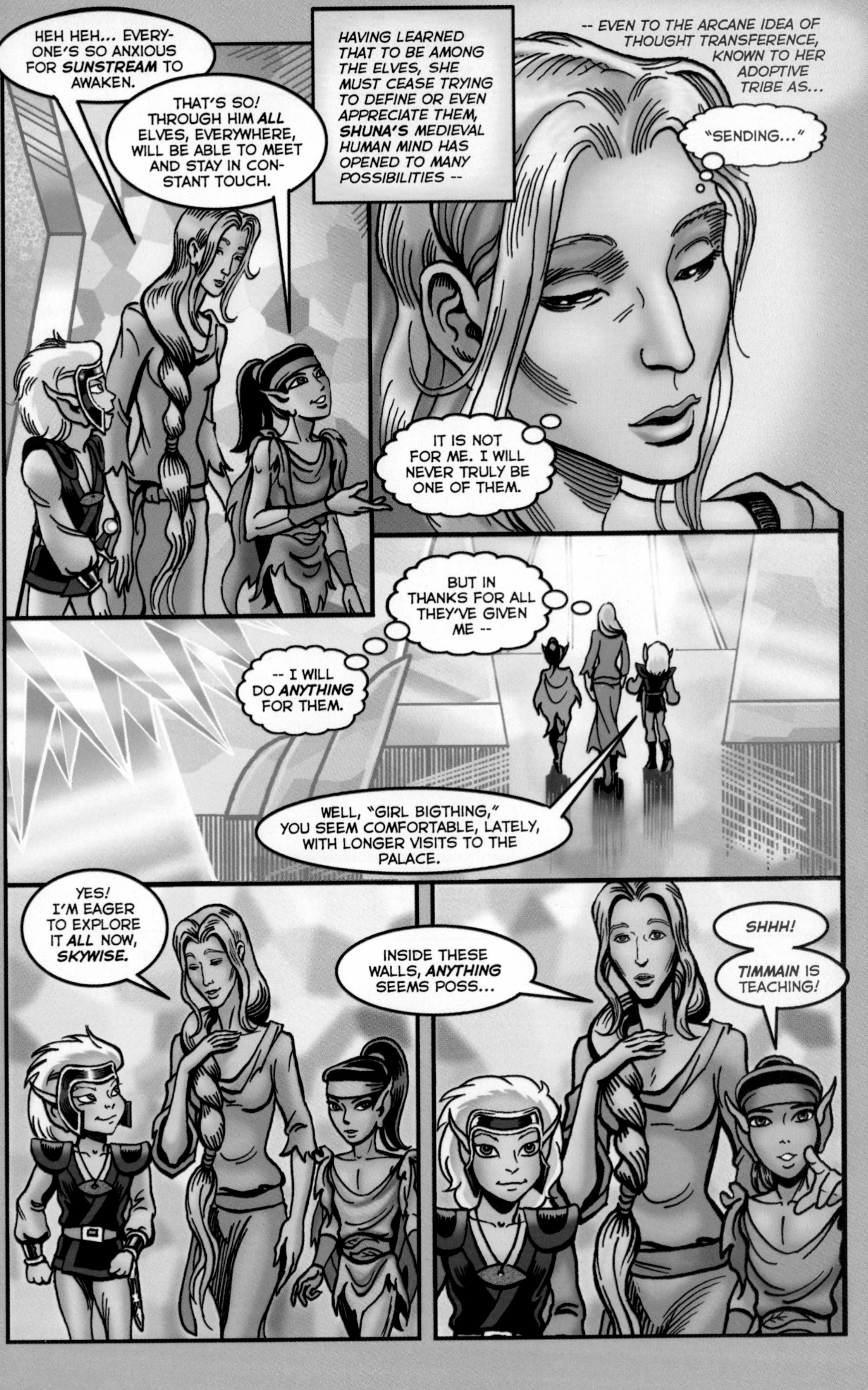
HEH HEH... EVERYONE'S SO ANXIOUS FOR SUNSTREAM TO AWAKEN.
THAT'S SO! THROUGH HIM ALL ELVES, EVERYWHERE, WILL BE ABLE TO MEET AND STAY IN CONSTANT TOUCH.
HAVING LEARNED THAT TO BE AMONG THE ELVES, SHE MUST CEASE TRYING TO DEFINE OR EVEN APPRECIATE THEM, SHUNA'S MEDIEVAL HUMAN MIND HAS OPENED TO MANY POSSIBILITIES --
-- EVEN TO THE ARCANE IDEA OF THOUGHT TRANSFERENCE, KNOWN TO HER ADOPTIVE TRIBE AS...
"SENDING..."
IT IS NOT FOR ME. I WILL NEVER TRULY BE ONE OF THEM.
BUT IN THANKS FOR ALL THEY'VE GIVEN ME --
-- I WILL DO ANYTHING FOR THEM.
WELL, "GIRL BIGTHING," YOU SEEM COMFORTABLE, LATELY, WITH LONGER VISITS TO THE PALACE.
YES! I'M EAGER TO EXPLORE IT ALL NOW, SKYWISE.
INSIDE THESE WALLS, ANYTHING SEEMS POSS...
SHHH!
TIMMAIN IS TEACHING!

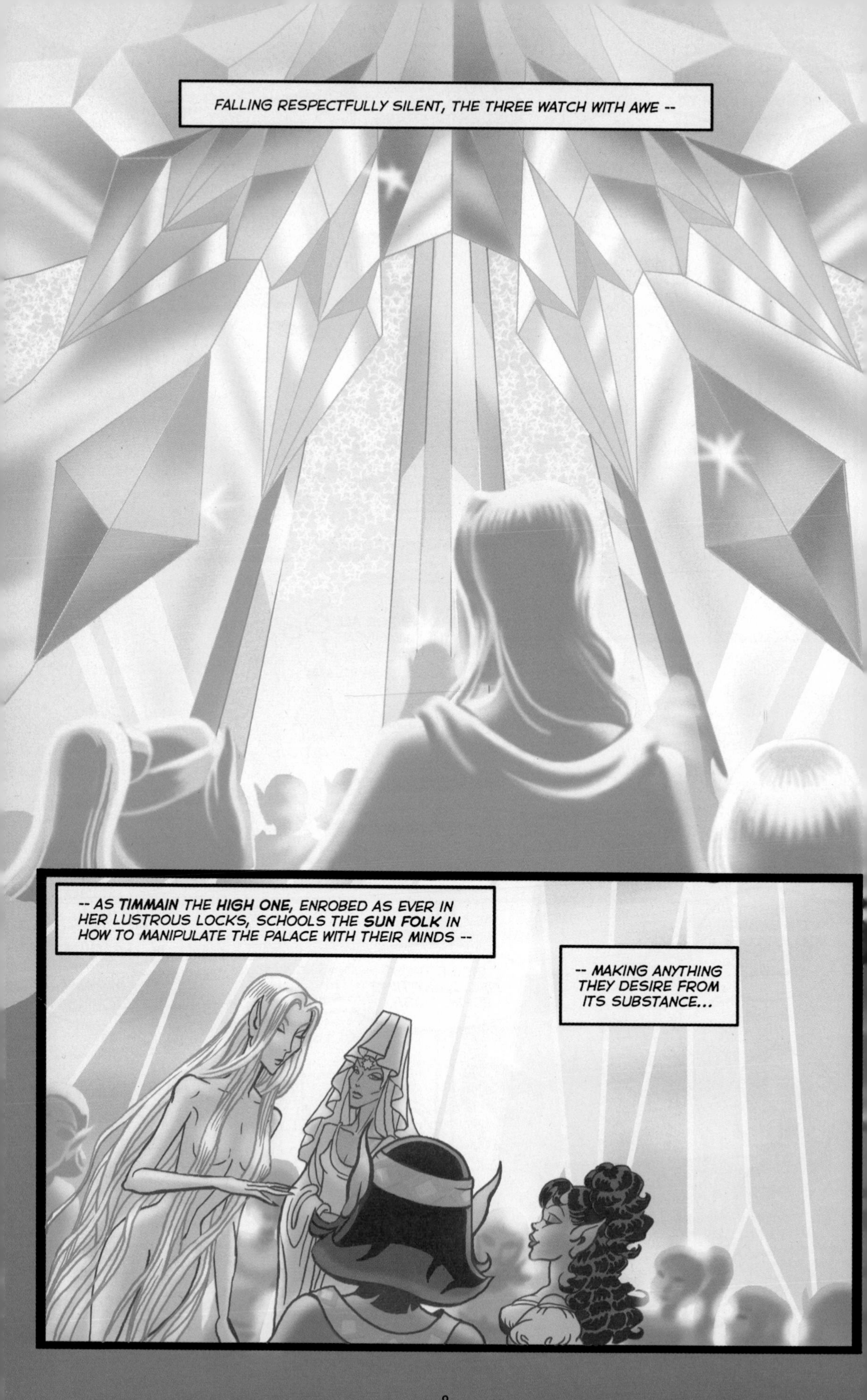
FALLING RESPECTFULLY SILENT, THE THREE WATCH WITH AWE --
-- AS TIMMAIN THE HIGH ONE, ENROBED AS EVER IN HER LUSTROUS LOCKS, SCHOOLS THE SUN FOLK IN HOW TO MANIPULATE THE PALACE WITH THEIR MINDS --
-- MAKING ANYTHING THEY DESIRE FROM ITS SUBSTANCE...

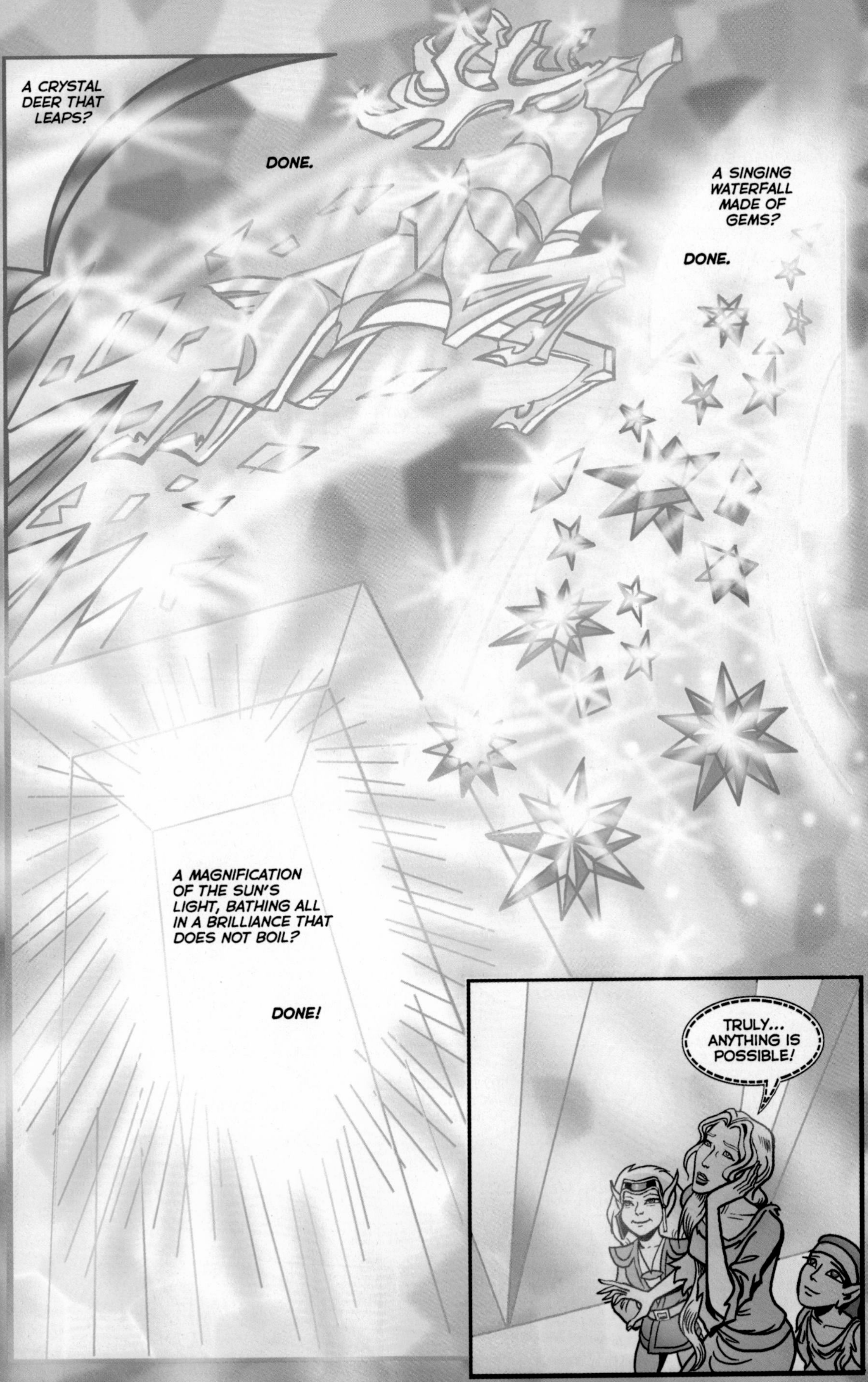
A CRYSTAL DEER THAT LEAPS?
DONE.
A SINGING WATERFALL MADE OF GEMS?
DONE.
A MAGNIFICATION OF THE SUN'S LIGHT, BATHING ALL IN A BRILLIANCE THAT DOES NOT BOIL?
DONE!
TRULY... ANYTHING IS POSSIBLE!

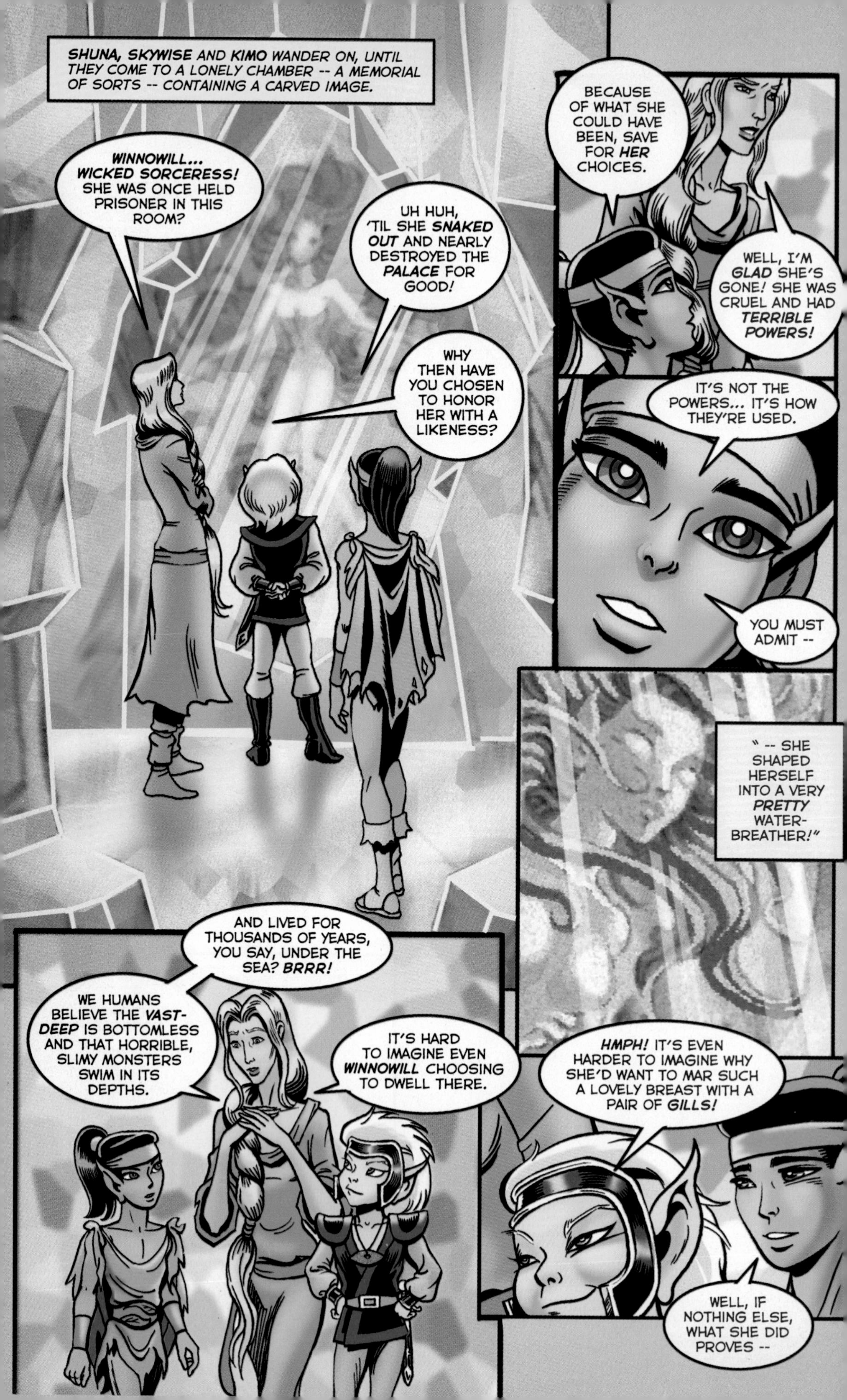
SHUNA, SKYWISE AND KIMO WANDER ON, UNTIL THEY COME TO A LONELY CHAMBER -- A MEMORIAL OF SORTS -- CONTAINING A CARVED IMAGE.
WINNOWILL... WICKED SORCERESS! SHE WAS ONCE HELD PRISONER IN THIS ROOM?
UH HUH, 'TIL SHE SNAKED OUT AND NEARLY DESTROYED THE PALACE FOR GOOD!
WHY THEN HAVE YOU CHOSEN TO HONOR HER WITH A LIKENESS?
BECAUSE OF WHAT SHE COULD HAVE BEEN, SAVE FOR HER CHOICES.
WELL, I'M GLAD SHE'S GONE! SHE WAS CRUEL AND HAD TERRIBLE POWERS!
IT'S NOT THE POWERS... IT'S HOW THEY'RE USED.
YOU MUST ADMIT --
" -- SHE SHAPED HERSELF INTO A VERY PRETTY WATER-BREATHER!"
AND LIVED FOR THOUSANDS OF YEARS, YOU SAY, UNDER THE SEA? BRRR!
WE HUMANS BELIEVE THE VAST-DEEP IS BOTTOMLESS AND THAT HORRIBLE, SLIMY MONSTERS SWIM IN ITS DEPTHS.
IT'S HARD TO IMAGINE EVEN WINNOWILL CHOOSING TO DWELL THERE.
HMPH! IT'S EVEN HARDER TO IMAGINE WHY SHE'D WANT TO MAR SUCH A LOVELY BREAST WITH A PAIR OF GILLS!
WELL, IF NOTHING ELSE, WHAT SHE DID PROVES --

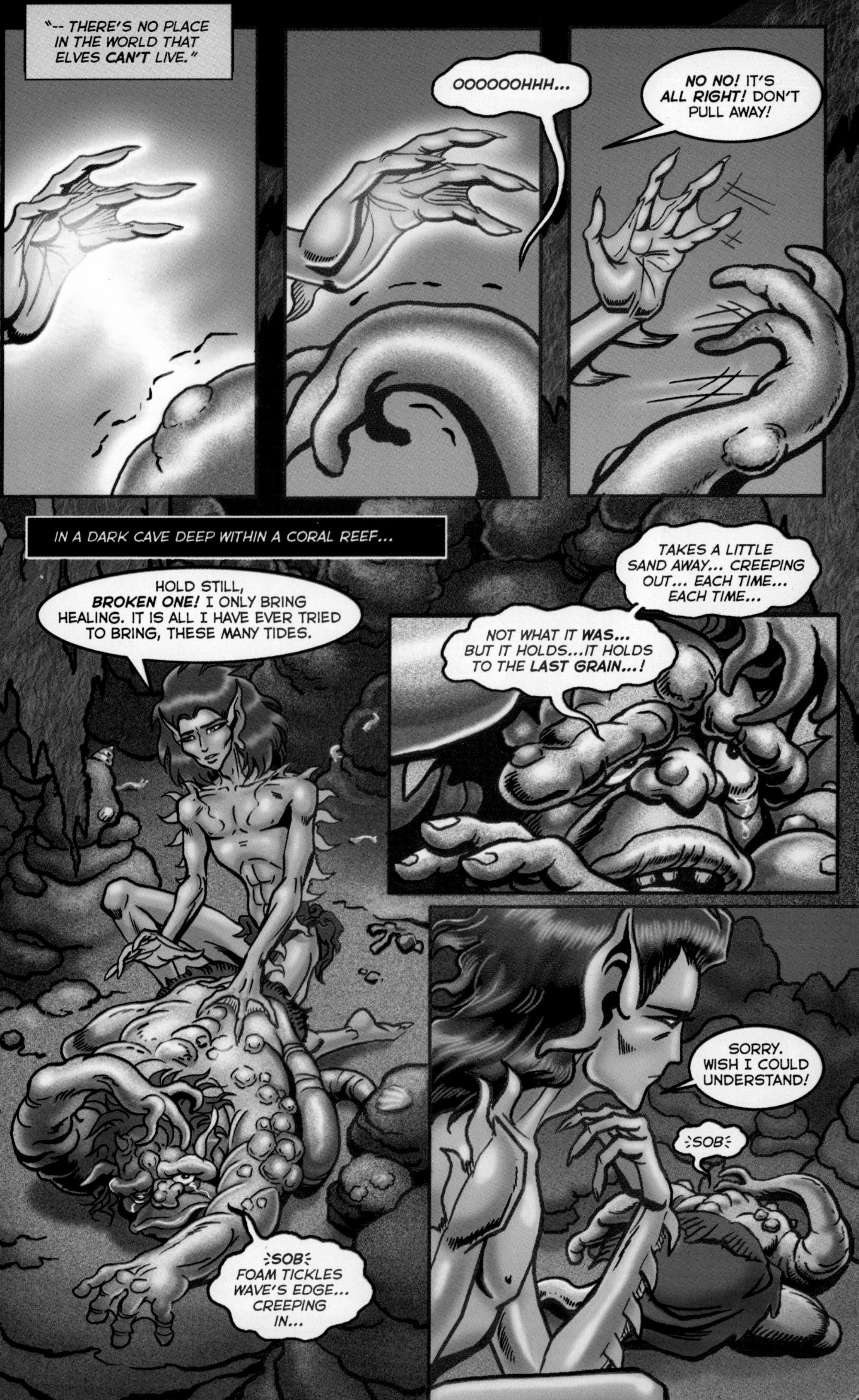
"-- THERE'S NO PLACE IN THE WORLD THAT ELVES CAN'T LIVE."
OOOOOOHHH...
NO NO! IT'S ALL RIGHT! DON'T PULL AWAY!
IN A DARK CAVE DEEP WITHIN A CORAL REEF...
HOLD STILL, BROKEN ONE! I ONLY BRING HEALING. IT IS ALL I HAVE EVER TRIED TO BRING, THESE MANY TIDES.
TAKES A LITTLE SAND AWAY... CREEPING OUT... EACH TIME... EACH TIME...
NOT WHAT IT WAS... BUT IT HOLDS...IT HOLDS TO THE LAST GRAIN...!
SOB FOAM TICKLES WAVE'S EDGE... CREEPING IN...
SORRY. WISH I COULD UNDERSTAND!
SOB

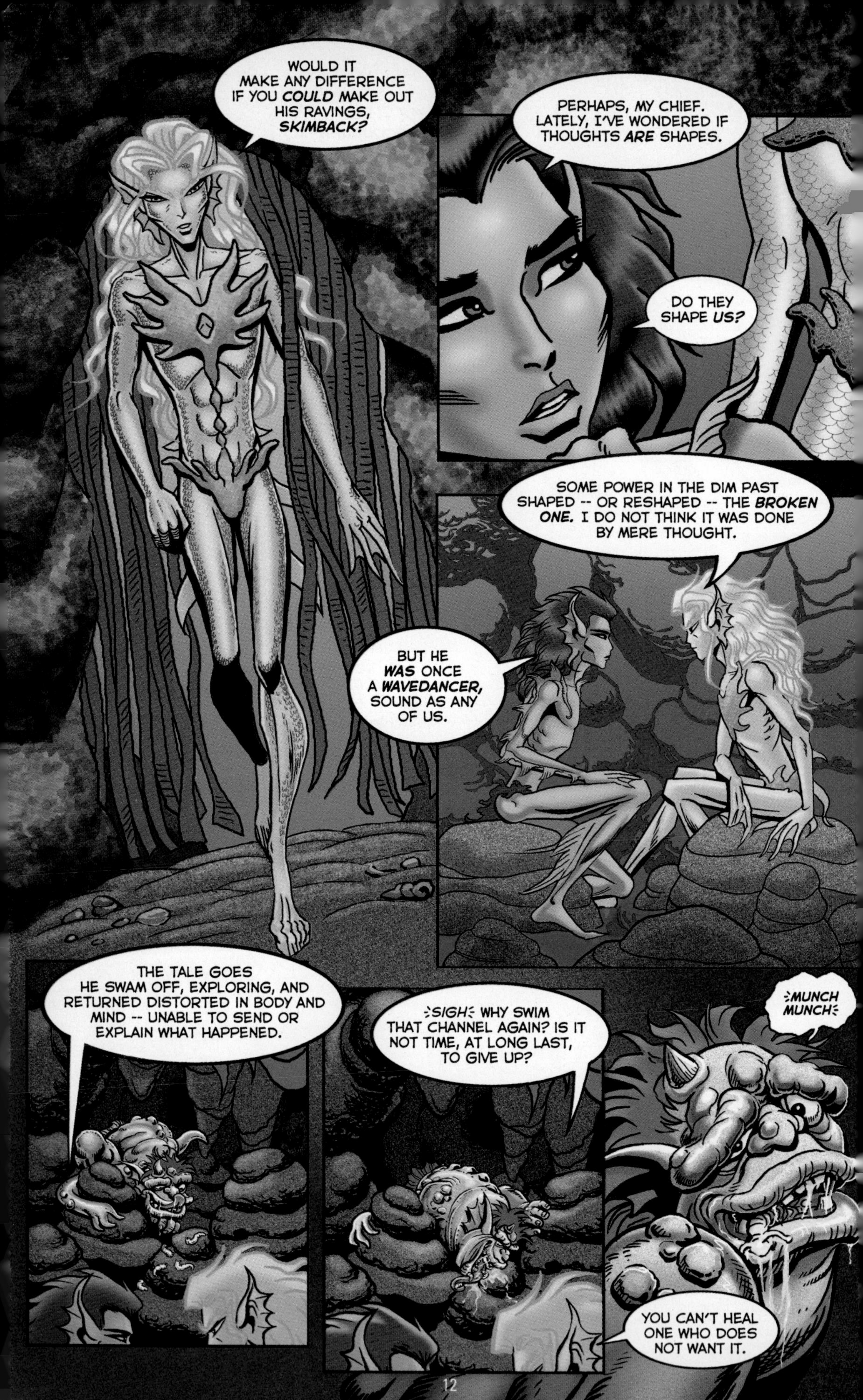
WOULD IT MAKE ANY DIFFERENCE IF YOU COULD MAKE OUT HIS RAVINGS, SKIMBACK?
PERHAPS, MY CHIEF. LATELY, I'VE WONDERED IF THOUGHTS ARE SHAPES.
DO THEY SHAPE US?
SOME POWER IN THE DIM PAST SHAPED -- OR RESHAPED -- THE BROKEN ONE. I DO NOT THINK IT WAS DONE BY MERE THOUGHT.
BUT HE WAS ONCE A WAVEDANCER, SOUND AS ANY OF US.
THE TALE GOES HE SWAM OFF, EXPLORING, AND RETURNED DISTORTED IN BODY AND MIND -- UNABLE TO SEND OR EXPLAIN WHAT HAPPENED.
SIGH WHY SWIM THAT CHANNEL AGAIN? IS IT NOT TIME, AT LONG LAST, TO GIVE UP?
MUNCH MUNCH
YOU CAN'T HEAL ONE WHO DOES NOT WANT IT.

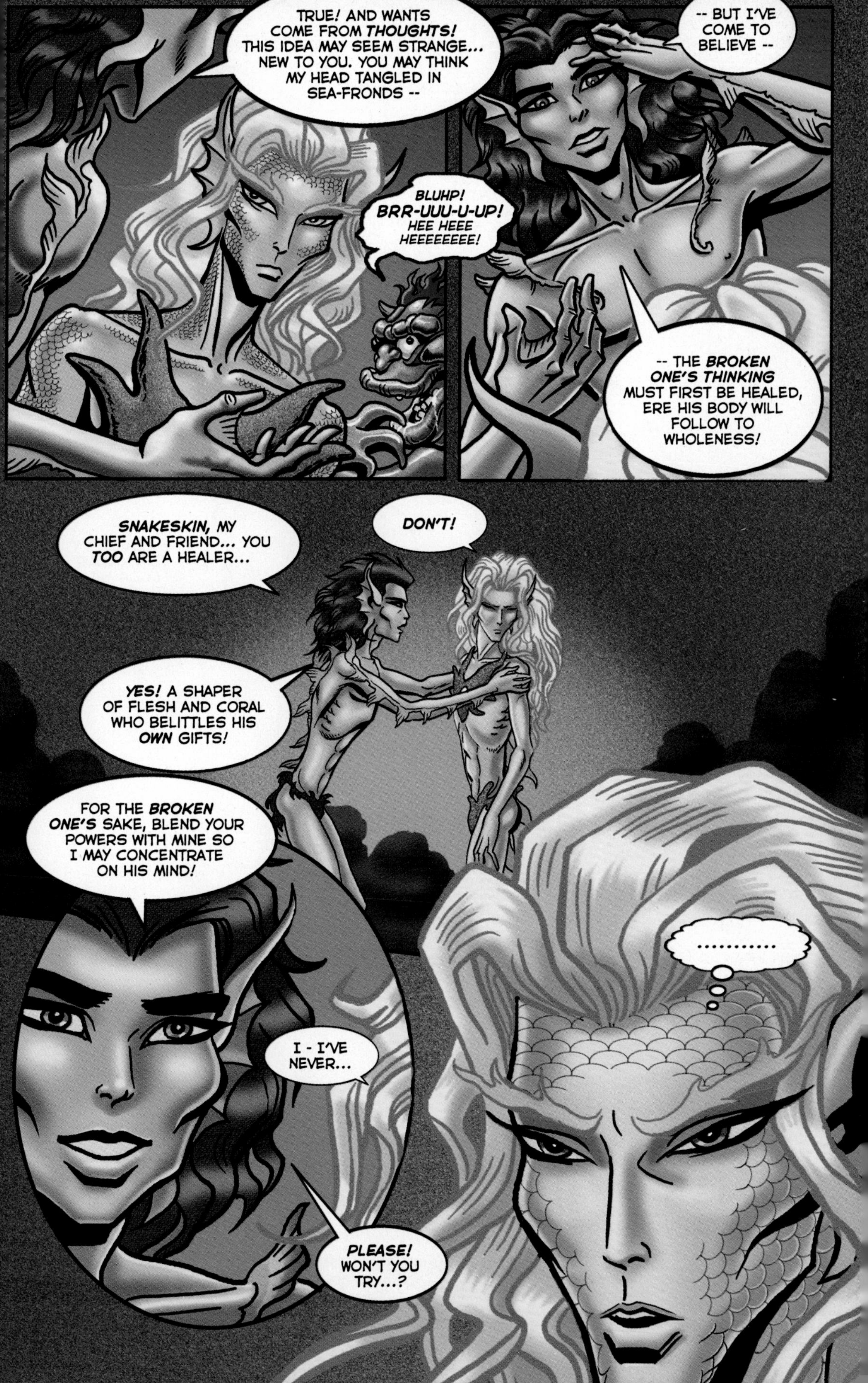
TRUE! AND WANTS COME FROM THOUGHTS! THIS IDEA MAY SEEM STRANGE... NEW TO YOU. YOU MAY THINK MY HEAD TANGLED IN SEA-FRONDS --
BLUHP! BRR-UUU-U-UP! HEE HEEE HEEEEEEEE!
-- BUT I'VE COME TO BELIEVE --
-- THE BROKEN ONE'S THINKING MUST FIRST BE HEALED, ERE HIS BODY WILL FOLLOW TO WHOLENESS!
SNAKESKIN, MY CHIEF AND FRIEND... YOU TOO ARE A HEALER...
DON'T!
YES! A SHAPER OF FLESH AND CORAL WHO BELITTLES HIS OWN GIFTS!
FOR THE BROKEN ONE'S SAKE, BLEND YOUR POWERS WITH MINE SO I MAY CONCENTRATE ON HIS MIND!
....
I - I'VE NEVER...
PLEASE! WON'T YOU TRY...?

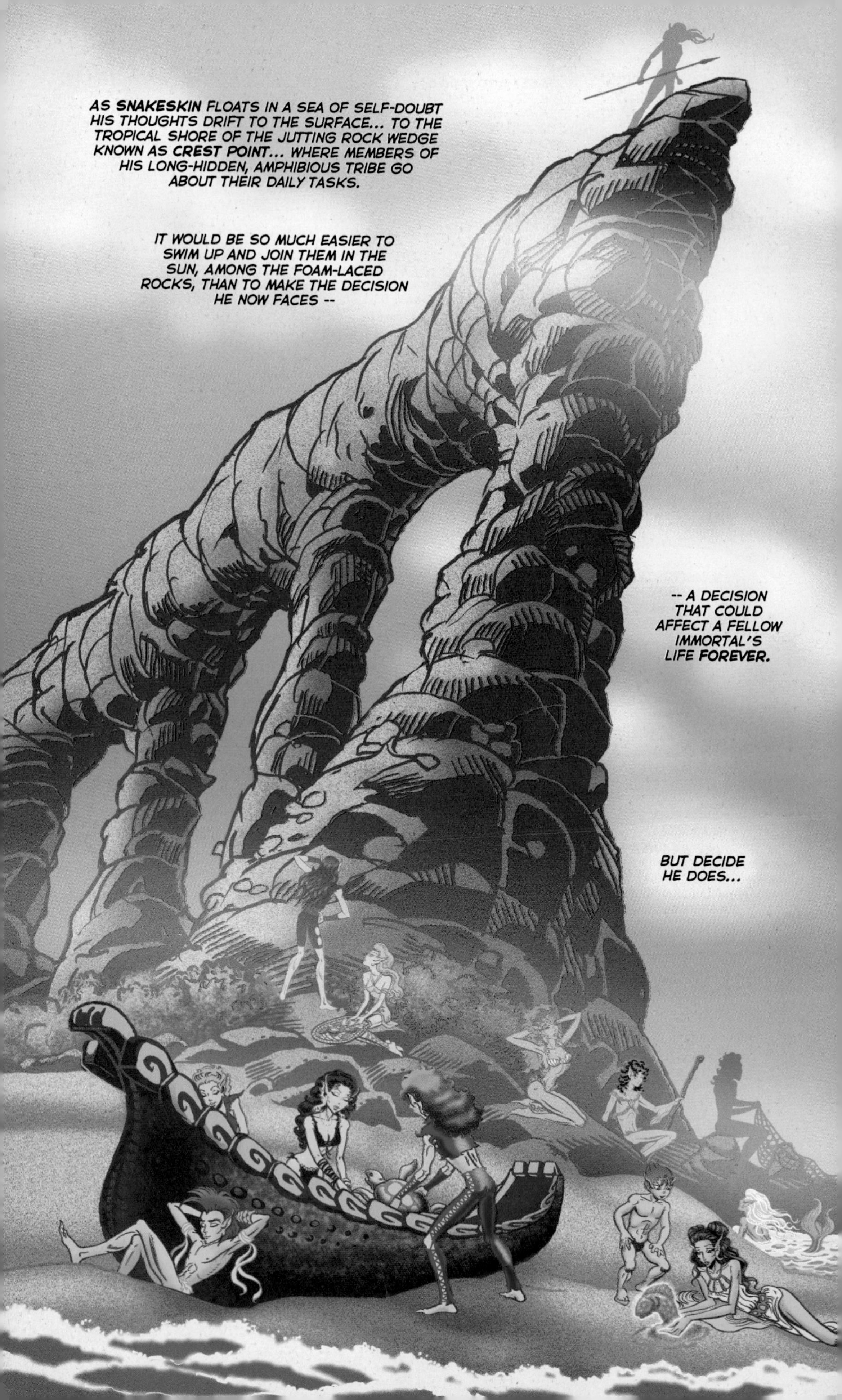
AS SNAKESKIN FLOATS IN A SEA OF SELF-DOUBT HIS THOUGHTS DRIFT TO THE SURFACE... TO THE TROPICAL SHORE OF THE JUTTING ROCK WEDGE KNOWN AS CREST POINT... WHERE MEMBERS OF HIS LONG-HIDDEN, AMPHIBIOUS TRIBE GO ABOUT THEIR DAILY TASKS.
IT WOULD BE SO MUCH EASIER TO SWIM UP AND JOIN THEM IN THE SUN, AMONG THE FOAM-LACED ROCKS, THAN TO MAKE THE DECISION HE NOW FACES --
-- A DECISION THAT COULD AFFECT A FELLOW IMMORTAL'S LIFE FOREVER.
BUT DECIDE HE DOES...

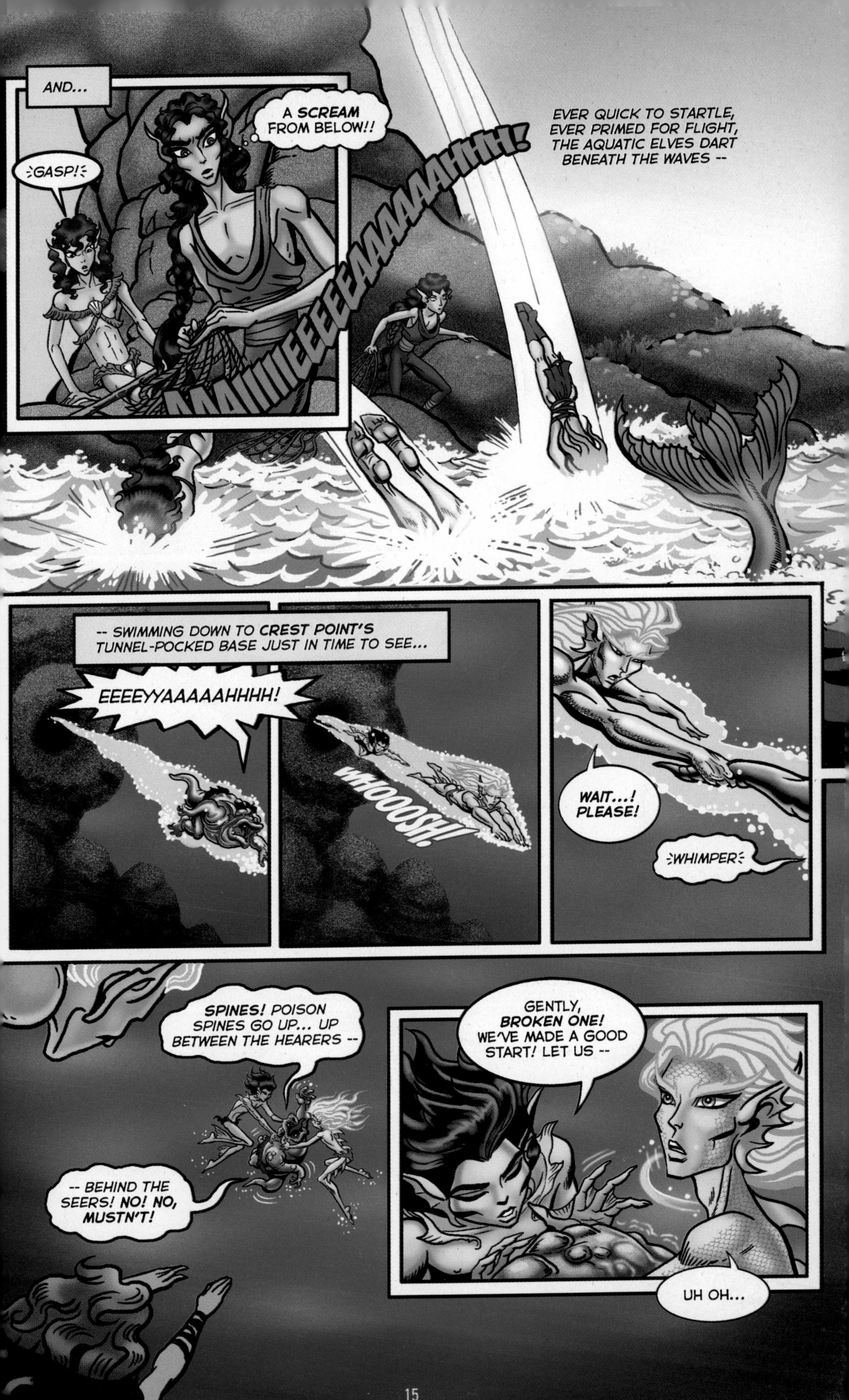
AND...
A SCREAM FROM BELOW!!
GASP!
AAAIIIIEEEEEEAAAAAAAHHHH!
EVER QUICK TO STARTLE, EVER PRIMED FOR FLIGHT, THE AQUATIC ELVES DART BENEATH THE WAVES --
-- SWIMMING DOWN TO CREST POINT'S TUNNEL-POCKED BASE JUST IN TIME TO SEE...
EEEEYYAAAAAHHHH!
WHOOOOSH!
WAIT...! PLEASE!
WHIMPER
SPINES! POISON SPINES GO UP... UP BETWEEN THE HEARERS --
-- BEHIND THE SEERS! NO! NO, MUSTN'T!
GENTLY, BROKEN ONE! WE'VE MADE A GOOD START! LET US --
UH OH...

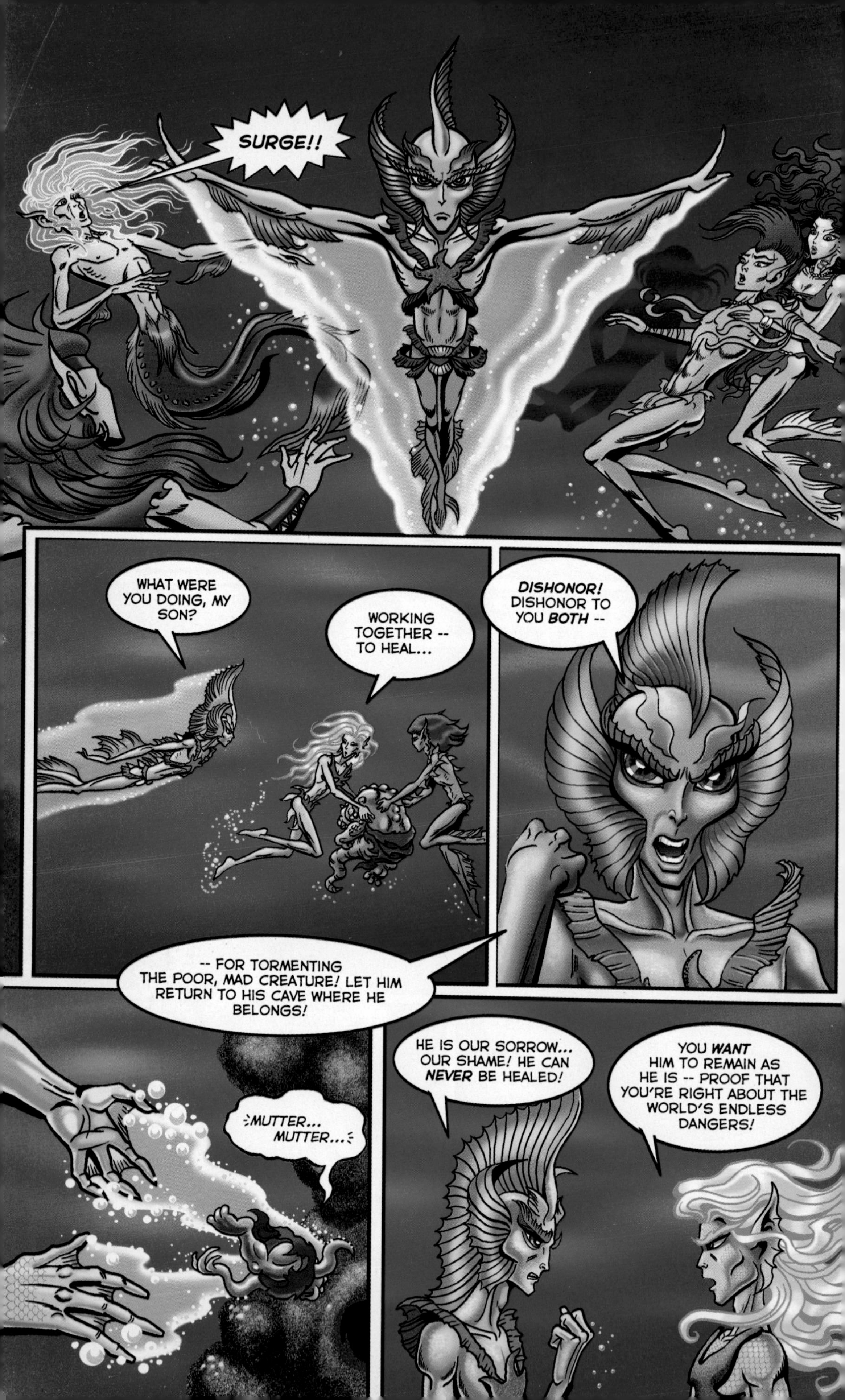
SURGE!!
WHAT WERE YOU DOING, MY SON?
WORKING TOGETHER -- TO HEAL...
DISHONOR! DISHONOR TO YOU BOTH --
-- FOR TORMENTING THE POOR, MAD CREATURE! LET HIM RETURN TO HIS CAVE WHERE HE BELONGS!
MUTTER... MUTTER...
HE IS OUR SORROW... OUR SHAME! HE CAN NEVER BE HEALED!
YOU WANT HIM TO REMAIN AS HE IS -- PROOF THAT YOU'RE RIGHT ABOUT THE WORLD'S ENDLESS DANGERS!

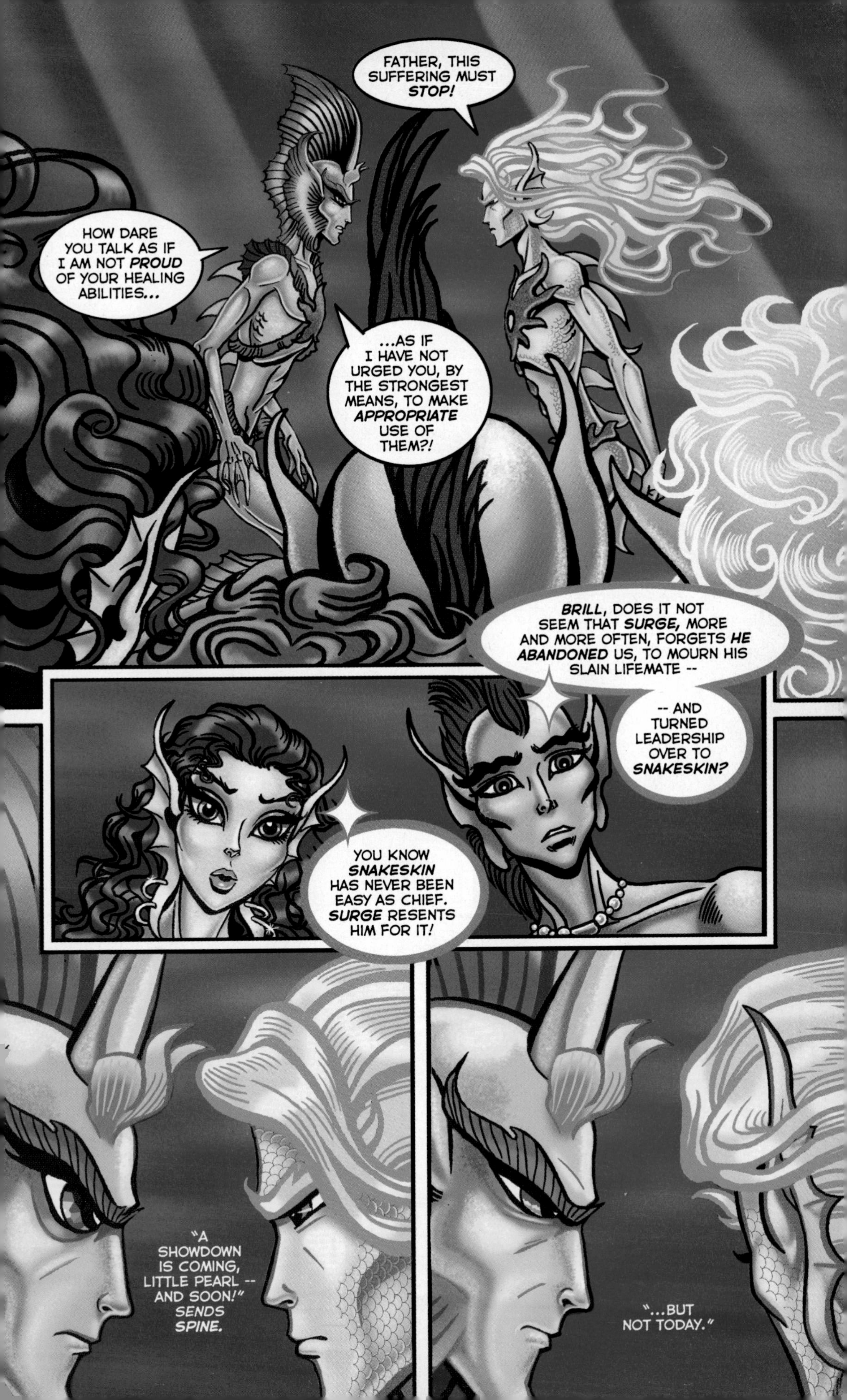
FATHER, THIS SUFFERING MUST STOP!
HOW DARE YOU TALK AS IF I AM NOT PROUD OF YOUR HEALING ABILITIES...
...AS IF I HAVE NOT URGED YOU, BY THE STRONGEST MEANS, TO MAKE APPROPRIATE USE OF THEM?!
BRILL, DOES IT NOT SEEM THAT SURGE, MORE AND MORE OFTEN, FORGETS HE ABANDONED US, TO MOURN HIS SLAIN LIFEMATE --
-- AND TURNED LEADERSHIP OVER TO SNAKESKIN?
YOU KNOW SNAKESKIN HAS NEVER BEEN EASY AS CHIEF. SURGE RESENTS HIM FOR IT!
"A SHOWDOWN IS COMING, LITTLE PEARL -- AND SOON!" SENDS SPINE.
"...BUT NOT TODAY."

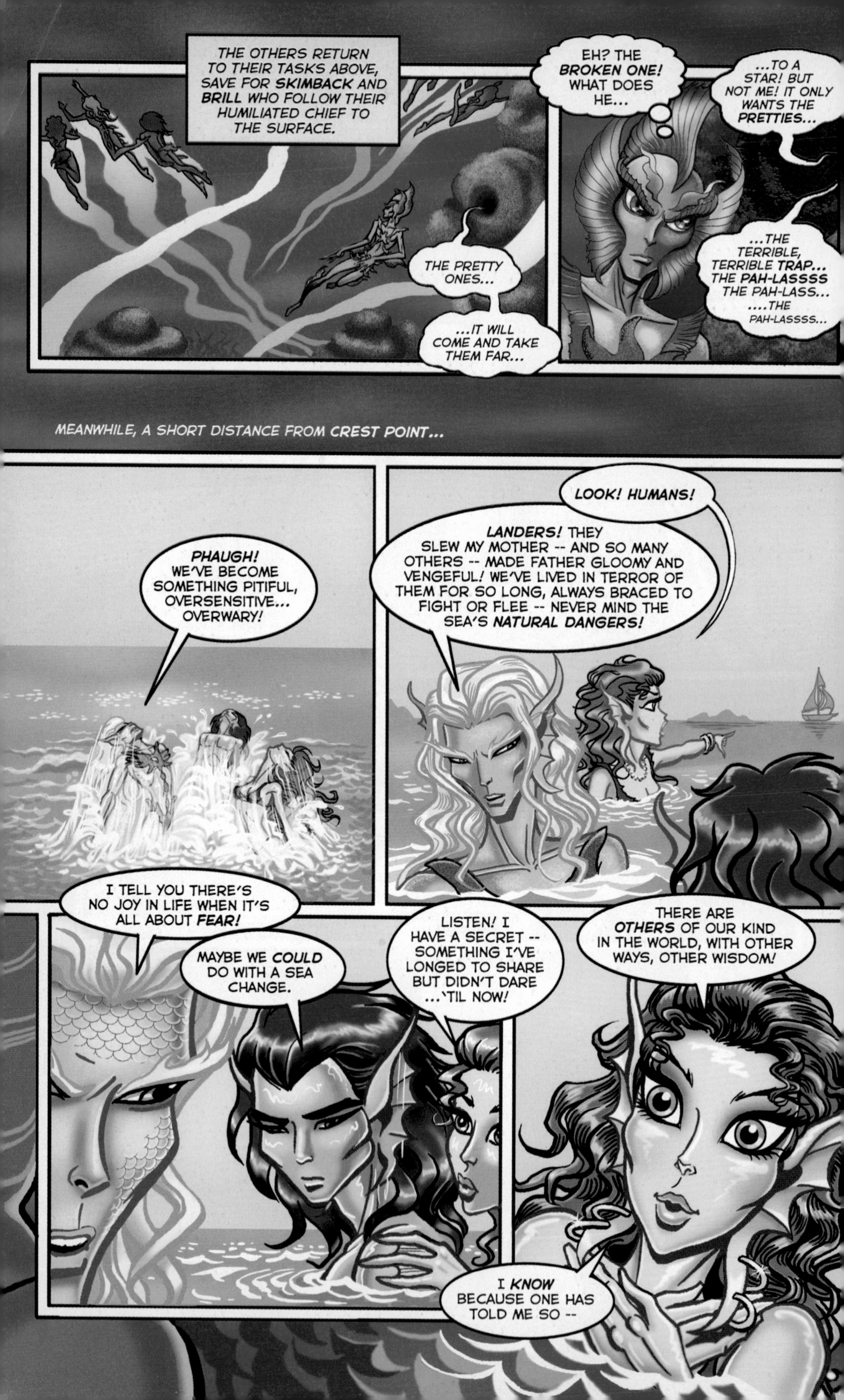
THE OTHERS RETURN TO THEIR TASKS ABOVE, SAVE FOR SKIMBACK AND BRILL WHO FOLLOW THEIR HUMILIATED CHIEF TO THE SURFACE.
THE PRETTY ONES...
...IT WILL COME AND TAKE THEM FAR...
EH? THE BROKEN ONE! WHAT DOES HE...
...TO A STAR! BUT NOT ME! IT ONLY WANTS THE PRETTIES...
...THE TERRIBLE, TERRIBLE TRAP... THE PAH-LASSSS THE PAH-LASS... ....THE PAH-LASSSS...
MEANWHILE, A SHORT DISTANCE FROM CREST POINT...
PHAUGH! WE'VE BECOME SOMETHING PITIFUL, OVERSENSITIVE... OVERWARY!
LOOK! HUMANS!
LANDERS! THEY SLEW MY MOTHER -- AND SO MANY OTHERS -- MADE FATHER GLOOMY AND VENGEFUL! WE'VE LIVED IN TERROR OF THEM FOR SO LONG, ALWAYS BRACED TO FIGHT OR FLEE -- NEVER MIND THE SEA'S NATURAL DANGERS!
I TELL YOU THERE'S NO JOY IN LIFE WHEN IT'S ALL ABOUT FEAR!
MAYBE WE COULD DO WITH A SEA CHANGE.
LISTEN! I HAVE A SECRET -- SOMETHING I'VE LONGED TO SHARE BUT DIDN'T DARE ...'TIL NOW!
THERE ARE OTHERS OF OUR KIND IN THE WORLD, WITH OTHER WAYS, OTHER WISDOM!
I KNOW BECAUSE ONE HAS TOLD ME SO --

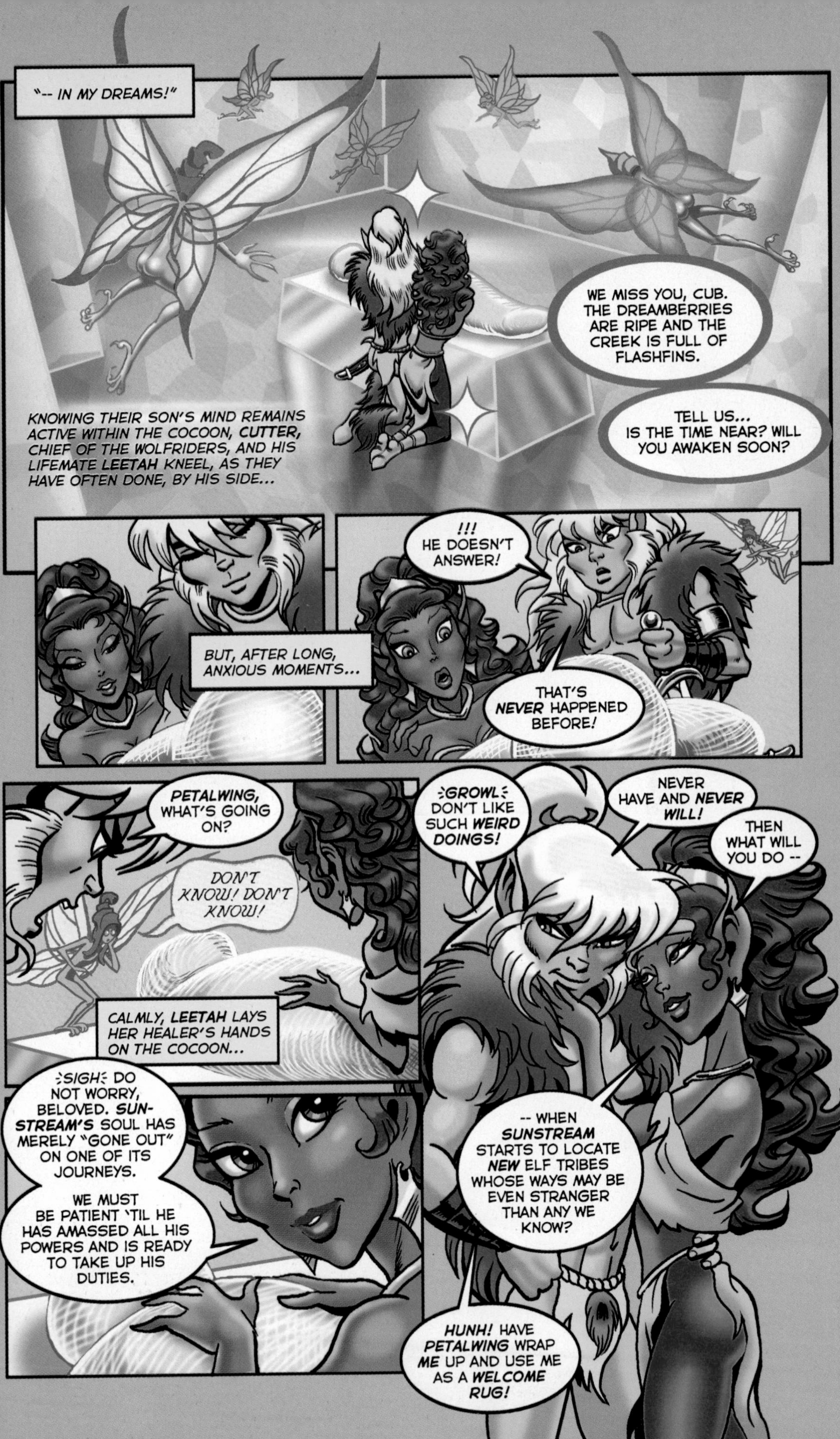

"-- IN MY DREAMS!"
KNOWING THEIR SON'S MIND REMAINS ACTIVE WITHIN THE COCOON, CUTTER, CHIEF OF THE WOLFRIDERS, AND HIS LIFEMATE LEETAH KNEEL, AS THEY HAVE OFTEN DONE, BY HIS SIDE...
WE MISS YOU, CUB. THE DREAMBERRIES ARE RIPE AND THE CREEK IS FULL OF FLASHFINS.
TELL US... IS THE TIME NEAR? WILL YOU AWAKEN SOON?
BUT, AFTER LONG, ANXIOUS MOMENTS...
!!! HE DOESN'T ANSWER!
THAT'S NEVER HAPPENED BEFORE!
PETALWING, WHAT'S GOING ON?
DON'T KNOW! DON'T KNOW!
CALMLY, LEETAH LAYS HER HEALER'S HANDS ON THE COCOON...
:SIGH: DO NOT WORRY, BELOVED. SUNSTREAM'S SOUL HAS MERELY "GONE OUT" ON ONE OF ITS JOURNEYS.
WE MUST BE PATIENT 'TIL HE HAS AMASSED ALL HIS POWERS AND IS READY TO TAKE UP HIS DUTIES.
:GROWL: DON'T LIKE SUCH WEIRD DOINGS!
NEVER HAVE AND NEVER WILL!
THEN WHAT WILL YOU DO --
-- WHEN SUNSTREAM STARTS TO LOCATE NEW ELF TRIBES WHOSE WAYS MAY BE EVEN STRANGER THAN ANY WE KNOW?
HUNH! HAVE PETALWING WRAP ME UP AND USE ME AS A WELCOME RUG!

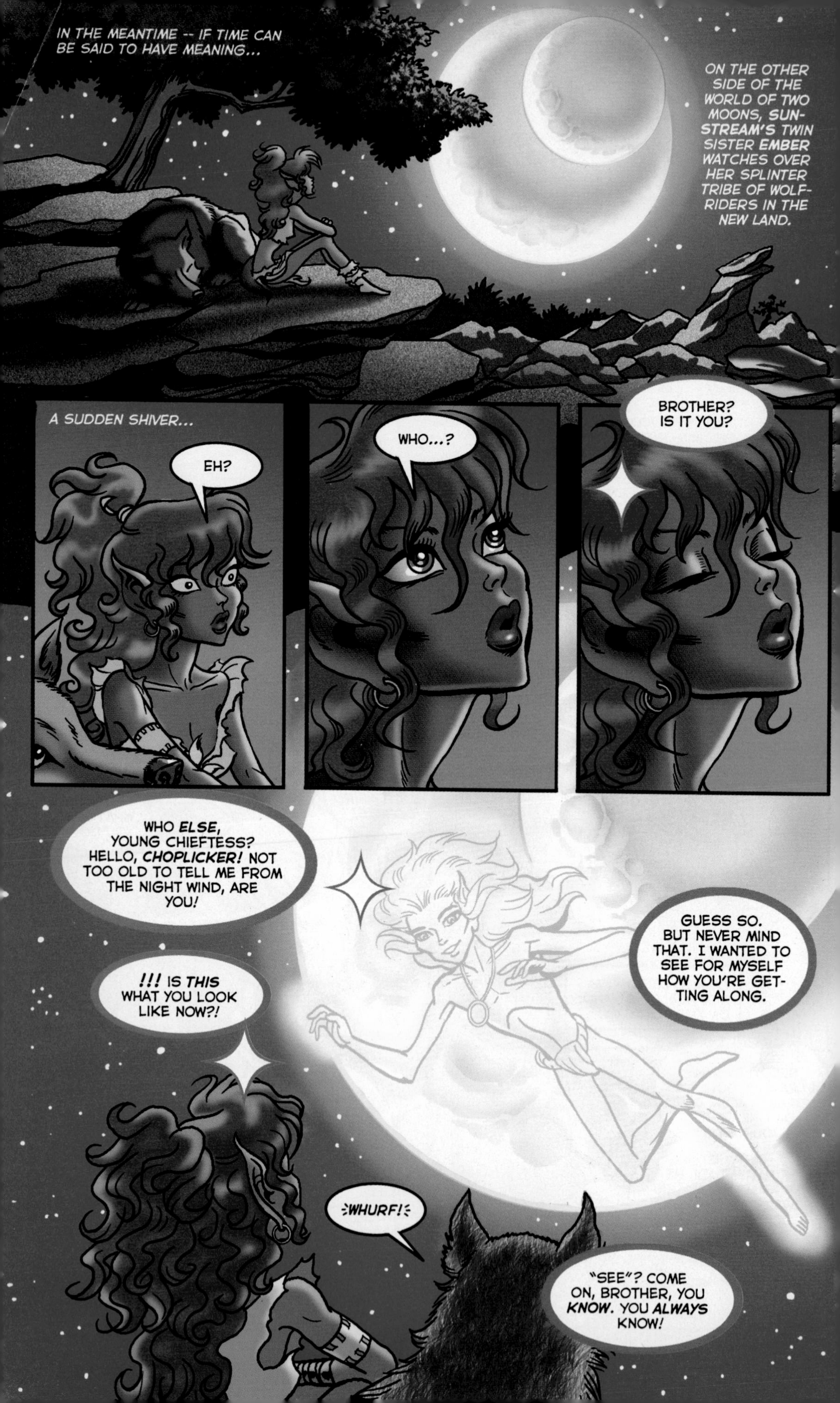
IN THE MEANTIME -- IF TIME CAN BE SAID TO HAVE MEANING...
ON THE OTHER SIDE OF THE WORLD OF TWO MOONS, SUNSTREAM'S TWIN SISTER EMBER WATCHES OVER HER SPLINTER TRIBE OF WOLF-RIDERS IN THE NEW LAND.
A SUDDEN SHIVER...
EH?
WHO...?
BROTHER? IS IT YOU?
WHO ELSE, YOUNG CHIEFTESS? HELLO, CHOPLICKER! NOT TOO OLD TO TELL ME FROM THE NIGHT WIND, ARE YOU!
!!! IS THIS WHAT YOU LOOK LIKE NOW?!
GUESS SO. BUT NEVER MIND THAT. I WANTED TO SEE FOR MYSELF HOW YOU'RE GETTING ALONG.
WHURF!
"SEE"? COME ON, BROTHER, YOU KNOW. YOU ALWAYS KNOW!

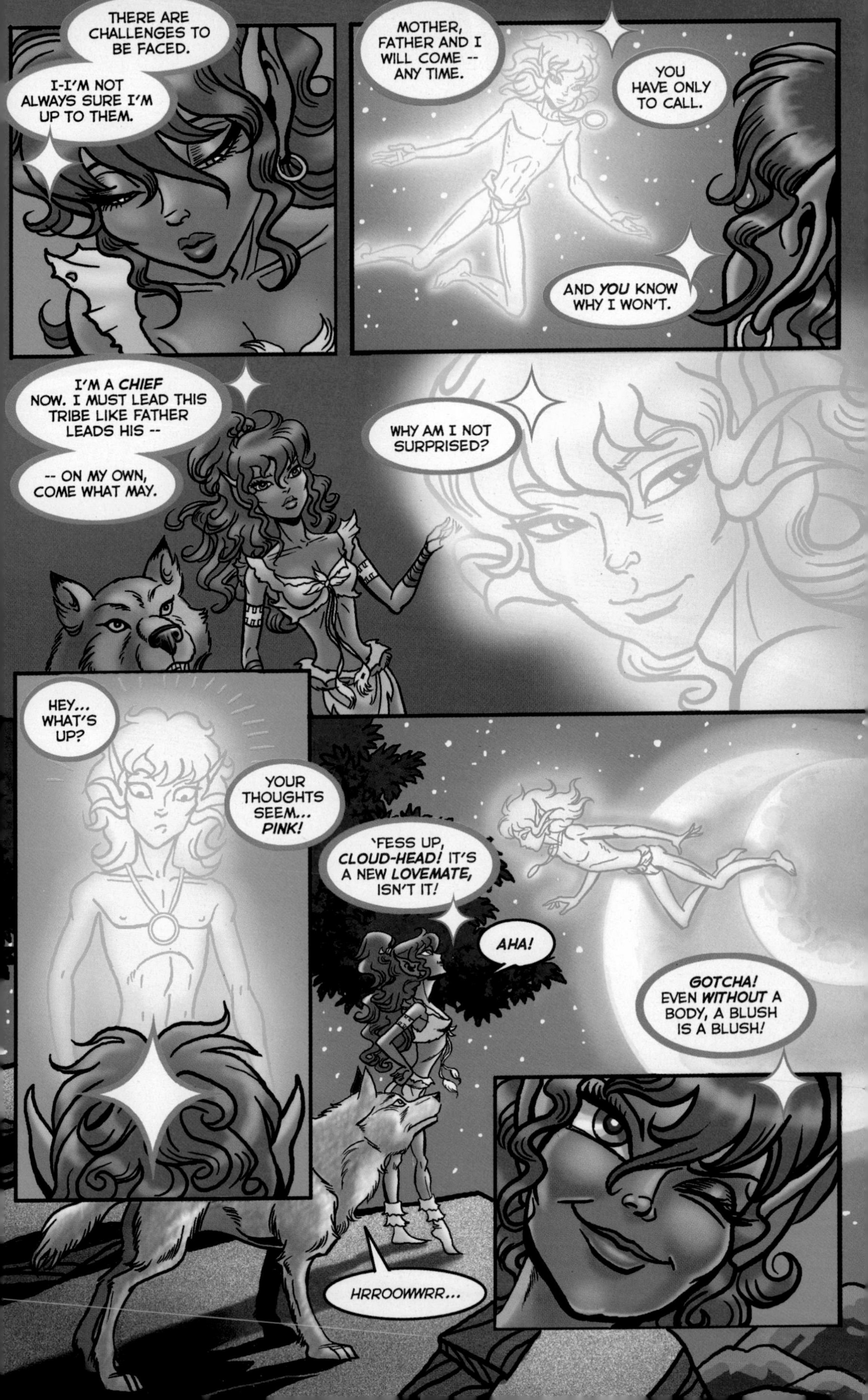

THERE ARE CHALLENGES TO BE FACED.
I-I'M NOT ALWAYS SURE I'M UP TO THEM.
MOTHER, FATHER AND I WILL COME -- ANY TIME.
YOU HAVE ONLY TO CALL.
AND *YOU* KNOW WHY I WON'T.
I'M A *CHIEF* NOW. I MUST LEAD THIS TRIBE LIKE FATHER LEADS HIS --
-- ON MY OWN, COME WHAT MAY.
WHY AM I NOT SURPRISED?
HEY... WHAT'S UP?
YOUR THOUGHTS SEEM... *PINK!*
'FESS UP, *CLOUD-HEAD!* IT'S A NEW *LOVEMATE,* ISN'T IT!
AHA!
GOTCHA! EVEN *WITHOUT* A BODY, A BLUSH IS A BLUSH!
HRROOWWRR...

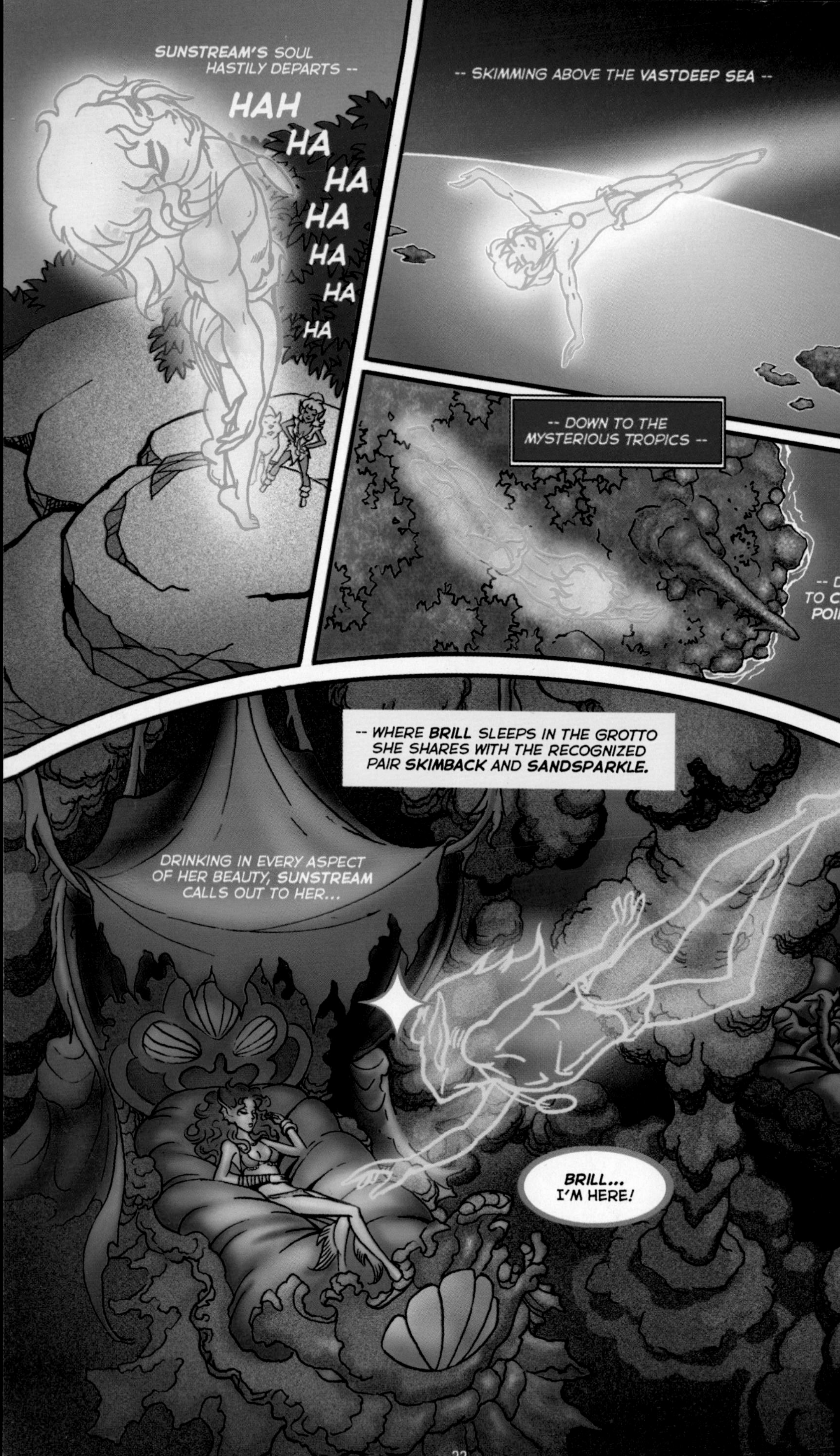
SUNSTREAM'S SOUL HASTILY DEPARTS --
HAH HA HA HA HA HA HA
-- SKIMMING ABOVE THE VASTDEEP SEA --
-- DOWN TO THE MYSTERIOUS TROPICS --
-- WHERE BRILL SLEEPS IN THE GROTTO SHE SHARES WITH THE RECOGNIZED PAIR SKIMBACK AND SANDSPARKLE.
DRINKING IN EVERY ASPECT OF HER BEAUTY, SUNSTREAM CALLS OUT TO HER...
BRILL... I'M HERE!

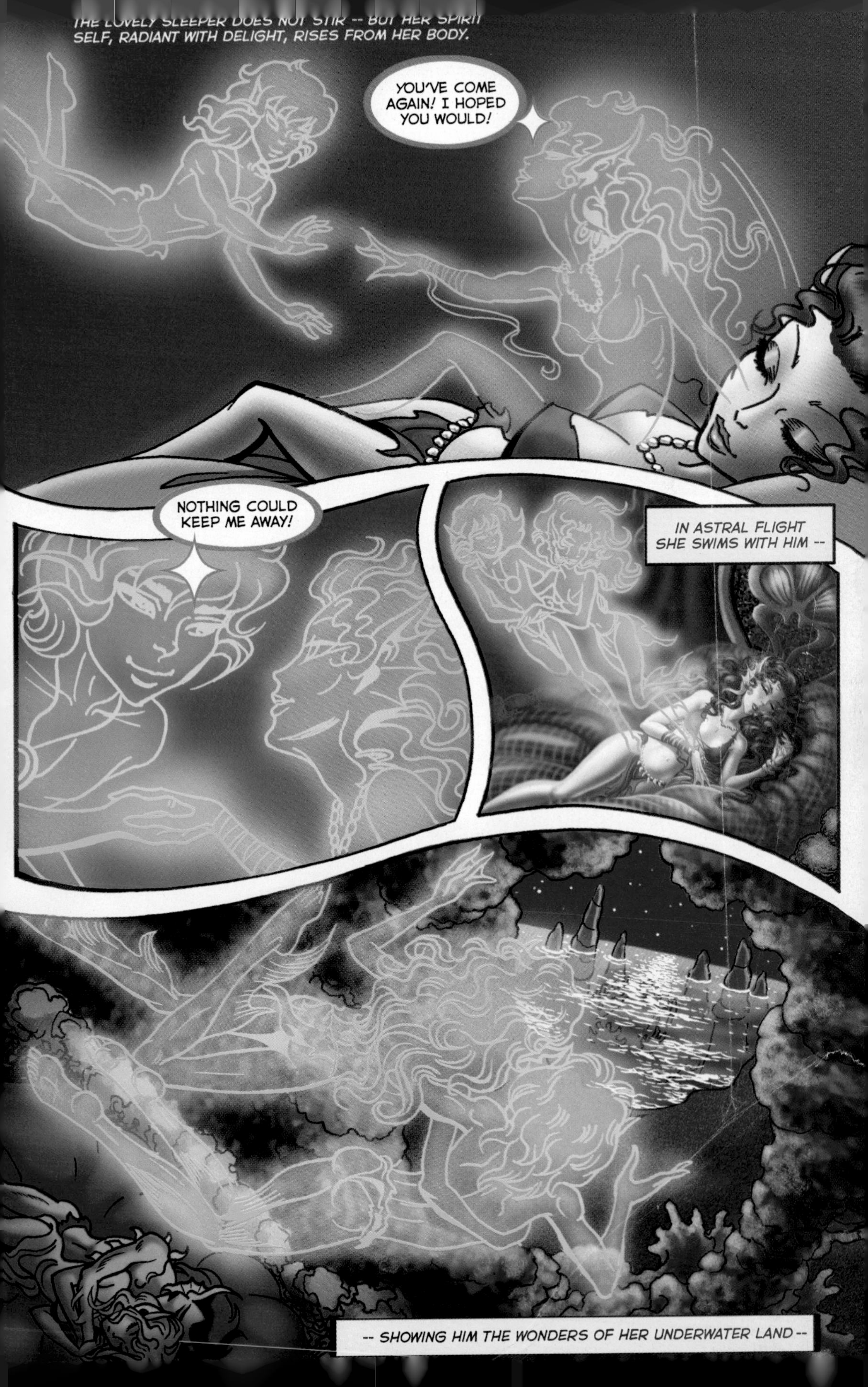
THE LOVELY SLEEPER DOES NOT STIR -- BUT HER SPIRIT SELF, RADIANT WITH DELIGHT, RISES FROM HER BODY.
YOU'VE COME AGAIN! I HOPED YOU WOULD!
NOTHING COULD KEEP ME AWAY!
IN ASTRAL FLIGHT SHE SWIMS WITH HIM --
-- SHOWING HIM THE WONDERS OF HER UNDERWATER LAND --

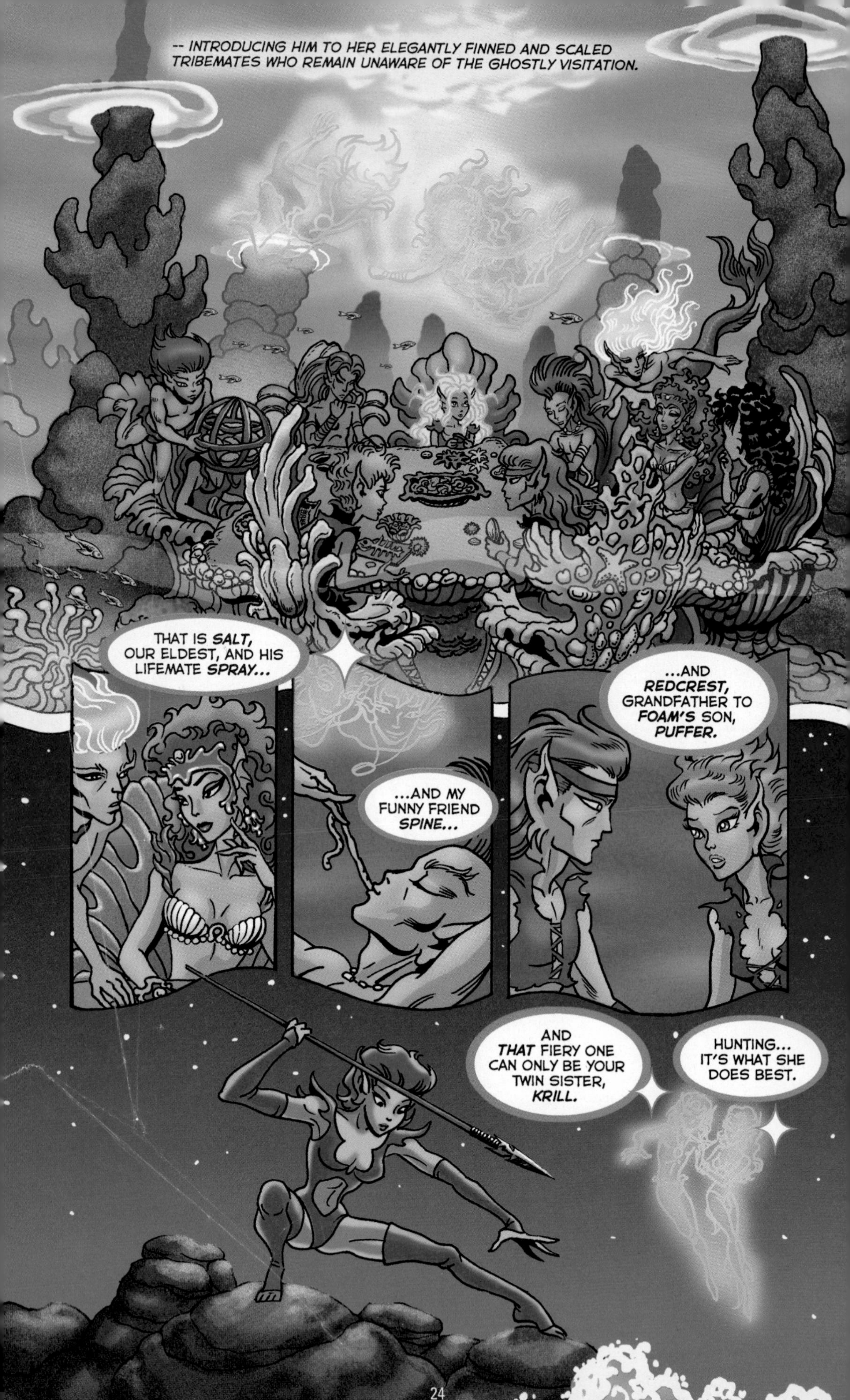

-- INTRODUCING HIM TO HER ELEGANTLY FINNED AND SCALED TRIBEMATES WHO REMAIN UNAWARE OF THE GHOSTLY VISITATION.
THAT IS SALT, OUR ELDEST, AND HIS LIFEMATE SPRAY...
...AND MY FUNNY FRIEND SPINE...
...AND REDCREST, GRANDFATHER TO FOAM'S SON, PUFFER.
AND THAT FIERY ONE CAN ONLY BE YOUR TWIN SISTER, KRILL.
HUNTING... IT'S WHAT SHE DOES BEST.

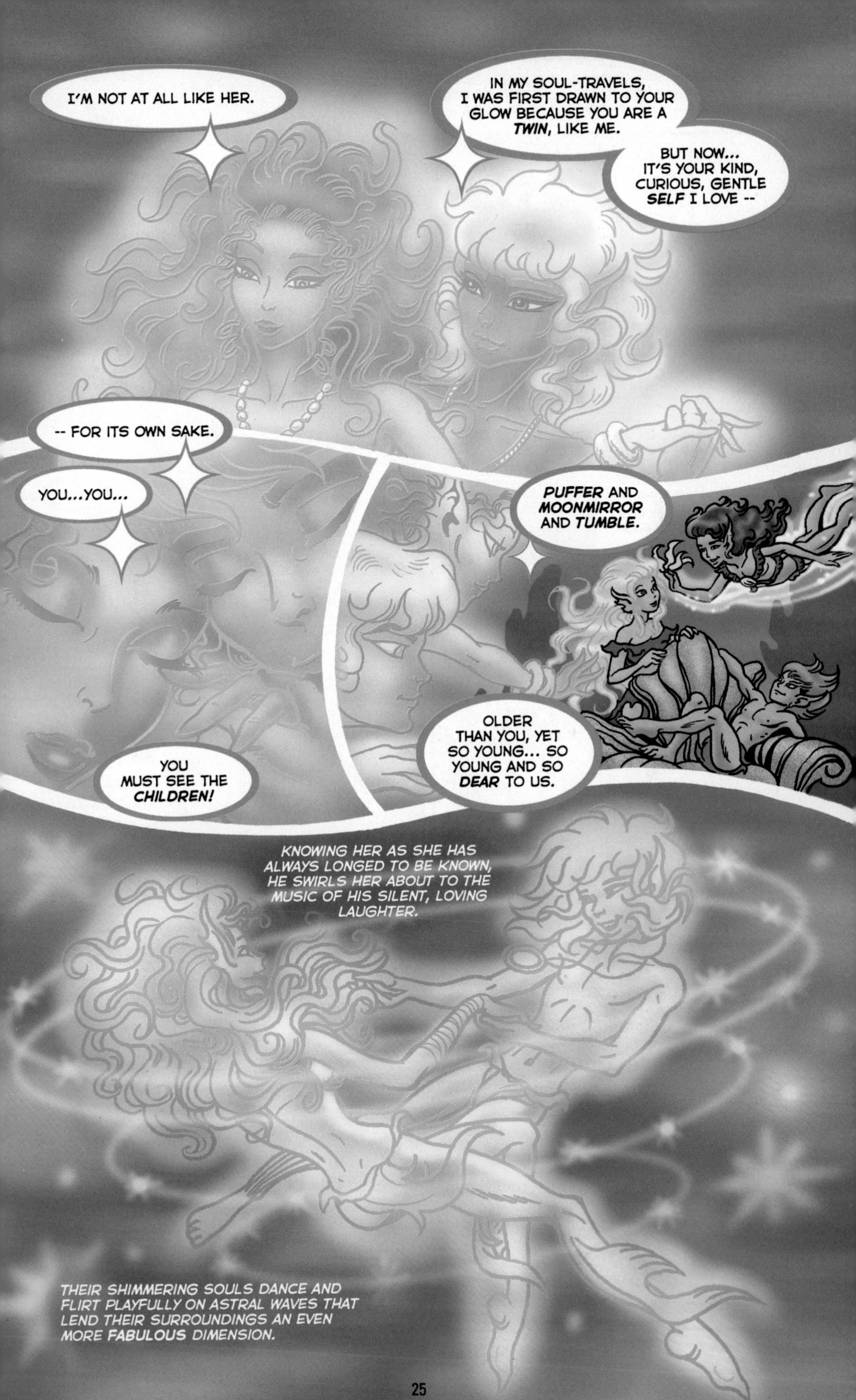
I'M NOT AT ALL LIKE HER.
IN MY SOUL-TRAVELS, I WAS FIRST DRAWN TO YOUR GLOW BECAUSE YOU ARE A TWIN, LIKE ME.
BUT NOW... IT'S YOUR KIND, CURIOUS, GENTLE SELF I LOVE --
-- FOR ITS OWN SAKE.
YOU...YOU...
YOU MUST SEE THE CHILDREN!
PUFFER AND MOONMIRROR AND TUMBLE.
OLDER THAN YOU, YET SO YOUNG... SO YOUNG AND SO DEAR TO US.
KNOWING HER AS SHE HAS ALWAYS LONGED TO BE KNOWN, HE SWIRLS HER ABOUT TO THE MUSIC OF HIS SILENT, LOVING LAUGHTER.
THEIR SHIMMERING SOULS DANCE AND FLIRT PLAYFULLY ON ASTRAL WAVES THAT LEND THEIR SURROUNDINGS AN EVEN MORE FABULOUS DIMENSION.

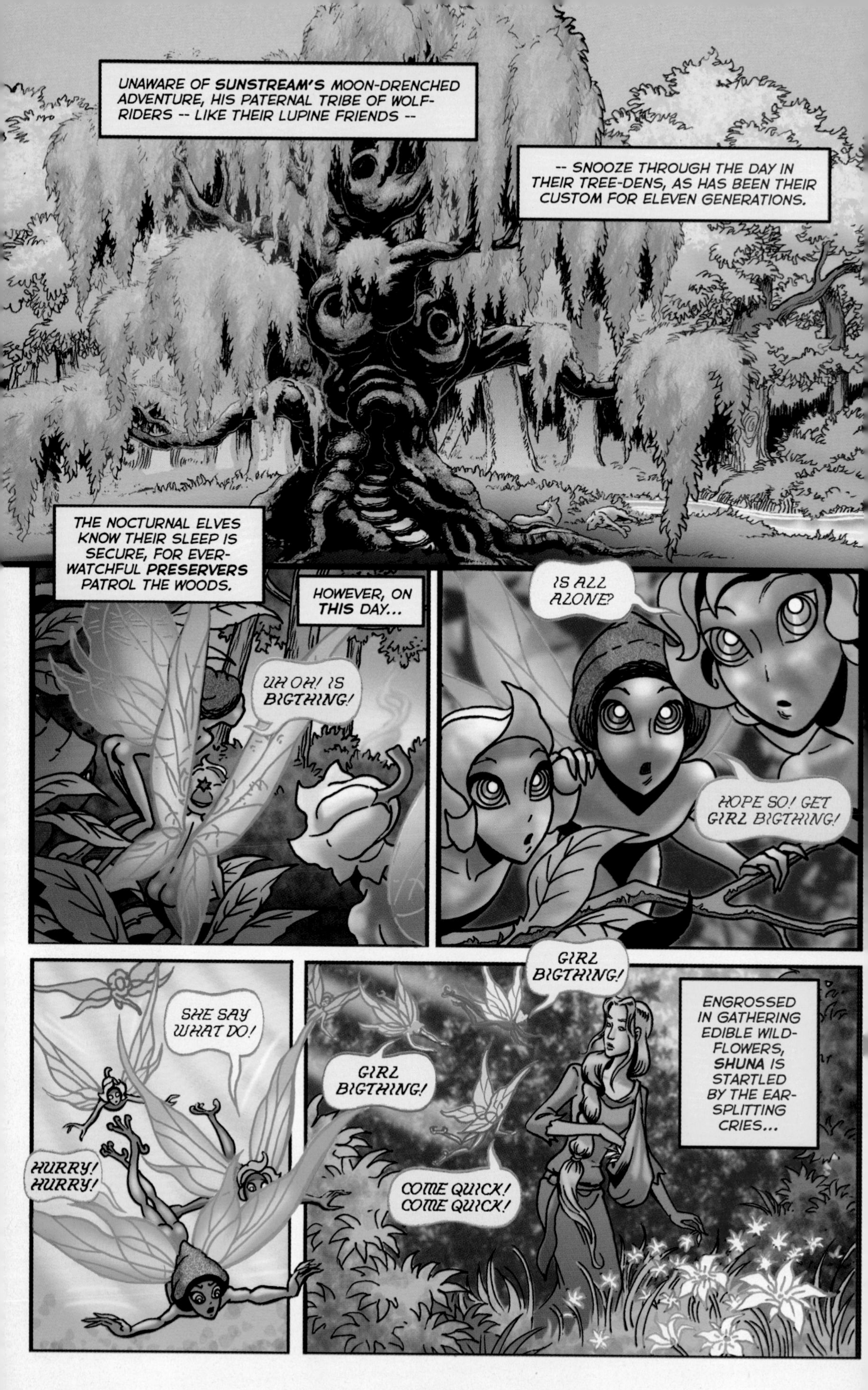
UNAWARE OF SUNSTREAM'S MOON-DRENCHED ADVENTURE, HIS PATERNAL TRIBE OF WOLF-RIDERS -- LIKE THEIR LUPINE FRIENDS --
-- SNOOZE THROUGH THE DAY IN THEIR TREE-DENS, AS HAS BEEN THEIR CUSTOM FOR ELEVEN GENERATIONS.
THE NOCTURNAL ELVES KNOW THEIR SLEEP IS SECURE, FOR EVER-WATCHFUL PRESERVERS PATROL THE WOODS.
HOWEVER, ON THIS DAY...
UH OH! IS BIGTHING!
IS ALL ALONE?
HOPE SO! GET GIRL BIGTHING!
SHE SAY WHAT DO!
HURRY! HURRY!
GIRL BIGTHING!
GIRL BIGTHING!
COME QUICK! COME QUICK!
ENGROSSED IN GATHERING EDIBLE WILD-FLOWERS, SHUNA IS STARTLED BY THE EAR-SPLITTING CRIES...

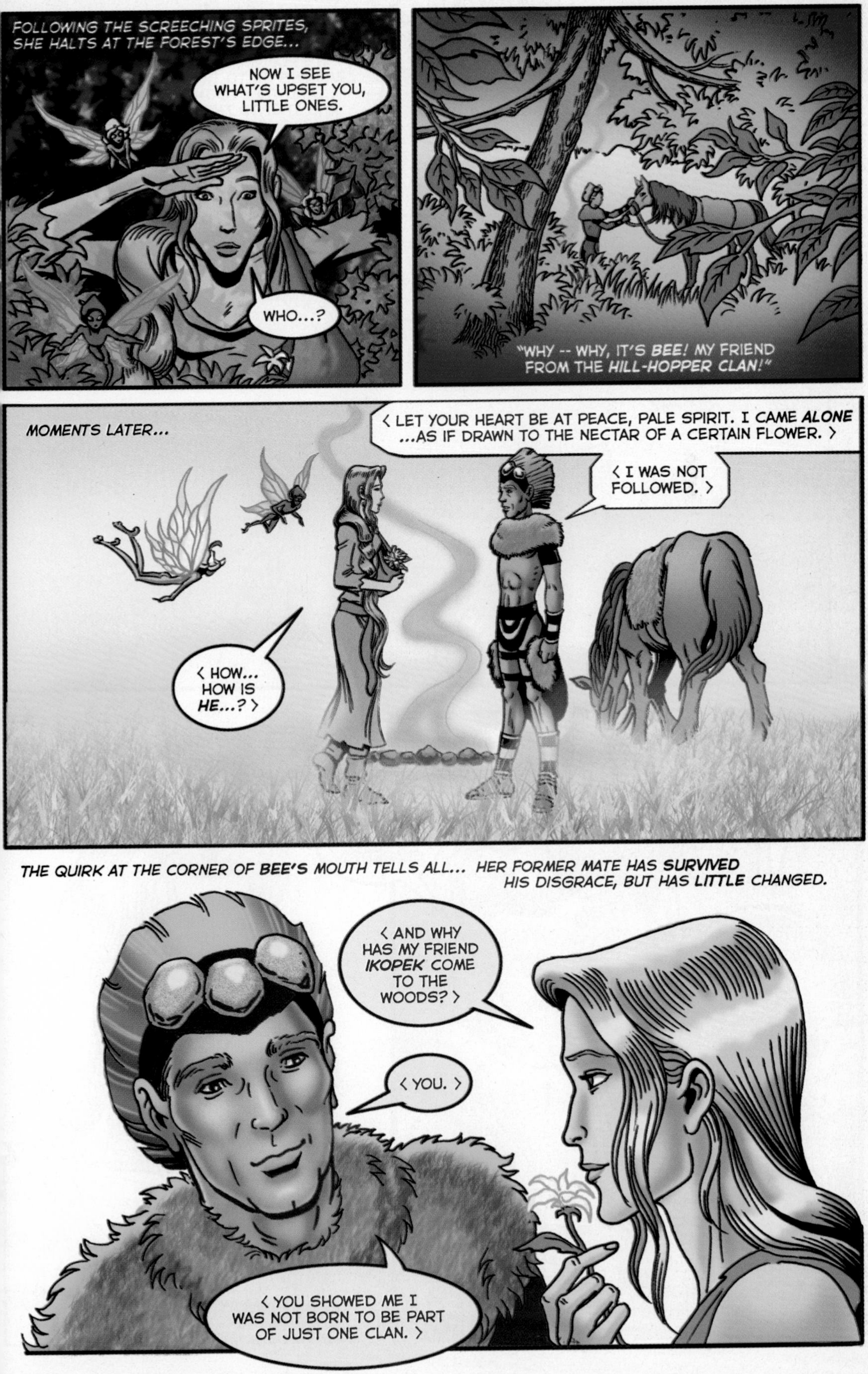
FOLLOWING THE SCREECHING SPRITES, SHE HALTS AT THE FOREST'S EDGE...
NOW I SEE WHAT'S UPSET YOU, LITTLE ONES.
WHO...?
"WHY -- WHY, IT'S BEE! MY FRIEND FROM THE HILL-HOPPER CLAN!"
MOMENTS LATER...
< LET YOUR HEART BE AT PEACE, PALE SPIRIT. I CAME ALONE ...AS IF DRAWN TO THE NECTAR OF A CERTAIN FLOWER. >
< I WAS NOT FOLLOWED. >
< HOW... HOW IS HE...? >
THE QUIRK AT THE CORNER OF BEE'S MOUTH TELLS ALL... HER FORMER MATE HAS SURVIVED HIS DISGRACE, BUT HAS LITTLE CHANGED.
< AND WHY HAS MY FRIEND IKOPEK COME TO THE WOODS? >
< YOU. >
< YOU SHOWED ME I WAS NOT BORN TO BE PART OF JUST ONE CLAN. >

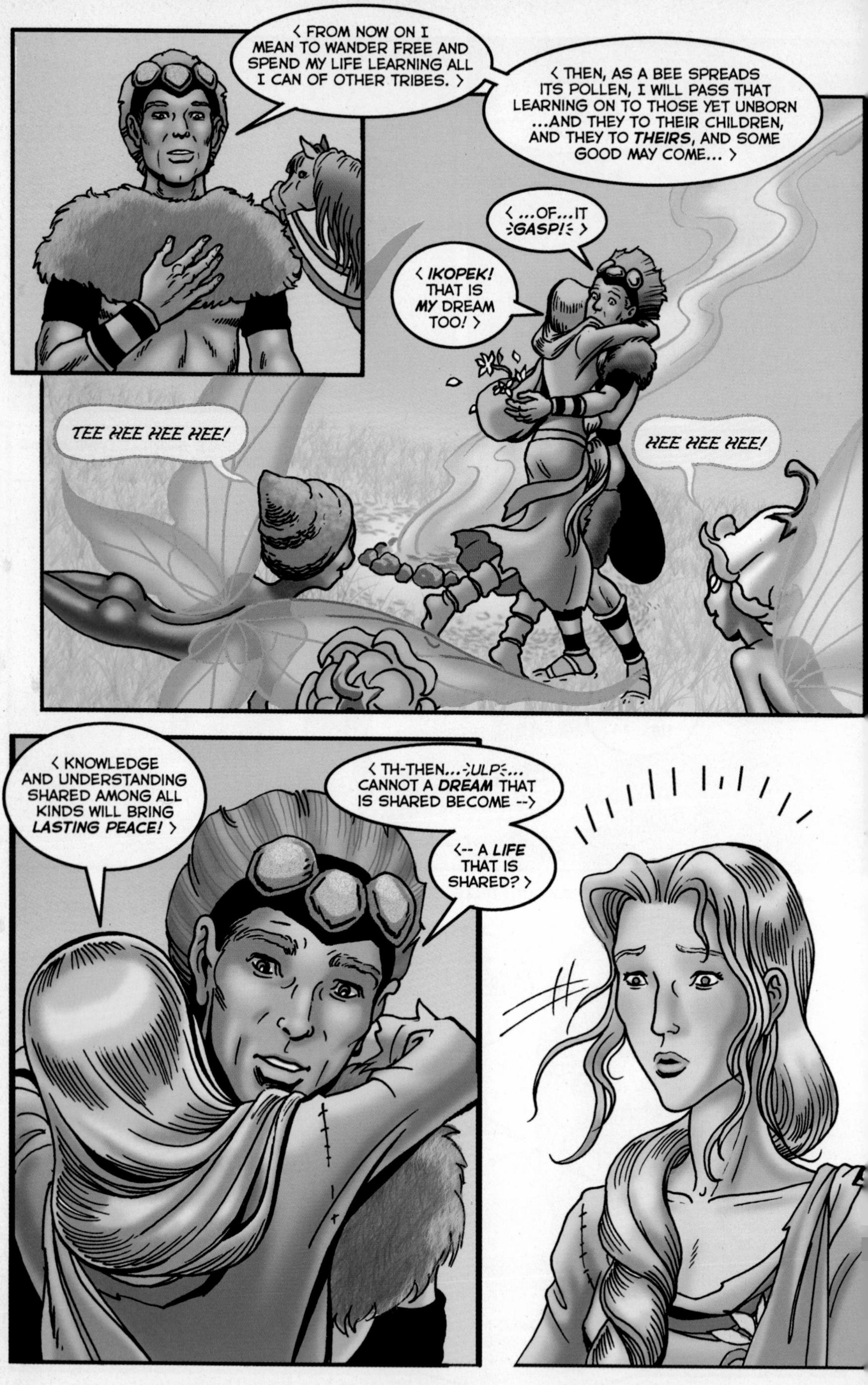

< FROM NOW ON I MEAN TO WANDER FREE AND SPEND MY LIFE LEARNING ALL I CAN OF OTHER TRIBES. >
< THEN, AS A BEE SPREADS ITS POLLEN, I WILL PASS THAT LEARNING ON TO THOSE YET UNBORN ...AND THEY TO THEIR CHILDREN, AND THEY TO *THEIRS*, AND SOME GOOD MAY COME... >
< ...OF...IT *GASP!* >
< *IKOPEK!* THAT IS *MY* DREAM TOO! >
TEE HEE HEE HEE!
HEE HEE HEE!
< KNOWLEDGE AND UNDERSTANDING SHARED AMONG ALL KINDS WILL BRING *LASTING PEACE!* >
< TH-THEN... *ULP*... CANNOT A *DREAM* THAT IS SHARED BECOME -->
<-- A *LIFE* THAT IS SHARED? >

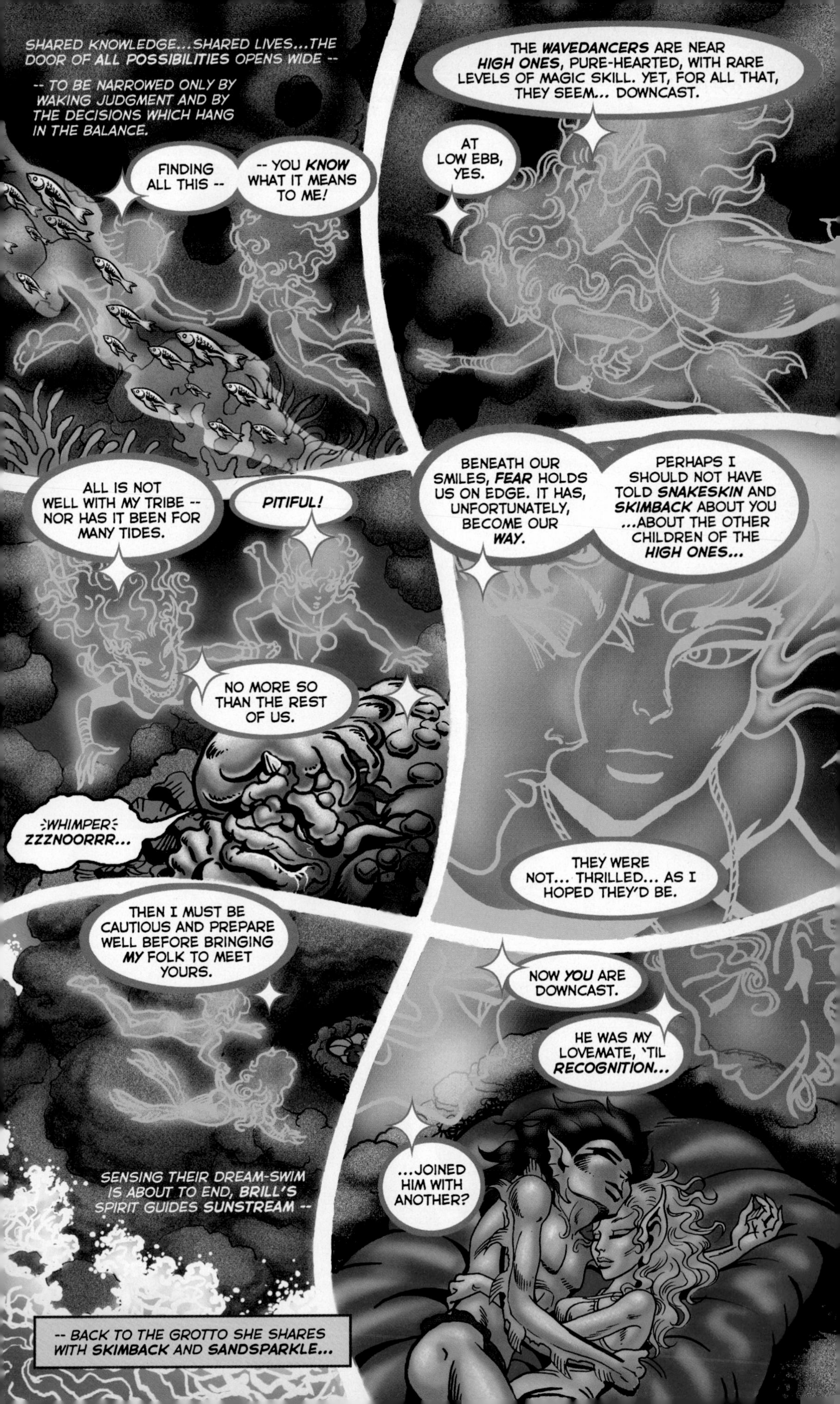

SHARED KNOWLEDGE...SHARED LIVES...THE DOOR OF ALL POSSIBILITIES OPENS WIDE --
-- TO BE NARROWED ONLY BY WAKING JUDGMENT AND BY THE DECISIONS WHICH HANG IN THE BALANCE.
FINDING ALL THIS --
-- YOU KNOW WHAT IT MEANS TO ME!
THE WAVEDANCERS ARE NEAR HIGH ONES, PURE-HEARTED, WITH RARE LEVELS OF MAGIC SKILL. YET, FOR ALL THAT, THEY SEEM... DOWNCAST.
AT LOW EBB, YES.
ALL IS NOT WELL WITH MY TRIBE -- NOR HAS IT BEEN FOR MANY TIDES.
PITIFUL!
NO MORE SO THAN THE REST OF US.
WHIMPER ZZZNOORRR...
BENEATH OUR SMILES, FEAR HOLDS US ON EDGE. IT HAS, UNFORTUNATELY, BECOME OUR WAY.
PERHAPS I SHOULD NOT HAVE TOLD SNAKESKIN AND SKIMBACK ABOUT YOU ...ABOUT THE OTHER CHILDREN OF THE HIGH ONES...
THEY WERE NOT... THRILLED... AS I HOPED THEY'D BE.
THEN I MUST BE CAUTIOUS AND PREPARE WELL BEFORE BRINGING MY FOLK TO MEET YOURS.
NOW YOU ARE DOWNCAST.
HE WAS MY LOVEMATE, 'TIL RECOGNITION...
...JOINED HIM WITH ANOTHER?
SENSING THEIR DREAM-SWIM IS ABOUT TO END, BRILL'S SPIRIT GUIDES SUNSTREAM --
-- BACK TO THE GROTTO SHE SHARES WITH SKIMBACK AND SANDSPARKLE...

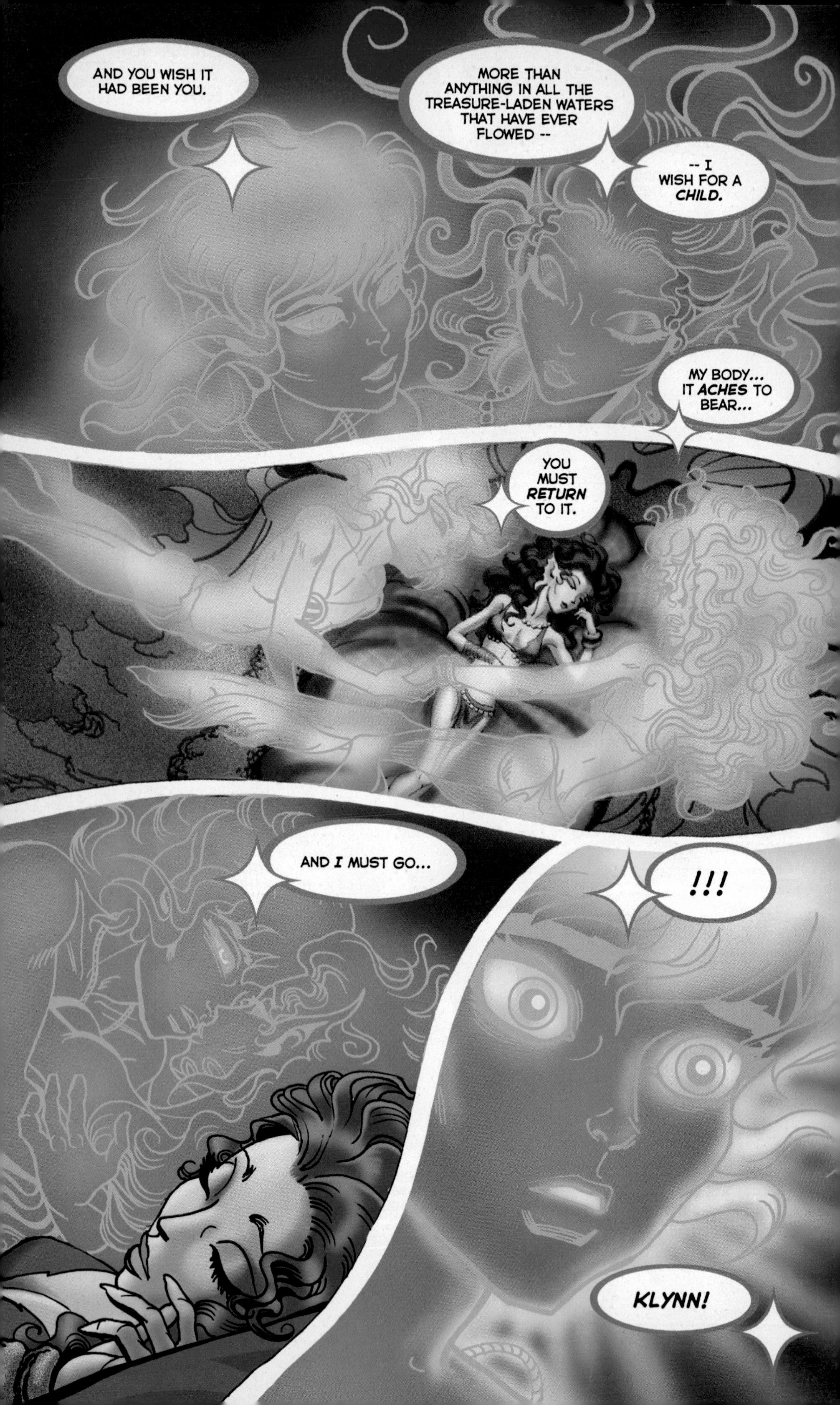
AND YOU WISH IT HAD BEEN YOU.
MORE THAN ANYTHING IN ALL THE TREASURE-LADEN WATERS THAT HAVE EVER FLOWED --
-- I WISH FOR A *CHILD.*
MY BODY... IT *ACHES* TO BEAR...
YOU MUST *RETURN* TO IT.
AND *I* MUST GO...
!!!
KLYNN!

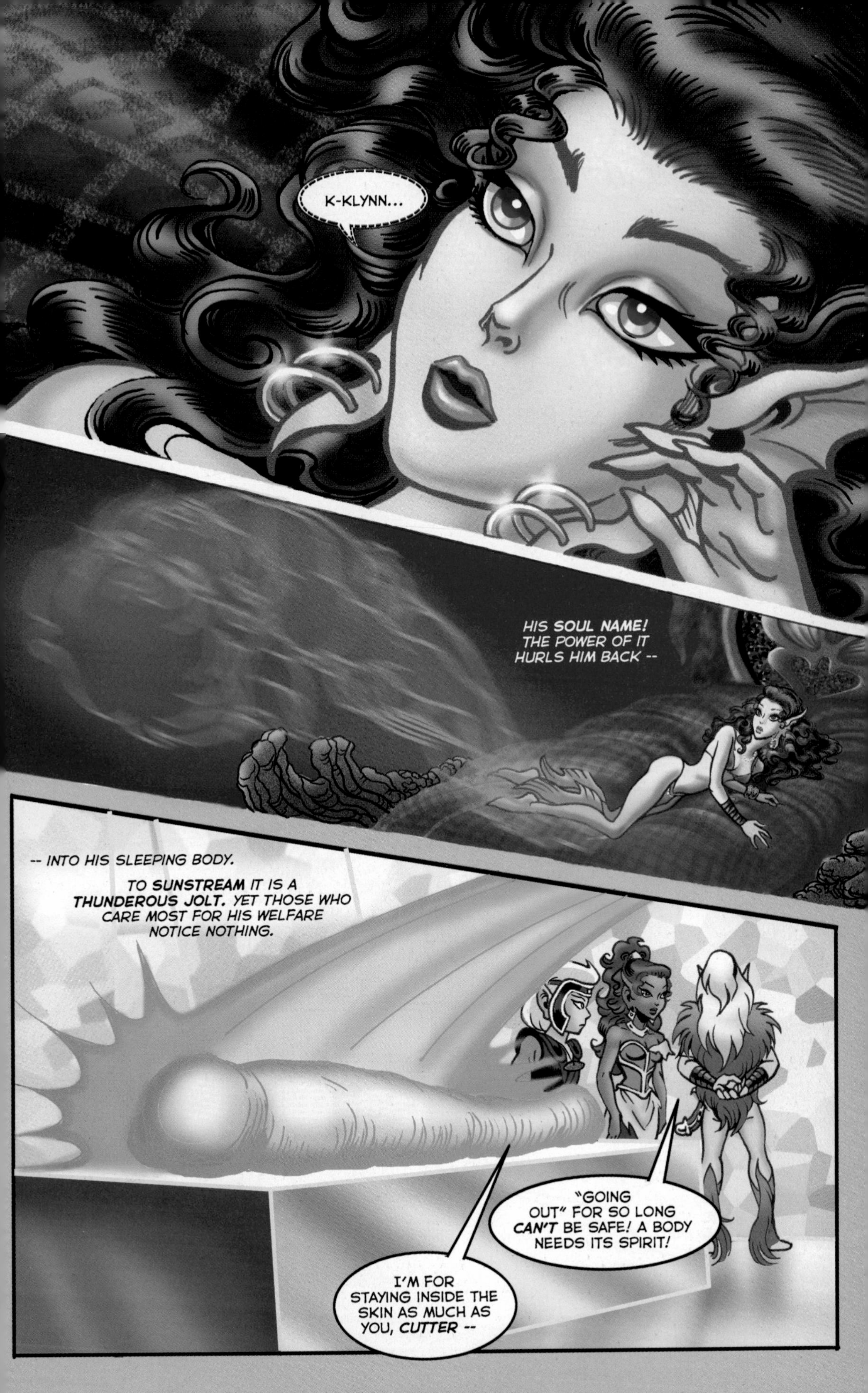
K-KLYNN...
HIS SOUL NAME! THE POWER OF IT HURLS HIM BACK --
-- INTO HIS SLEEPING BODY.
TO SUNSTREAM IT IS A THUNDEROUS JOLT. YET THOSE WHO CARE MOST FOR HIS WELFARE NOTICE NOTHING.
"GOING OUT" FOR SO LONG CAN'T BE SAFE! A BODY NEEDS ITS SPIRIT!
I'M FOR STAYING INSIDE THE SKIN AS MUCH AS YOU, CUTTER --

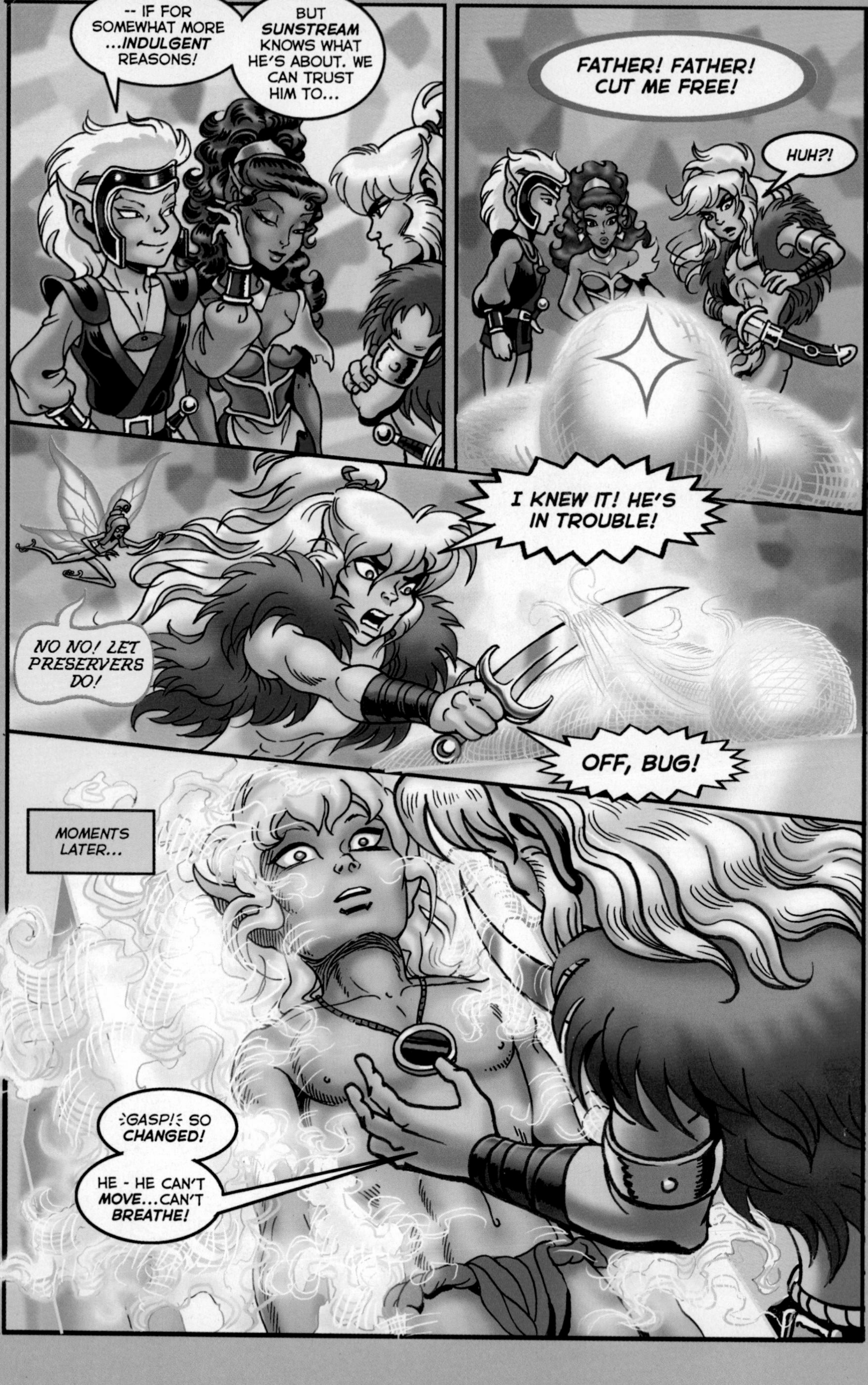

-- IF FOR SOMEWHAT MORE ...INDULGENT REASONS!
BUT SUNSTREAM KNOWS WHAT HE'S ABOUT. WE CAN TRUST HIM TO...
FATHER! FATHER! CUT ME FREE!
HUH?!
I KNEW IT! HE'S IN TROUBLE!
NO NO! LET PRESERVERS DO!
OFF, BUG!
MOMENTS LATER...
GASP! SO CHANGED!
HE - HE CAN'T MOVE...CAN'T BREATHE!

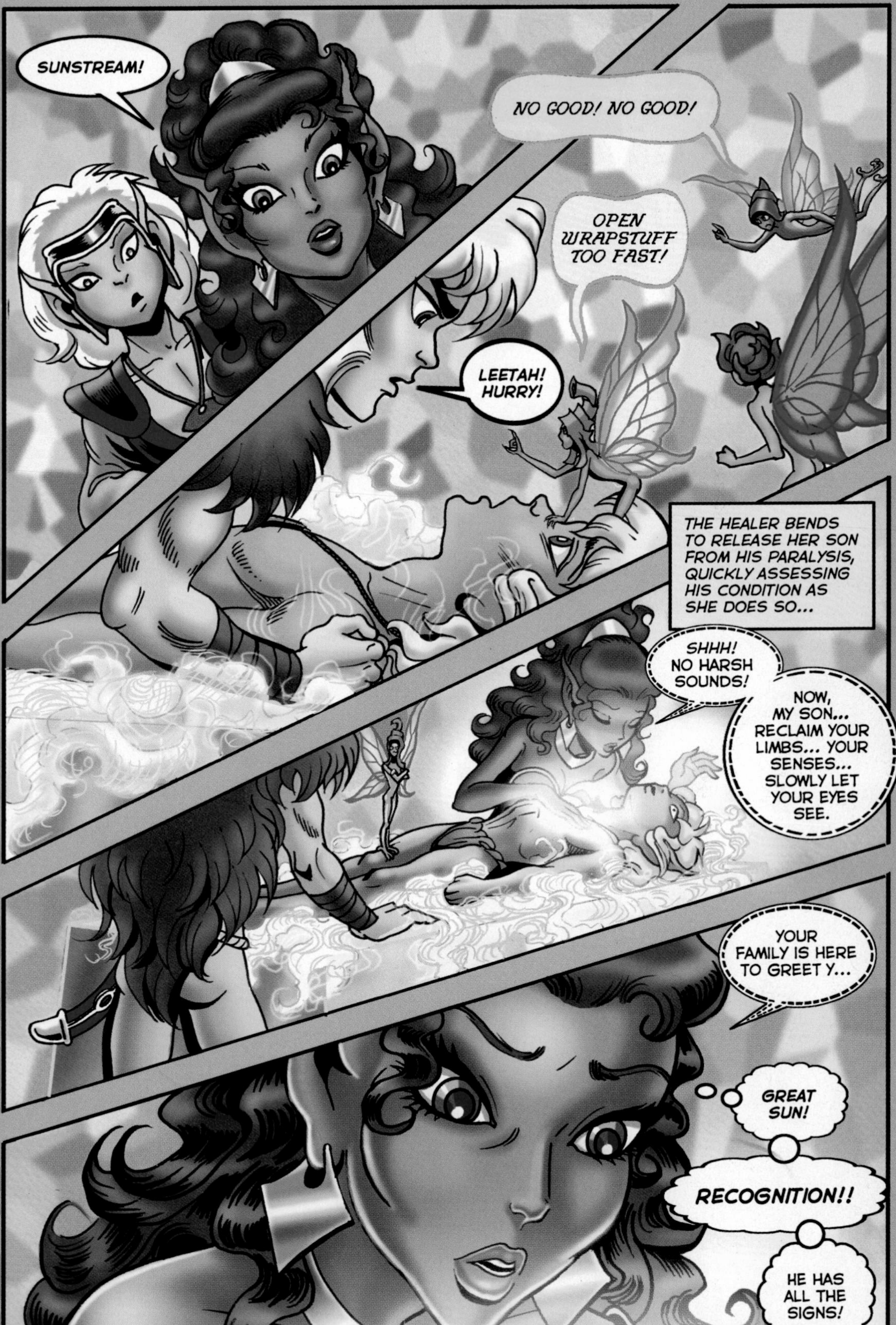
SUNSTREAM!
NO GOOD! NO GOOD!
OPEN WRAPSTUFF TOO FAST!
LEETAH! HURRY!
THE HEALER BENDS TO RELEASE HER SON FROM HIS PARALYSIS, QUICKLY ASSESSING HIS CONDITION AS SHE DOES SO...
SHHH! NO HARSH SOUNDS!
NOW, MY SON... RECLAIM YOUR LIMBS... YOUR SENSES... SLOWLY LET YOUR EYES SEE.
YOUR FAMILY IS HERE TO GREET Y...
GREAT SUN!
RECOGNITION!!
HE HAS ALL THE SIGNS!

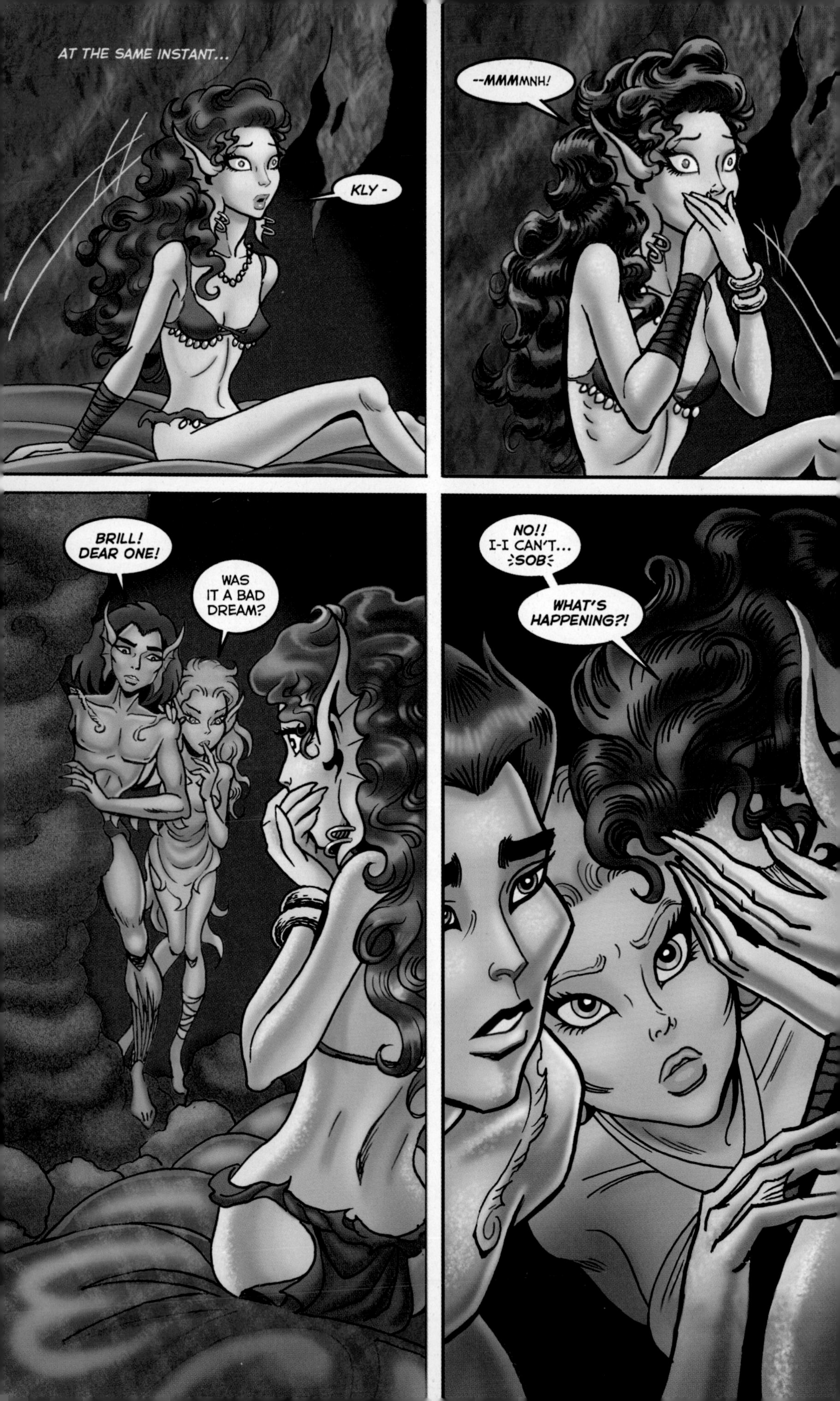
AT THE SAME INSTANT...
KLY -
--MMMMNH!
BRILL! DEAR ONE!
WAS IT A BAD DREAM?
NO!! I-I CAN'T... SOB
WHAT'S HAPPENING?!

CHAPTER TWO

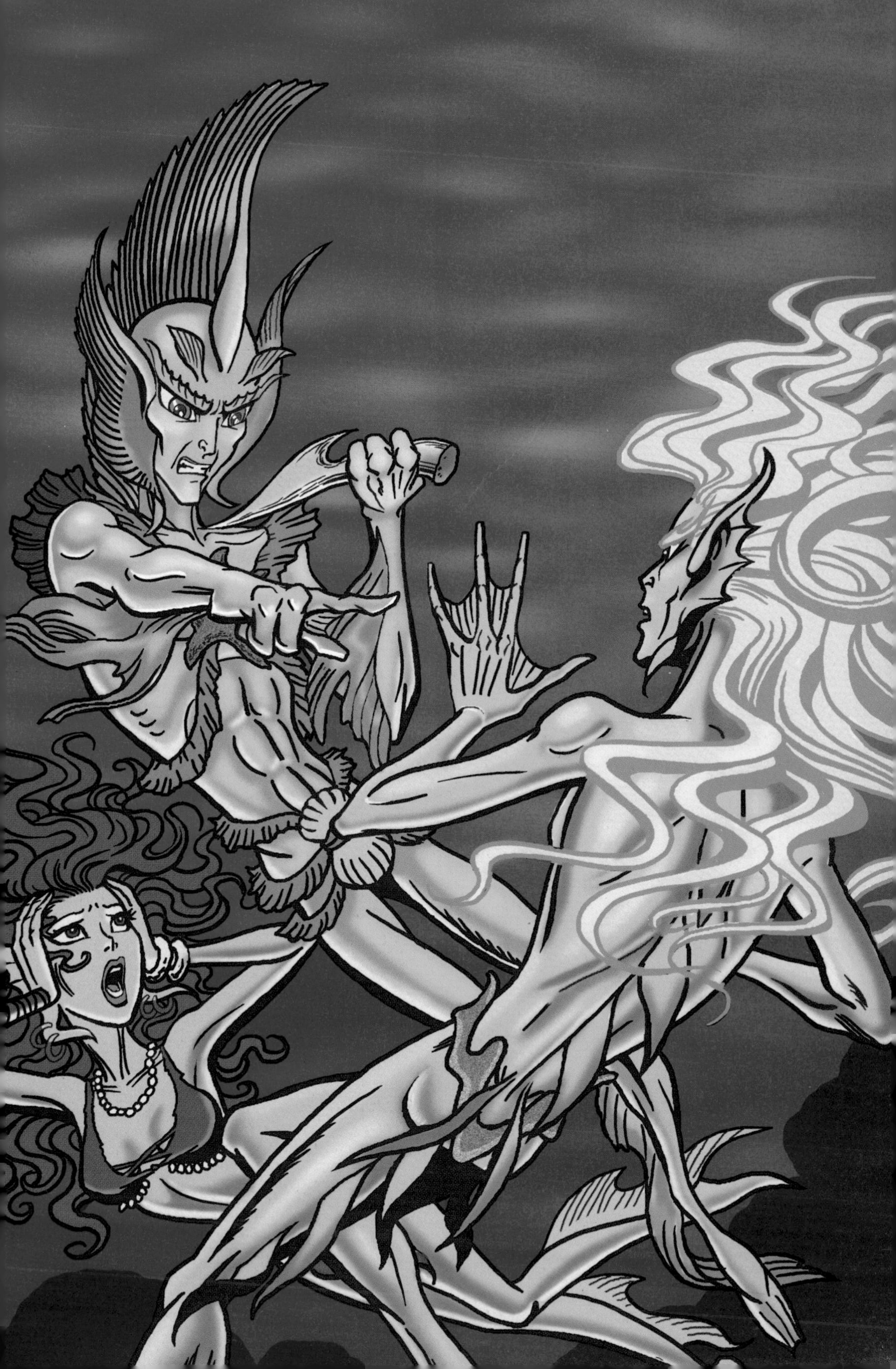

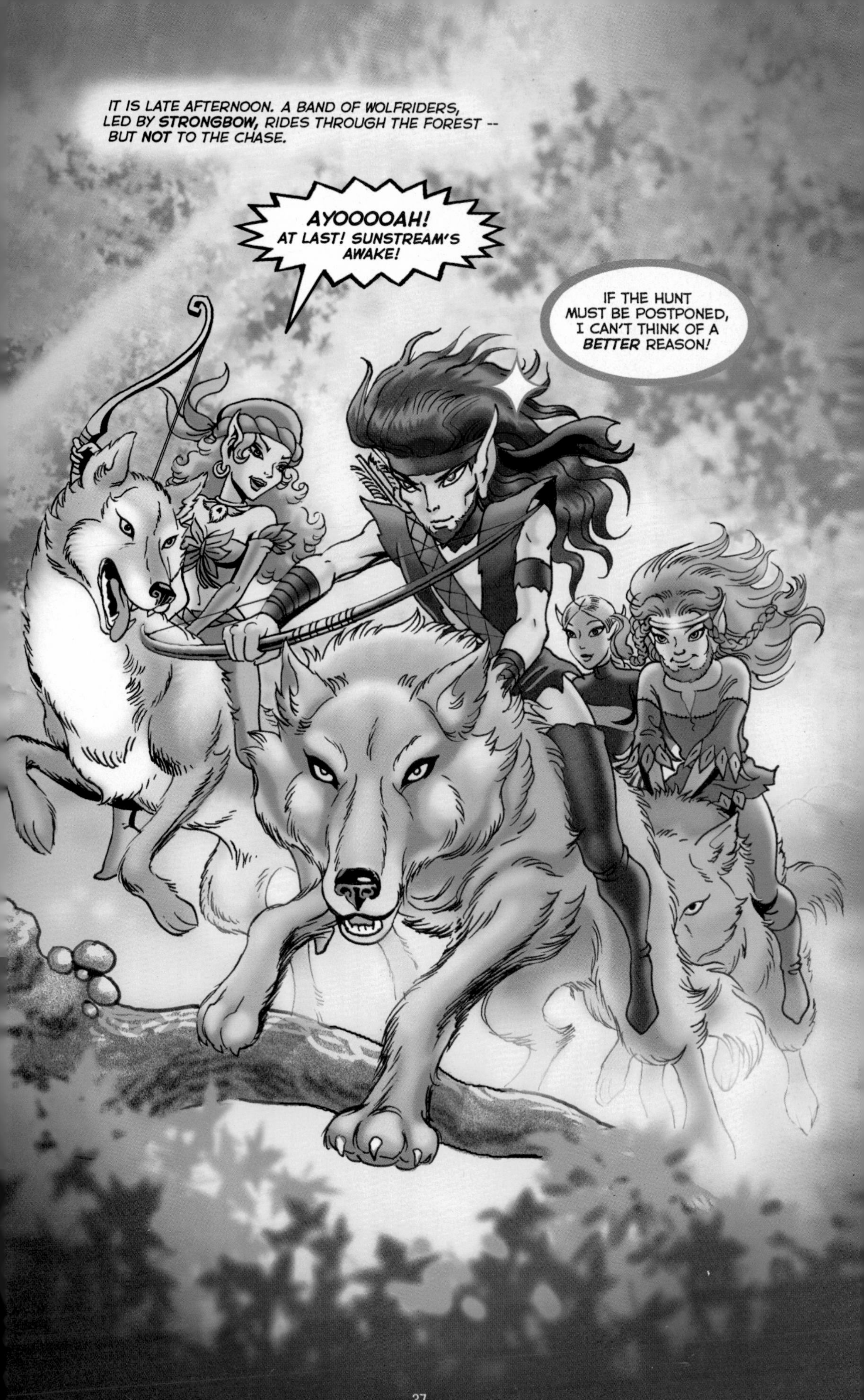
IT IS LATE AFTERNOON. A BAND OF WOLFRIDERS, LED BY **STRONGBOW,** RIDES THROUGH THE FOREST -- BUT ***NOT*** TO THE CHASE.
AYOOOOAH! AT LAST! SUNSTREAM'S AWAKE!
IF THE HUNT MUST BE POSTPONED, I CAN'T THINK OF A *BETTER* REASON!

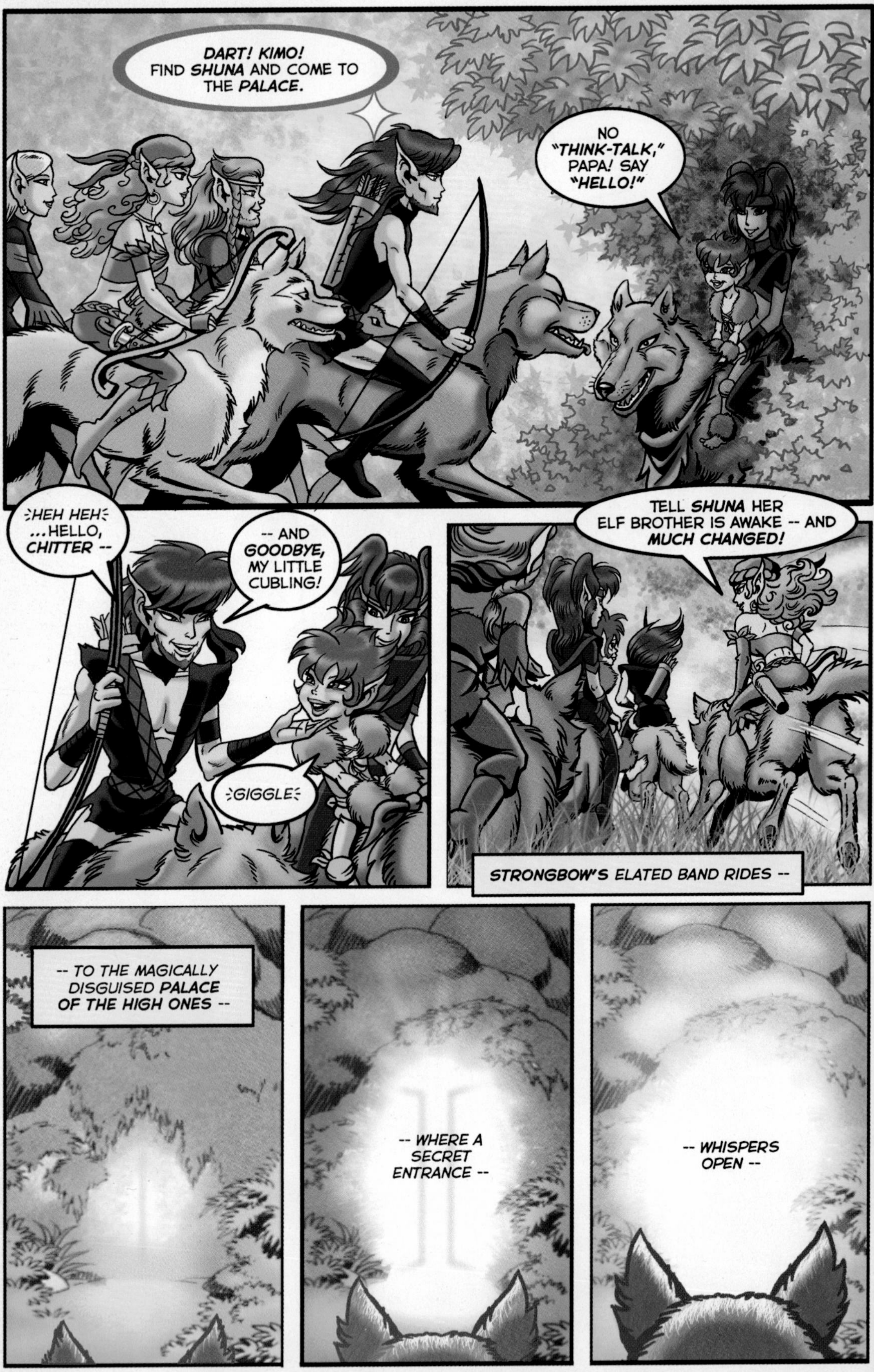
DART! KIMO! FIND SHUNA AND COME TO THE PALACE.
NO "THINK-TALK," PAPA! SAY "HELLO!"
HEH HEH ...HELLO, CHITTER --
-- AND GOODBYE, MY LITTLE CUBLING!
GIGGLE
TELL SHUNA HER ELF BROTHER IS AWAKE -- AND MUCH CHANGED!
STRONGBOW'S ELATED BAND RIDES --
-- TO THE MAGICALLY DISGUISED PALACE OF THE HIGH ONES --
-- WHERE A SECRET ENTRANCE --
-- WHISPERS OPEN --

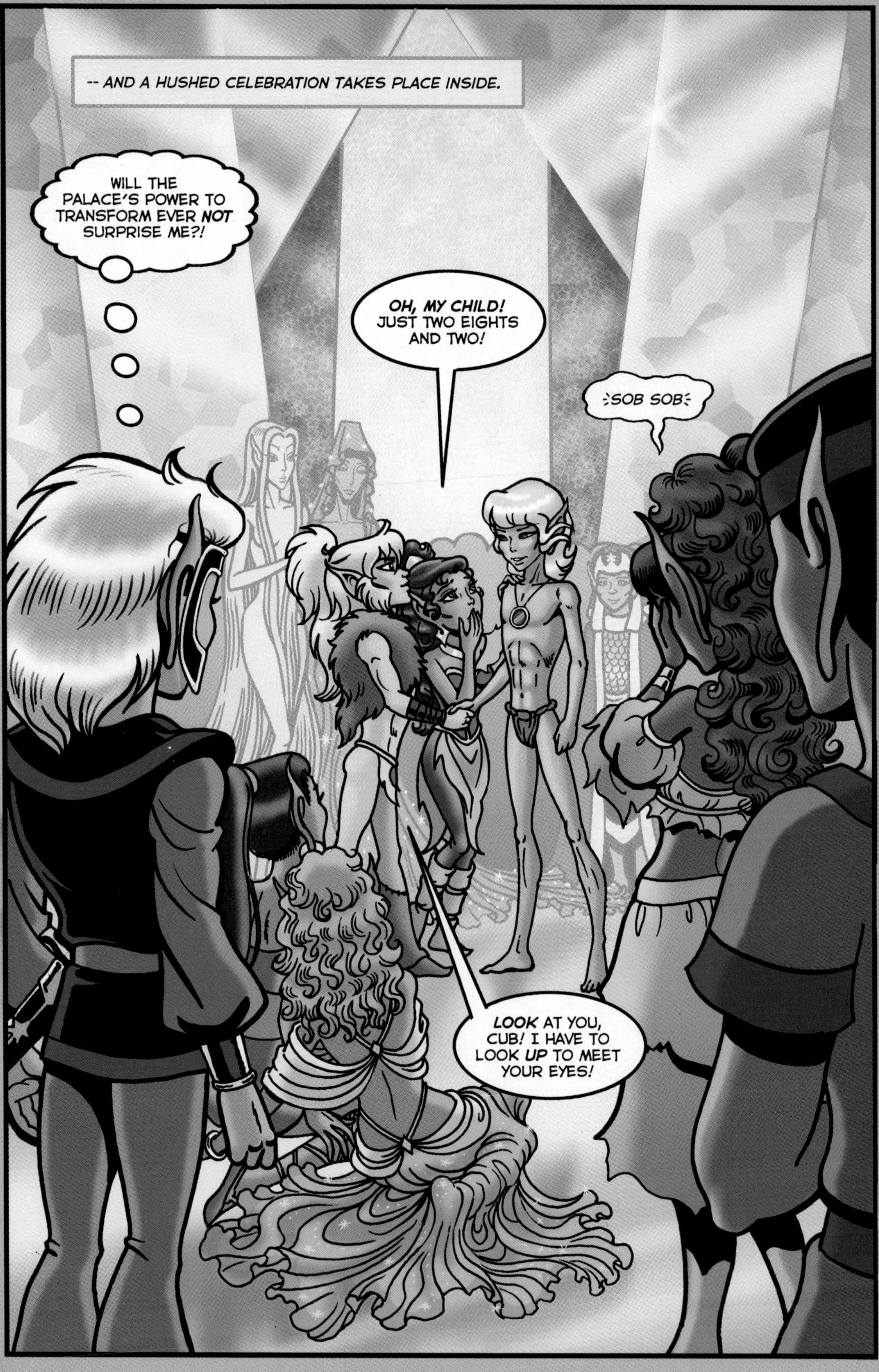
-- AND A HUSHED CELEBRATION TAKES PLACE INSIDE.
WILL THE PALACE'S POWER TO TRANSFORM EVER *NOT* SURPRISE ME?!
OH, MY CHILD! JUST TWO EIGHTS AND TWO!
SOB SOB
LOOK AT YOU, CUB! I HAVE TO LOOK *UP* TO MEET YOUR EYES!

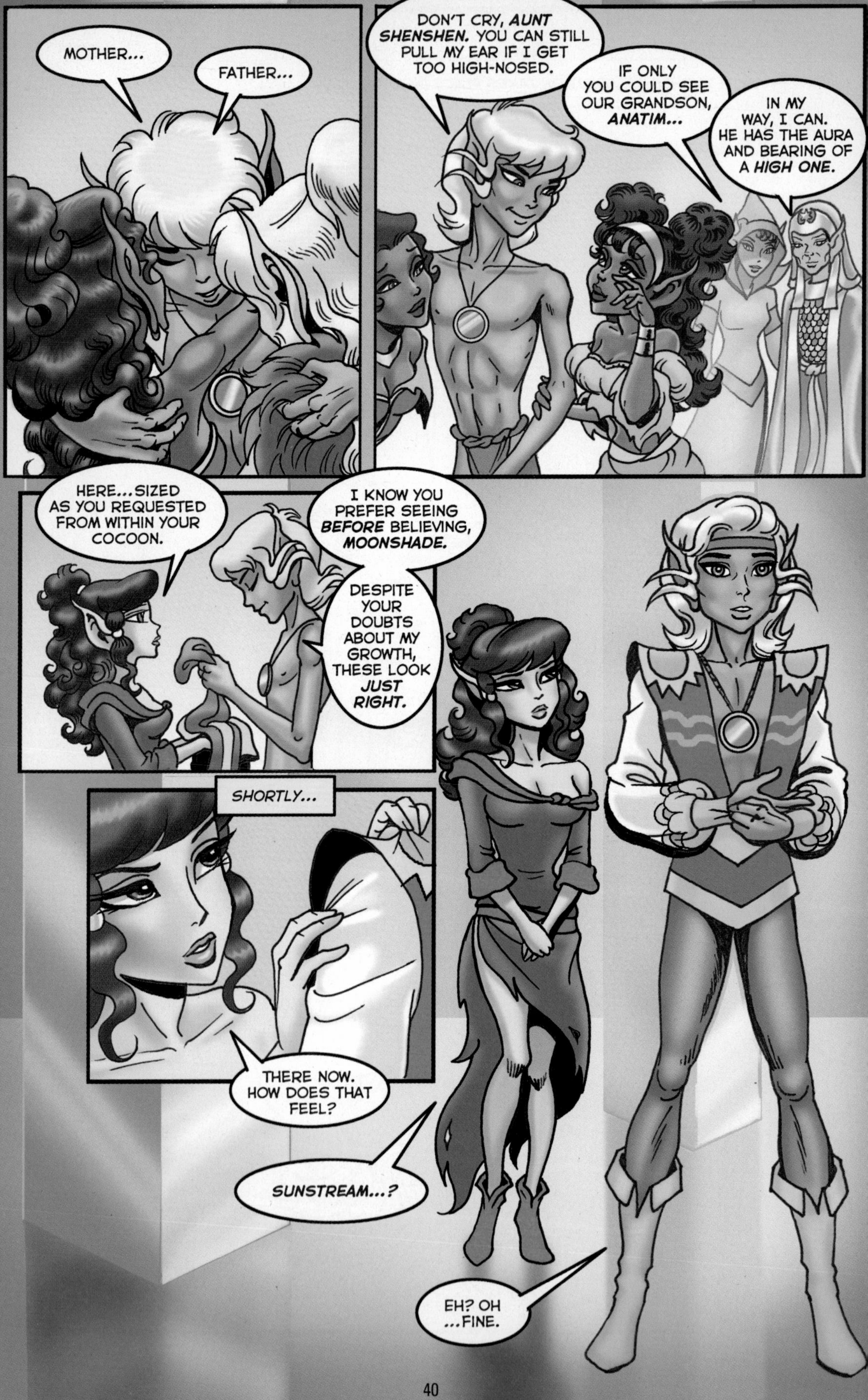
MOTHER...
FATHER...
DON'T CRY, AUNT SHENSHEN. YOU CAN STILL PULL MY EAR IF I GET TOO HIGH-NOSED.
IF ONLY YOU COULD SEE OUR GRANDSON, ANATIM...
IN MY WAY, I CAN. HE HAS THE AURA AND BEARING OF A HIGH ONE.
HERE...SIZED AS YOU REQUESTED FROM WITHIN YOUR COCOON.
I KNOW YOU PREFER SEEING BEFORE BELIEVING, MOONSHADE.
DESPITE YOUR DOUBTS ABOUT MY GROWTH, THESE LOOK JUST RIGHT.
SHORTLY...
THERE NOW. HOW DOES THAT FEEL?
SUNSTREAM...?
EH? OH ...FINE.

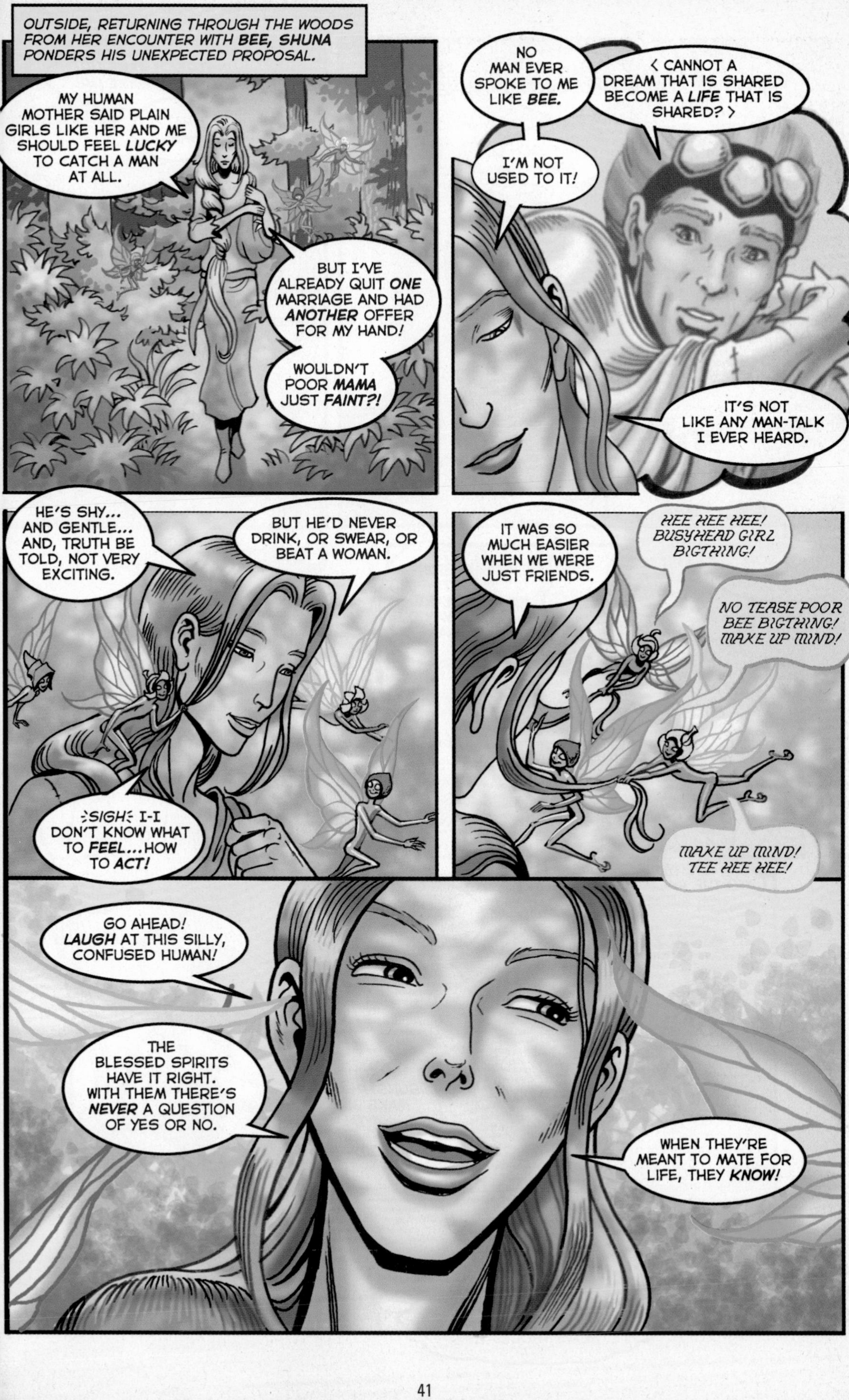
OUTSIDE, RETURNING THROUGH THE WOODS FROM HER ENCOUNTER WITH BEE, SHUNA PONDERS HIS UNEXPECTED PROPOSAL.
MY HUMAN MOTHER SAID PLAIN GIRLS LIKE HER AND ME SHOULD FEEL LUCKY TO CATCH A MAN AT ALL.
BUT I'VE ALREADY QUIT ONE MARRIAGE AND HAD ANOTHER OFFER FOR MY HAND!
WOULDN'T POOR MAMA JUST FAINT?!
NO MAN EVER SPOKE TO ME LIKE BEE.
I'M NOT USED TO IT!
< CANNOT A DREAM THAT IS SHARED BECOME A LIFE THAT IS SHARED? >
IT'S NOT LIKE ANY MAN-TALK I EVER HEARD.
HE'S SHY... AND GENTLE... AND, TRUTH BE TOLD, NOT VERY EXCITING.
BUT HE'D NEVER DRINK, OR SWEAR, OR BEAT A WOMAN.
SIGH I-I DON'T KNOW WHAT TO FEEL...HOW TO ACT!
IT WAS SO MUCH EASIER WHEN WE WERE JUST FRIENDS.
HEE HEE HEE! BUSYHEAD GIRL BIGTHING!
NO TEASE POOR BEE BIGTHING! MAKE UP MIND!
MAKE UP MIND! TEE HEE HEE!
GO AHEAD! LAUGH AT THIS SILLY, CONFUSED HUMAN!
THE BLESSED SPIRITS HAVE IT RIGHT. WITH THEM THERE'S NEVER A QUESTION OF YES OR NO.
WHEN THEY'RE MEANT TO MATE FOR LIFE, THEY KNOW!

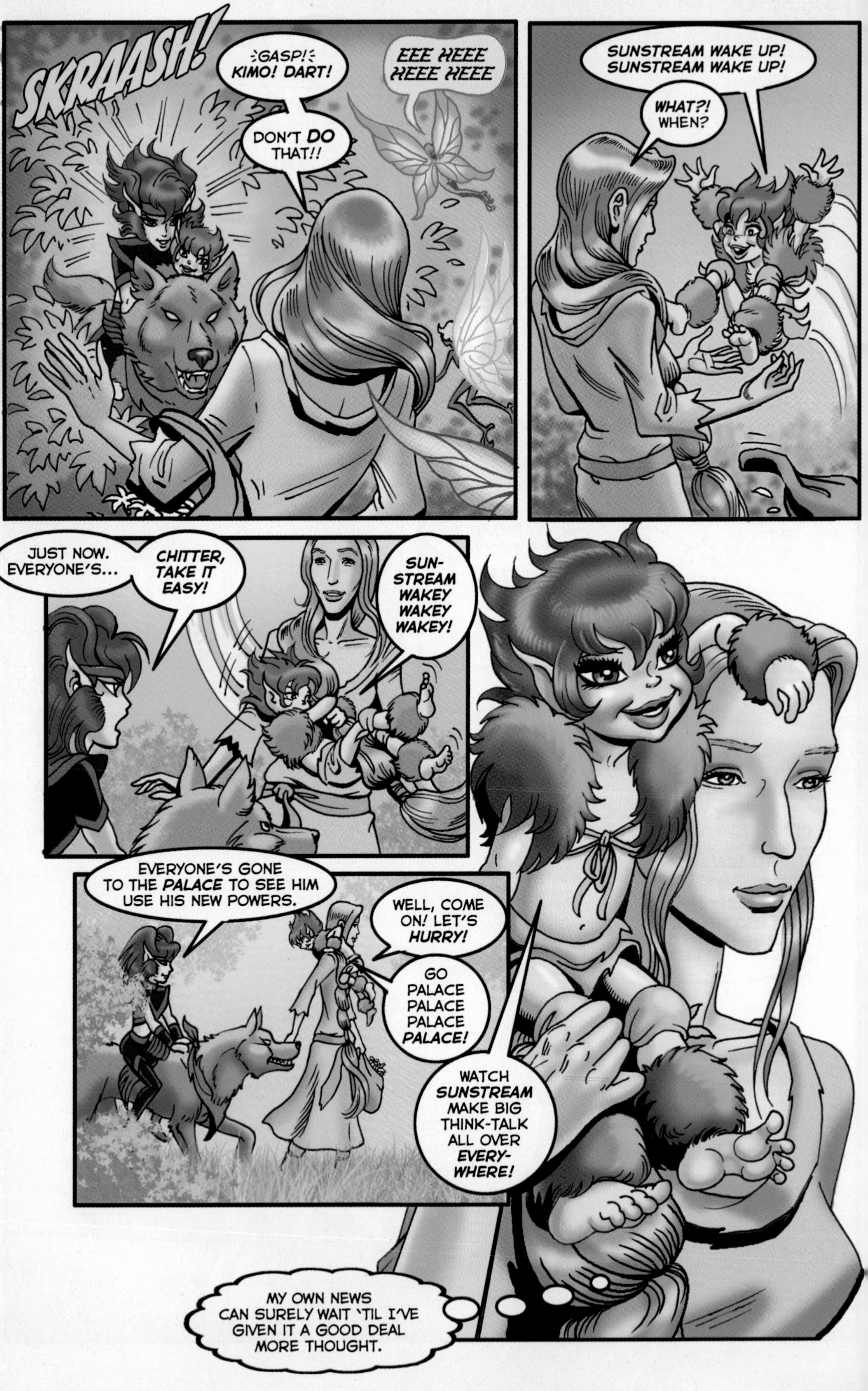
SKRAASH!
GASP! KIMO! DART!
DON'T DO THAT!!
EEE HEEE HEEE HEEE
SUNSTREAM WAKE UP! SUNSTREAM WAKE UP!
WHAT?! WHEN?
JUST NOW. EVERYONE'S...
CHITTER, TAKE IT EASY!
SUN-STREAM WAKEY WAKEY WAKEY!
EVERYONE'S GONE TO THE PALACE TO SEE HIM USE HIS NEW POWERS.
WELL, COME ON! LET'S HURRY!
GO PALACE PALACE PALACE PALACE!
WATCH SUNSTREAM MAKE BIG THINK-TALK ALL OVER EVERY-WHERE!
MY OWN NEWS CAN SURELY WAIT 'TIL I'VE GIVEN IT A GOOD DEAL MORE THOUGHT.

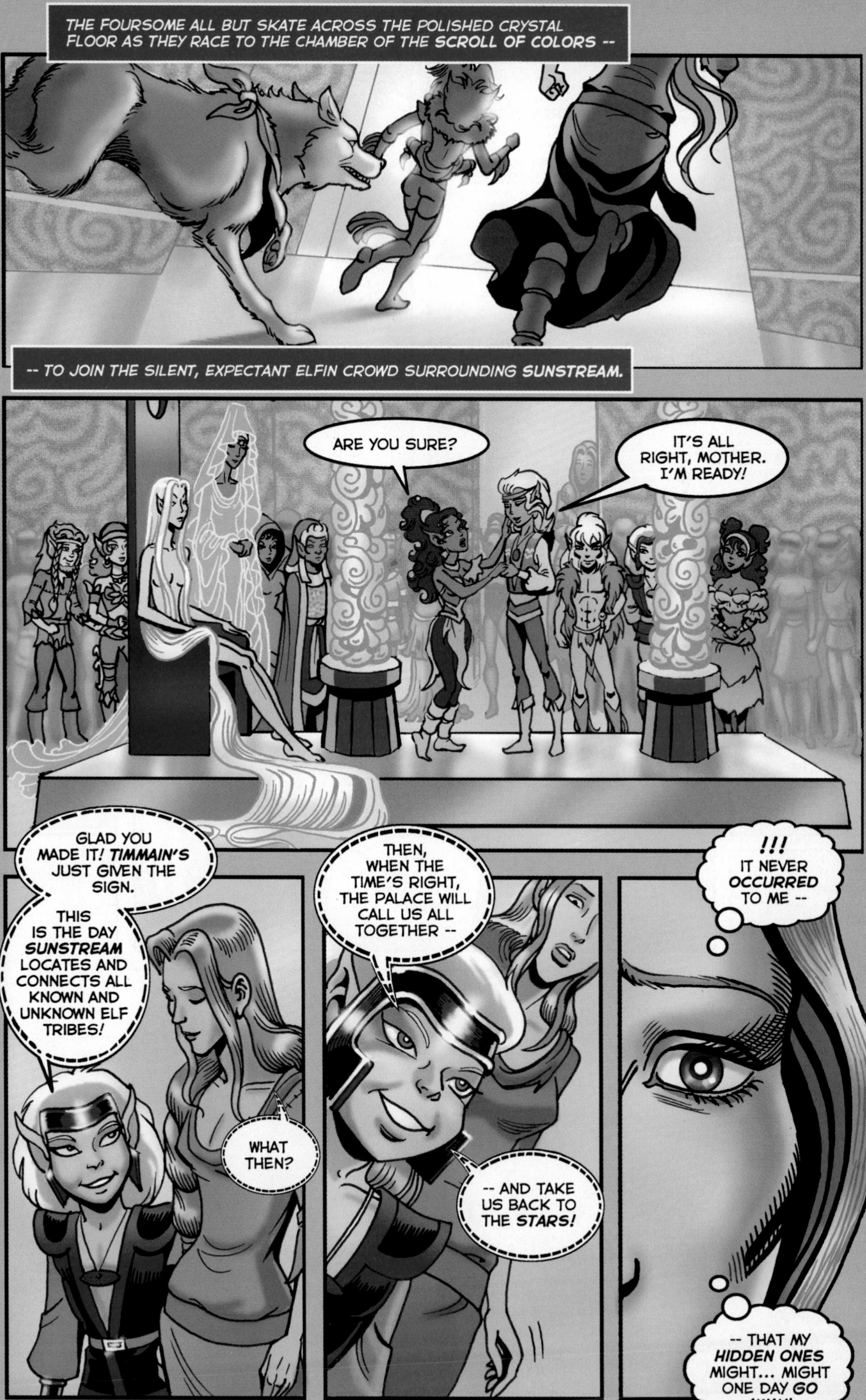
THE FOURSOME ALL BUT SKATE ACROSS THE POLISHED CRYSTAL FLOOR AS THEY RACE TO THE CHAMBER OF THE SCROLL OF COLORS --
-- TO JOIN THE SILENT, EXPECTANT ELFIN CROWD SURROUNDING SUNSTREAM.
ARE YOU SURE?
IT'S ALL RIGHT, MOTHER. I'M READY!
GLAD YOU MADE IT! TIMMAIN'S JUST GIVEN THE SIGN.
THIS IS THE DAY SUNSTREAM LOCATES AND CONNECTS ALL KNOWN AND UNKNOWN ELF TRIBES!
WHAT THEN?
THEN, WHEN THE TIME'S RIGHT, THE PALACE WILL CALL US ALL TOGETHER --
-- AND TAKE US BACK TO THE STARS!
!!! IT NEVER OCCURRED TO ME --
-- THAT MY HIDDEN ONES MIGHT... MIGHT ONE DAY GO AWAY!

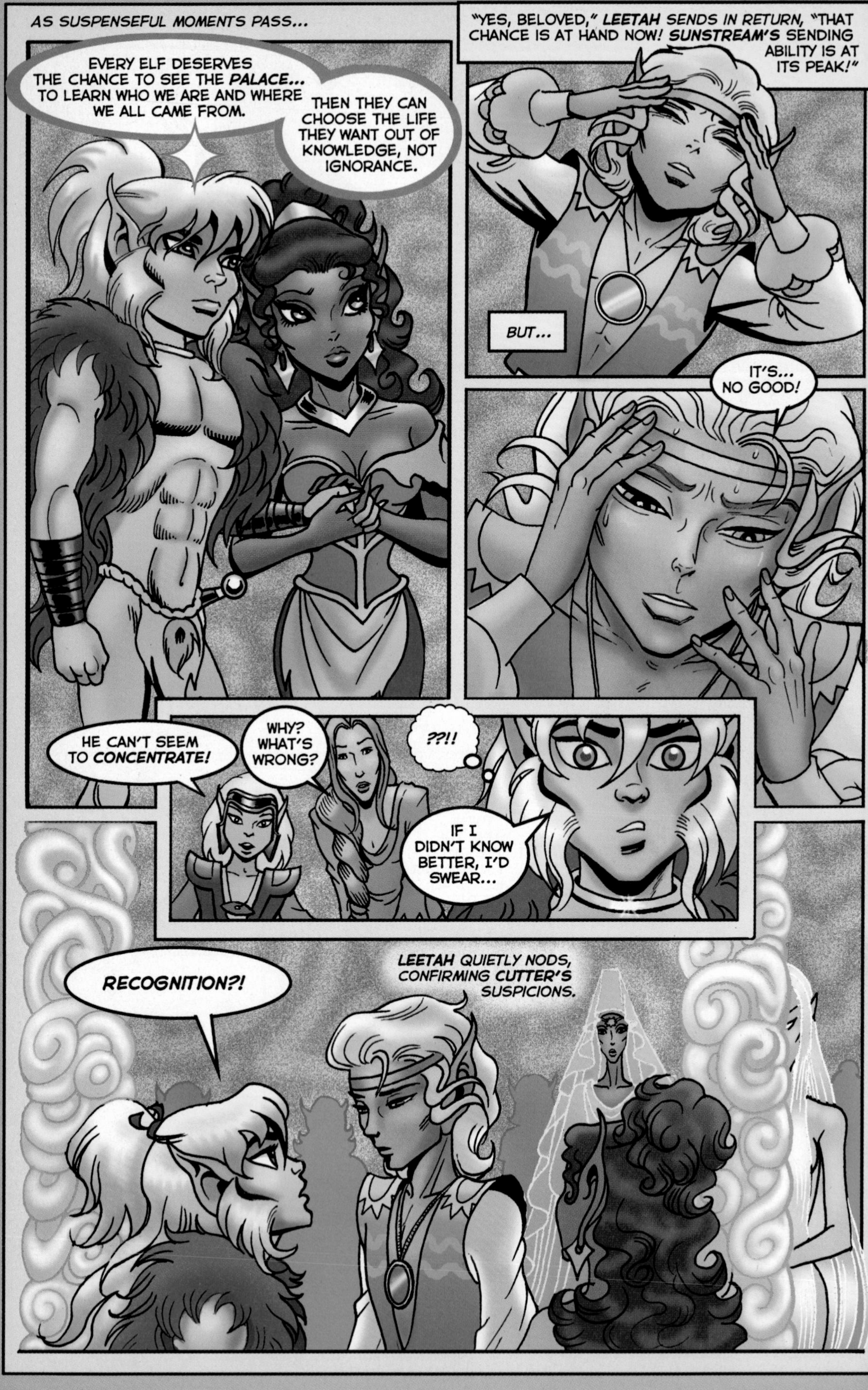
AS SUSPENSEFUL MOMENTS PASS...
EVERY ELF DESERVES THE CHANCE TO SEE THE PALACE... TO LEARN WHO WE ARE AND WHERE WE ALL CAME FROM.
THEN THEY CAN CHOOSE THE LIFE THEY WANT OUT OF KNOWLEDGE, NOT IGNORANCE.
"YES, BELOVED," LEETAH SENDS IN RETURN, "THAT CHANCE IS AT HAND NOW! SUNSTREAM'S SENDING ABILITY IS AT ITS PEAK!"
BUT...
IT'S... NO GOOD!
HE CAN'T SEEM TO CONCENTRATE!
WHY? WHAT'S WRONG?
??!!
IF I DIDN'T KNOW BETTER, I'D SWEAR...
RECOGNITION?!
LEETAH QUIETLY NODS, CONFIRMING CUTTER'S SUSPICIONS.

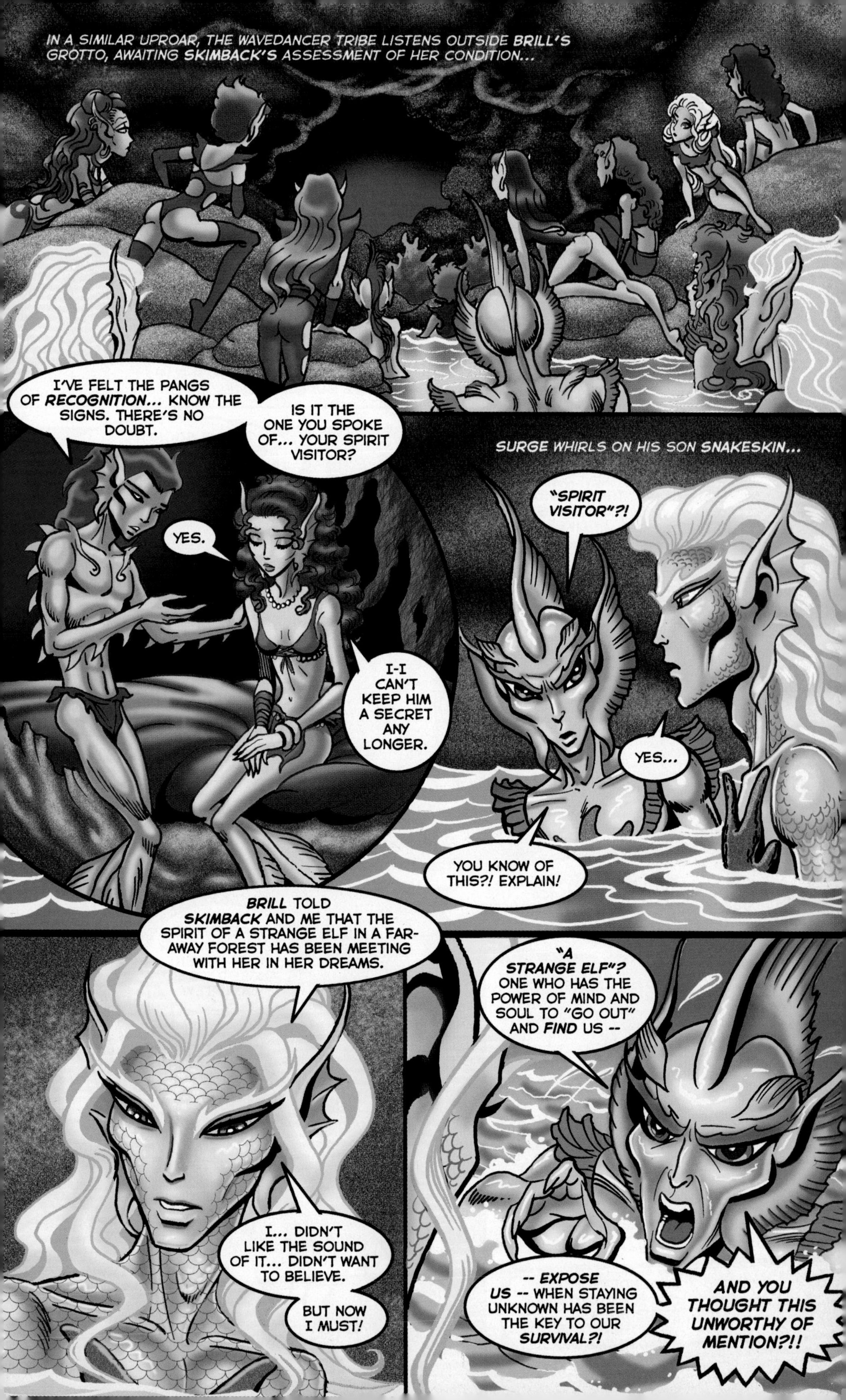
IN A SIMILAR UPROAR, THE WAVEDANCER TRIBE LISTENS OUTSIDE BRILL'S GROTTO, AWAITING SKIMBACK'S ASSESSMENT OF HER CONDITION...
I'VE FELT THE PANGS OF RECOGNITION... KNOW THE SIGNS. THERE'S NO DOUBT.
IS IT THE ONE YOU SPOKE OF... YOUR SPIRIT VISITOR?
YES.
I-I CAN'T KEEP HIM A SECRET ANY LONGER.
SURGE WHIRLS ON HIS SON SNAKESKIN...
"SPIRIT VISITOR"?!
YES...
YOU KNOW OF THIS?! EXPLAIN!
BRILL TOLD SKIMBACK AND ME THAT THE SPIRIT OF A STRANGE ELF IN A FAR-AWAY FOREST HAS BEEN MEETING WITH HER IN HER DREAMS.
I... DIDN'T LIKE THE SOUND OF IT... DIDN'T WANT TO BELIEVE.
BUT NOW I MUST!
"A STRANGE ELF"? ONE WHO HAS THE POWER OF MIND AND SOUL TO "GO OUT" AND FIND US --
-- EXPOSE US -- WHEN STAYING UNKNOWN HAS BEEN THE KEY TO OUR SURVIVAL?!
AND YOU THOUGHT THIS UNWORTHY OF MENTION?!!

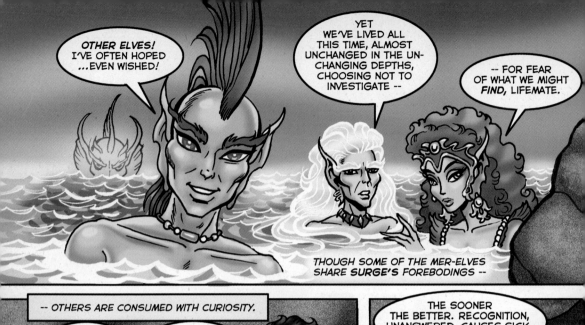

OTHER ELVES! I'VE OFTEN HOPED ...EVEN WISHED!

YET WE'VE LIVED ALL THIS TIME, ALMOST UNCHANGED IN THE UN-CHANGING DEPTHS, CHOOSING NOT TO INVESTIGATE --

-- FOR FEAR OF WHAT WE MIGHT *FIND*, LIFEMATE.

THOUGH SOME OF THE MER-ELVES SHARE SURGE'S FOREBODINGS --

-- OTHERS ARE CONSUMED WITH CURIOSITY.

WHAT'S A *LAND* FOREST LIKE?

NEVER MIND *THAT!* WHAT ARE THE *STRANGERS* LIKE?

HOW SOON CAN WE MEET THEM?

THE SOONER THE BETTER. RECOGNITION, UNANSWERED, CAUSES SICK-NESS AND PAIN.

FOR *BRILL'S* SAKE, SHE *MUST* MEET AND JOIN WITH THE ONE CALLED *SUNSTREAM!*

BUT *HOW?*

MY LOVE HAS TOLD ME OF THE *CRYSTAL PALACE*...THE VESSEL THAT BROUGHT THE *HIGH ONES*, COUNTLESS TIDES AGO, TO THIS WORLD.

HE IS SO WONDERFUL! HE CAN FLY IT *ANYWHERE* IN THE FLICK OF A FIN ...TO THE STARS...OR UNDER THE SEA!

IRREVERENT TO MENTION OUR MOST ANCIENT ANCESTORS SO *CASUALLY!*

"PAH-LASSS... PAH-LASSS..." THE PALACE!

THIS STRANGER *COMMANDS* IT, SHE SAYS!

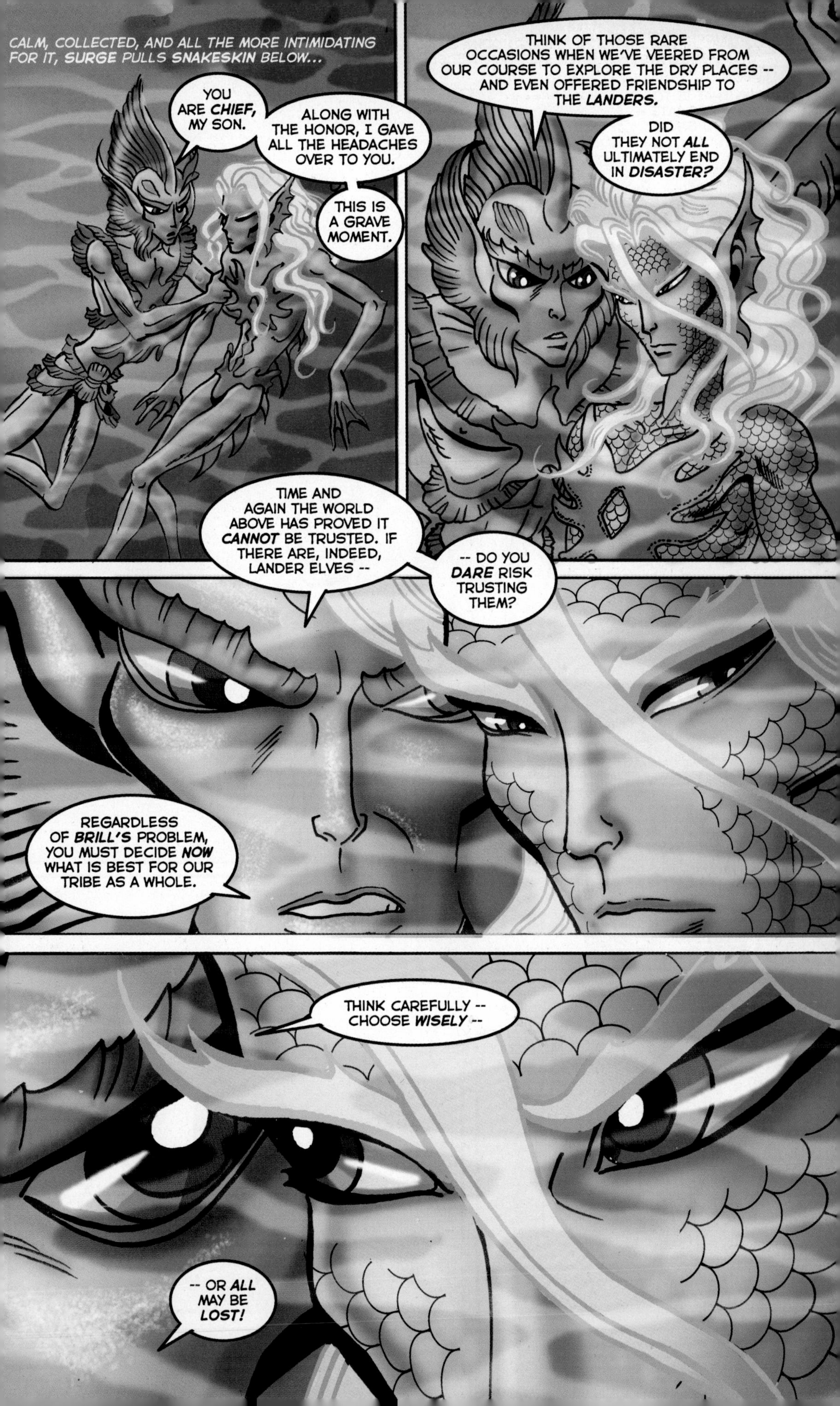
CALM, COLLECTED, AND ALL THE MORE INTIMIDATING FOR IT, SURGE PULLS SNAKESKIN BELOW...
YOU ARE CHIEF, MY SON.
ALONG WITH THE HONOR, I GAVE ALL THE HEADACHES OVER TO YOU.
THIS IS A GRAVE MOMENT.
THINK OF THOSE RARE OCCASIONS WHEN WE'VE VEERED FROM OUR COURSE TO EXPLORE THE DRY PLACES -- AND EVEN OFFERED FRIENDSHIP TO THE LANDERS.
DID THEY NOT ALL ULTIMATELY END IN DISASTER?
TIME AND AGAIN THE WORLD ABOVE HAS PROVED IT CANNOT BE TRUSTED. IF THERE ARE, INDEED, LANDER ELVES --
-- DO YOU DARE RISK TRUSTING THEM?
REGARDLESS OF BRILL'S PROBLEM, YOU MUST DECIDE NOW WHAT IS BEST FOR OUR TRIBE AS A WHOLE.
THINK CAREFULLY -- CHOOSE WISELY --
-- OR ALL MAY BE LOST!

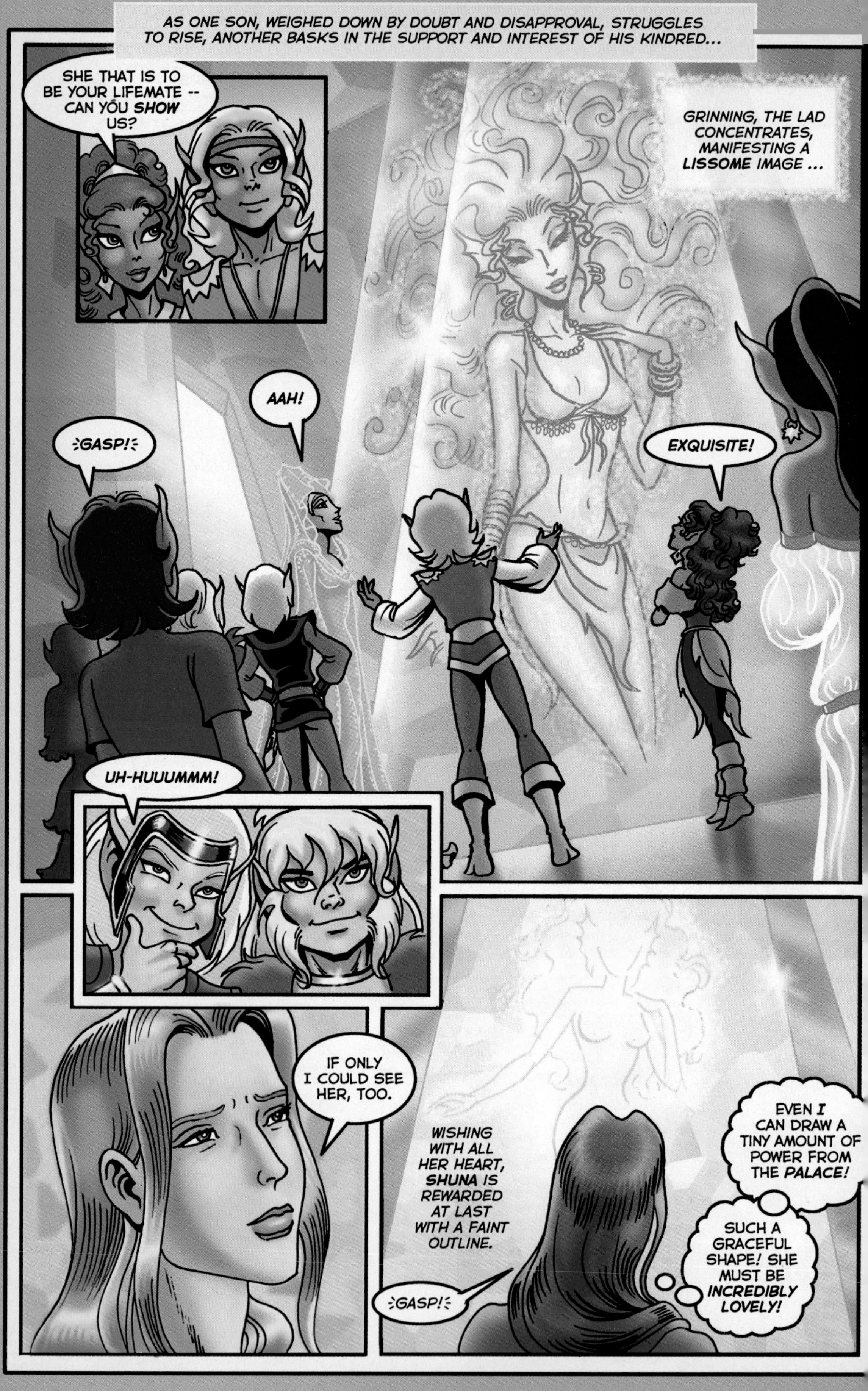
AS ONE SON, WEIGHED DOWN BY DOUBT AND DISAPPROVAL, STRUGGLES TO RISE, ANOTHER BASKS IN THE SUPPORT AND INTEREST OF HIS KINDRED...
SHE THAT IS TO BE YOUR LIFEMATE -- CAN YOU SHOW US?
GRINNING, THE LAD CONCENTRATES, MANIFESTING A LISSOME IMAGE ...
AAH!
GASP!
EXQUISITE!
UH-HUUUMMM!
IF ONLY I COULD SEE HER, TOO.
WISHING WITH ALL HER HEART, SHUNA IS REWARDED AT LAST WITH A FAINT OUTLINE.
GASP!
EVEN I CAN DRAW A TINY AMOUNT OF POWER FROM THE PALACE!
SUCH A GRACEFUL SHAPE! SHE MUST BE INCREDIBLY LOVELY!

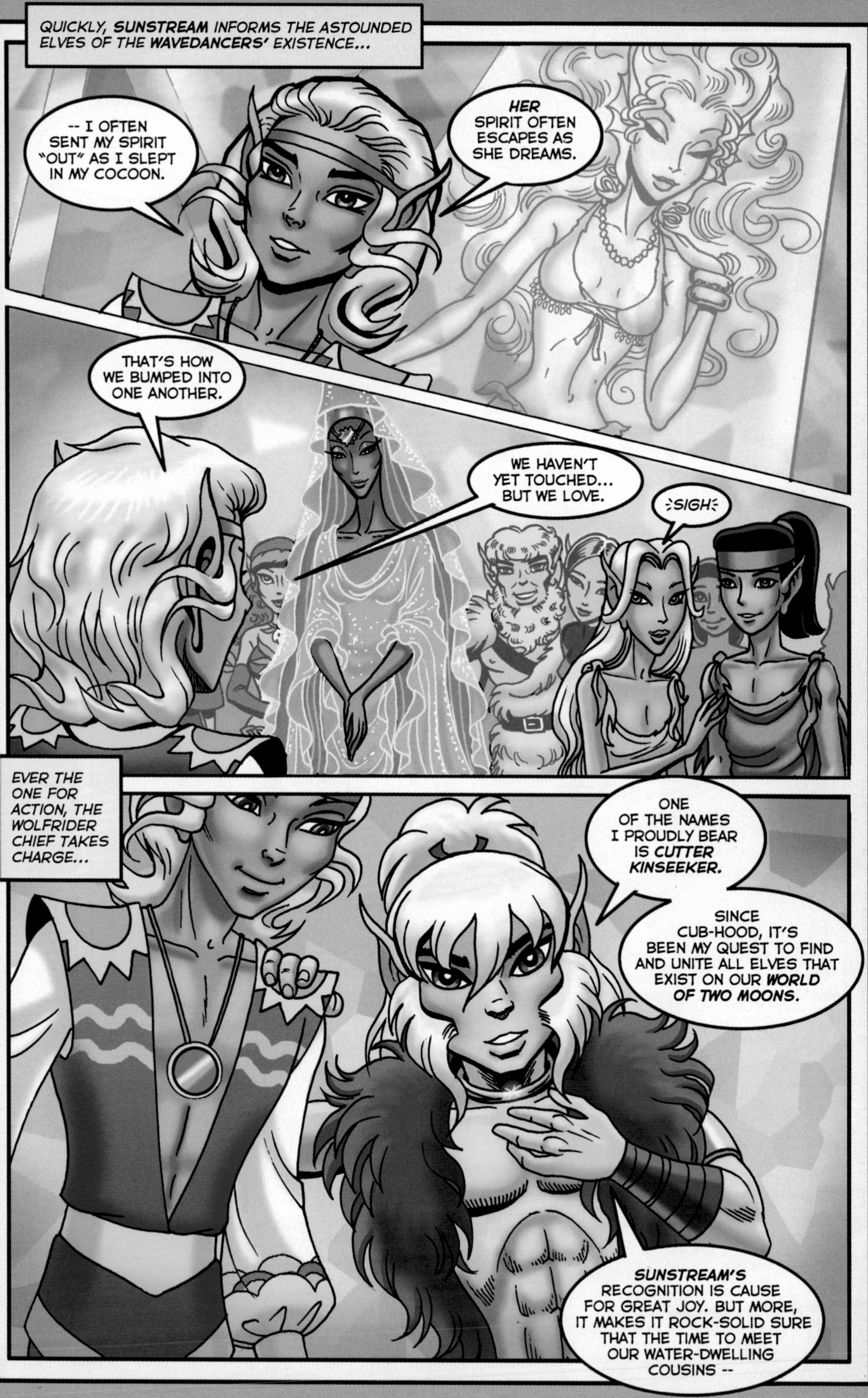
QUICKLY, SUNSTREAM INFORMS THE ASTOUNDED ELVES OF THE WAVEDANCERS' EXISTENCE...
-- I OFTEN SENT MY SPIRIT "OUT" AS I SLEPT IN MY COCOON.
HER SPIRIT OFTEN ESCAPES AS SHE DREAMS.
THAT'S HOW WE BUMPED INTO ONE ANOTHER.
WE HAVEN'T YET TOUCHED... BUT WE LOVE.
SIGH
EVER THE ONE FOR ACTION, THE WOLFRIDER CHIEF TAKES CHARGE...
ONE OF THE NAMES I PROUDLY BEAR IS CUTTER KINSEEKER.
SINCE CUB-HOOD, IT'S BEEN MY QUEST TO FIND AND UNITE ALL ELVES THAT EXIST ON OUR WORLD OF TWO MOONS.
SUNSTREAM'S RECOGNITION IS CAUSE FOR GREAT JOY. BUT MORE, IT MAKES IT ROCK-SOLID SURE THAT THE TIME TO MEET OUR WATER-DWELLING COUSINS --

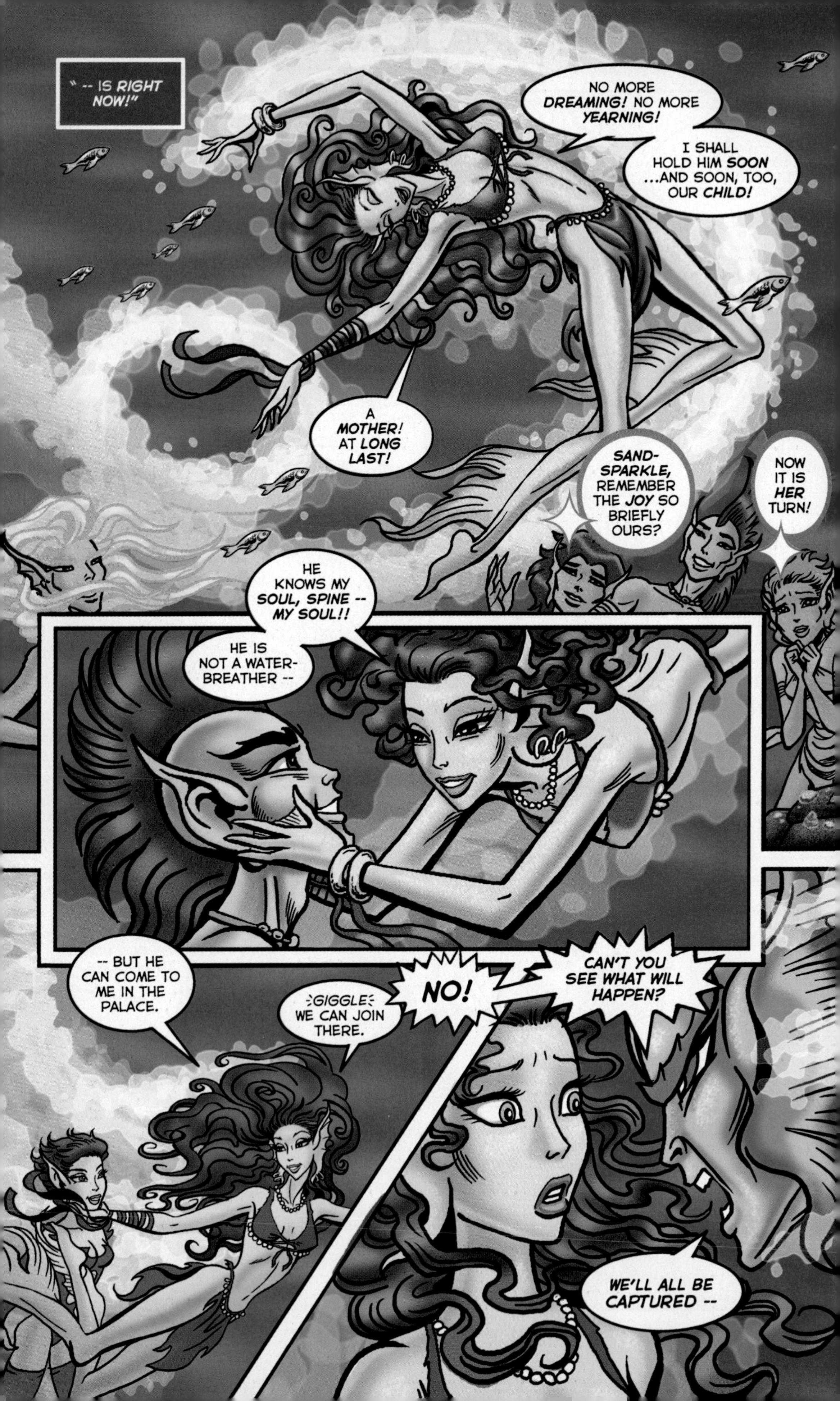

"-- IS RIGHT NOW!"
NO MORE DREAMING! NO MORE YEARNING!
I SHALL HOLD HIM SOON ...AND SOON, TOO, OUR CHILD!
A MOTHER! AT LONG LAST!
SAND-SPARKLE, REMEMBER THE JOY SO BRIEFLY OURS?
NOW IT IS HER TURN!
HE KNOWS MY SOUL, SPINE -- MY SOUL!!
HE IS NOT A WATER-BREATHER --
-- BUT HE CAN COME TO ME IN THE PALACE.
GIGGLE WE CAN JOIN THERE.
NO!
CAN'T YOU SEE WHAT WILL HAPPEN?
WE'LL ALL BE CAPTURED --

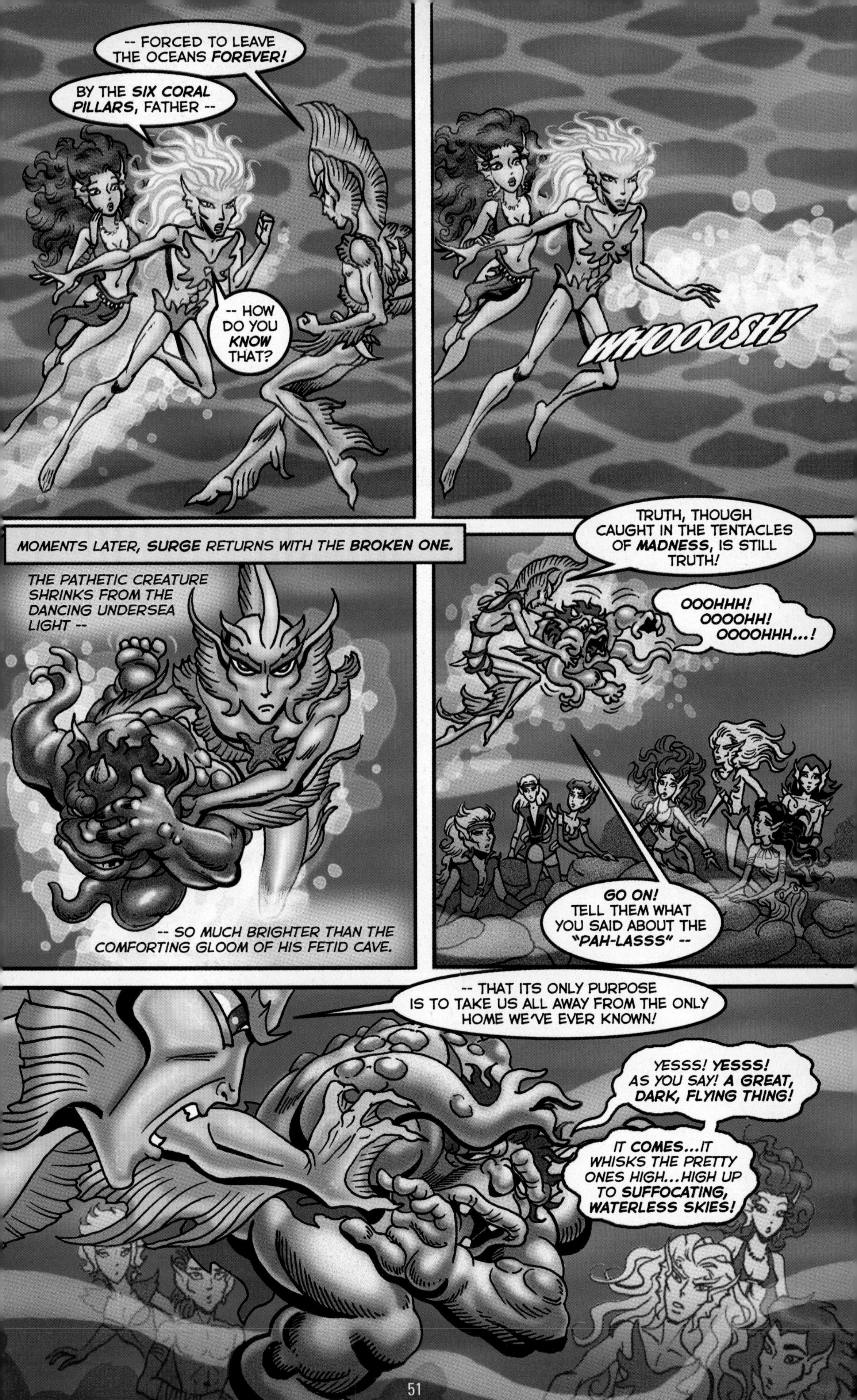
-- FORCED TO LEAVE THE OCEANS FOREVER!
BY THE SIX CORAL PILLARS, FATHER --
-- HOW DO YOU KNOW THAT?
WHOOOOSH!
MOMENTS LATER, SURGE RETURNS WITH THE BROKEN ONE.
THE PATHETIC CREATURE SHRINKS FROM THE DANCING UNDERSEA LIGHT --
-- SO MUCH BRIGHTER THAN THE COMFORTING GLOOM OF HIS FETID CAVE.
TRUTH, THOUGH CAUGHT IN THE TENTACLES OF MADNESS, IS STILL TRUTH!
OOOHHH! OOOOHH! OOOOHHH...!
GO ON! TELL THEM WHAT YOU SAID ABOUT THE "PAH-LASSS" --
-- THAT ITS ONLY PURPOSE IS TO TAKE US ALL AWAY FROM THE ONLY HOME WE'VE EVER KNOWN!
YESSS! YESSS! AS YOU SAY! A GREAT, DARK, FLYING THING!
IT COMES...IT WHISKS THE PRETTY ONES HIGH...HIGH UP TO SUFFOCATING, WATERLESS SKIES!

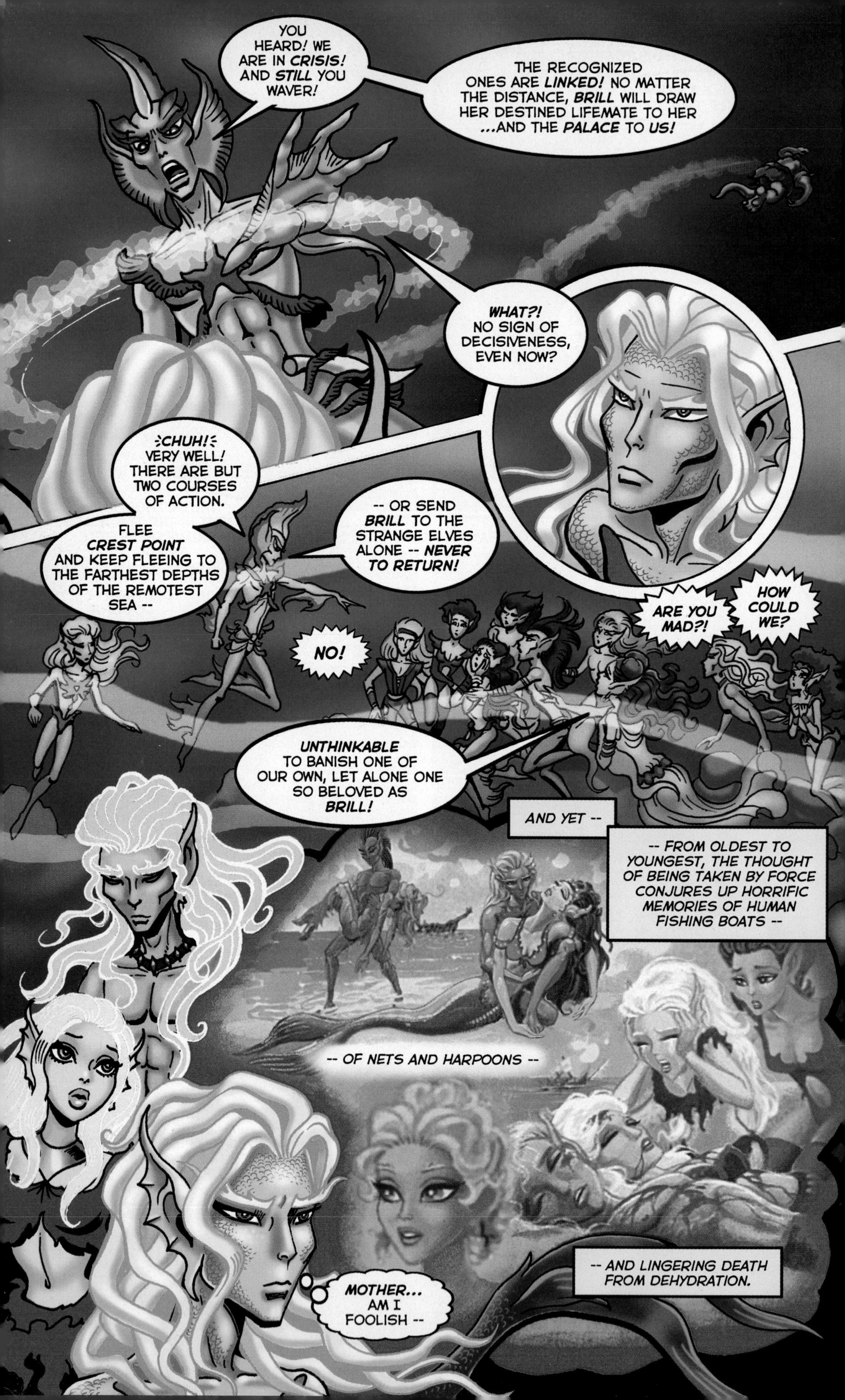
YOU HEARD! WE ARE IN CRISIS! AND STILL YOU WAVER!
THE RECOGNIZED ONES ARE LINKED! NO MATTER THE DISTANCE, BRILL WILL DRAW HER DESTINED LIFEMATE TO HER ...AND THE PALACE TO US!
WHAT?! NO SIGN OF DECISIVENESS, EVEN NOW?
CHUH! VERY WELL! THERE ARE BUT TWO COURSES OF ACTION.
FLEE CREST POINT AND KEEP FLEEING TO THE FARTHEST DEPTHS OF THE REMOTEST SEA --
-- OR SEND BRILL TO THE STRANGE ELVES ALONE -- NEVER TO RETURN!
NO!
ARE YOU MAD?!
HOW COULD WE?
UNTHINKABLE TO BANISH ONE OF OUR OWN, LET ALONE ONE SO BELOVED AS BRILL!
AND YET --
-- FROM OLDEST TO YOUNGEST, THE THOUGHT OF BEING TAKEN BY FORCE CONJURES UP HORRIFIC MEMORIES OF HUMAN FISHING BOATS --
-- OF NETS AND HARPOONS --
-- AND LINGERING DEATH FROM DEHYDRATION.
MOTHER... AM I FOOLISH --

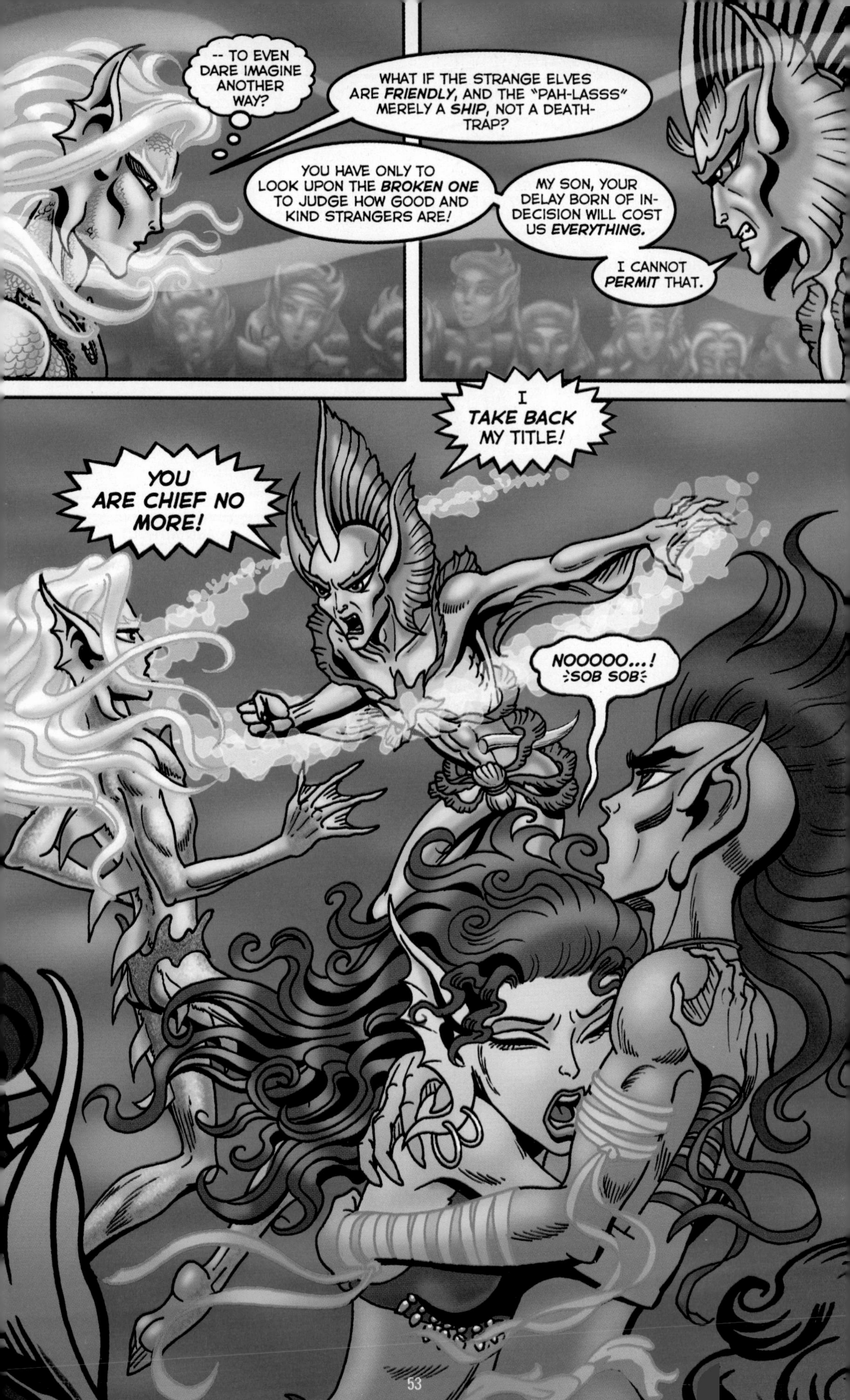
-- TO EVEN DARE IMAGINE ANOTHER WAY?
WHAT IF THE STRANGE ELVES ARE FRIENDLY, AND THE "PAH-LASSS" MERELY A SHIP, NOT A DEATH-TRAP?
YOU HAVE ONLY TO LOOK UPON THE BROKEN ONE TO JUDGE HOW GOOD AND KIND STRANGERS ARE!
MY SON, YOUR DELAY BORN OF IN-DECISION WILL COST US EVERYTHING.
I CANNOT PERMIT THAT.
I TAKE BACK MY TITLE!
YOU ARE CHIEF NO MORE!
NOOOOO...! SOB SOB

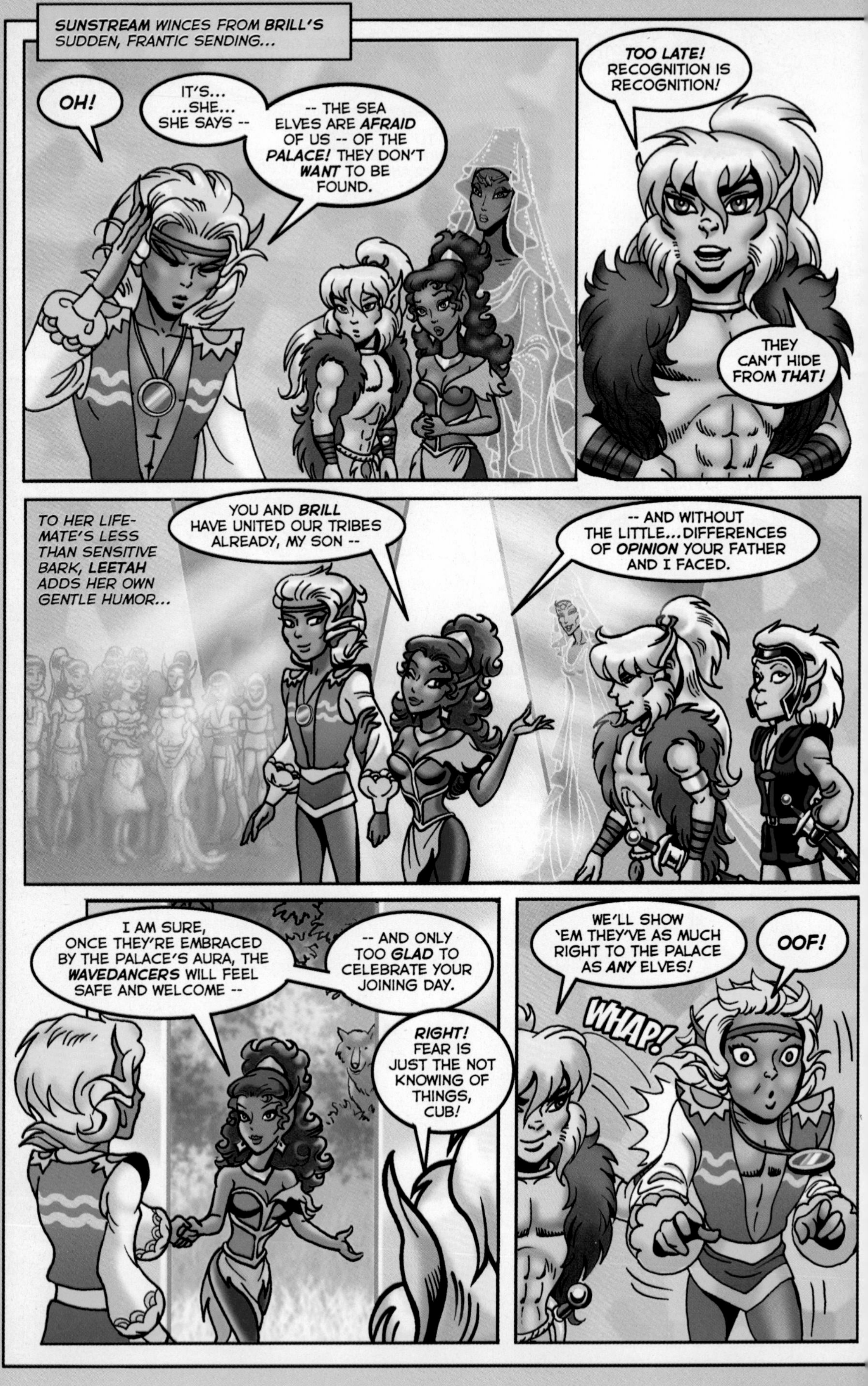

SUNSTREAM WINCES FROM BRILL'S SUDDEN, FRANTIC SENDING...
OH!
IT'S... ...SHE... SHE SAYS --
-- THE SEA ELVES ARE AFRAID OF US -- OF THE PALACE! THEY DON'T WANT TO BE FOUND.
TOO LATE! RECOGNITION IS RECOGNITION!
THEY CAN'T HIDE FROM THAT!
TO HER LIFE-MATE'S LESS THAN SENSITIVE BARK, LEETAH ADDS HER OWN GENTLE HUMOR...
YOU AND BRILL HAVE UNITED OUR TRIBES ALREADY, MY SON --
-- AND WITHOUT THE LITTLE...DIFFERENCES OF OPINION YOUR FATHER AND I FACED.
I AM SURE, ONCE THEY'RE EMBRACED BY THE PALACE'S AURA, THE WAVEDANCERS WILL FEEL SAFE AND WELCOME --
-- AND ONLY TOO GLAD TO CELEBRATE YOUR JOINING DAY.
RIGHT! FEAR IS JUST THE NOT KNOWING OF THINGS, CUB!
WE'LL SHOW 'EM THEY'VE AS MUCH RIGHT TO THE PALACE AS ANY ELVES!
WHAP!
OOF!

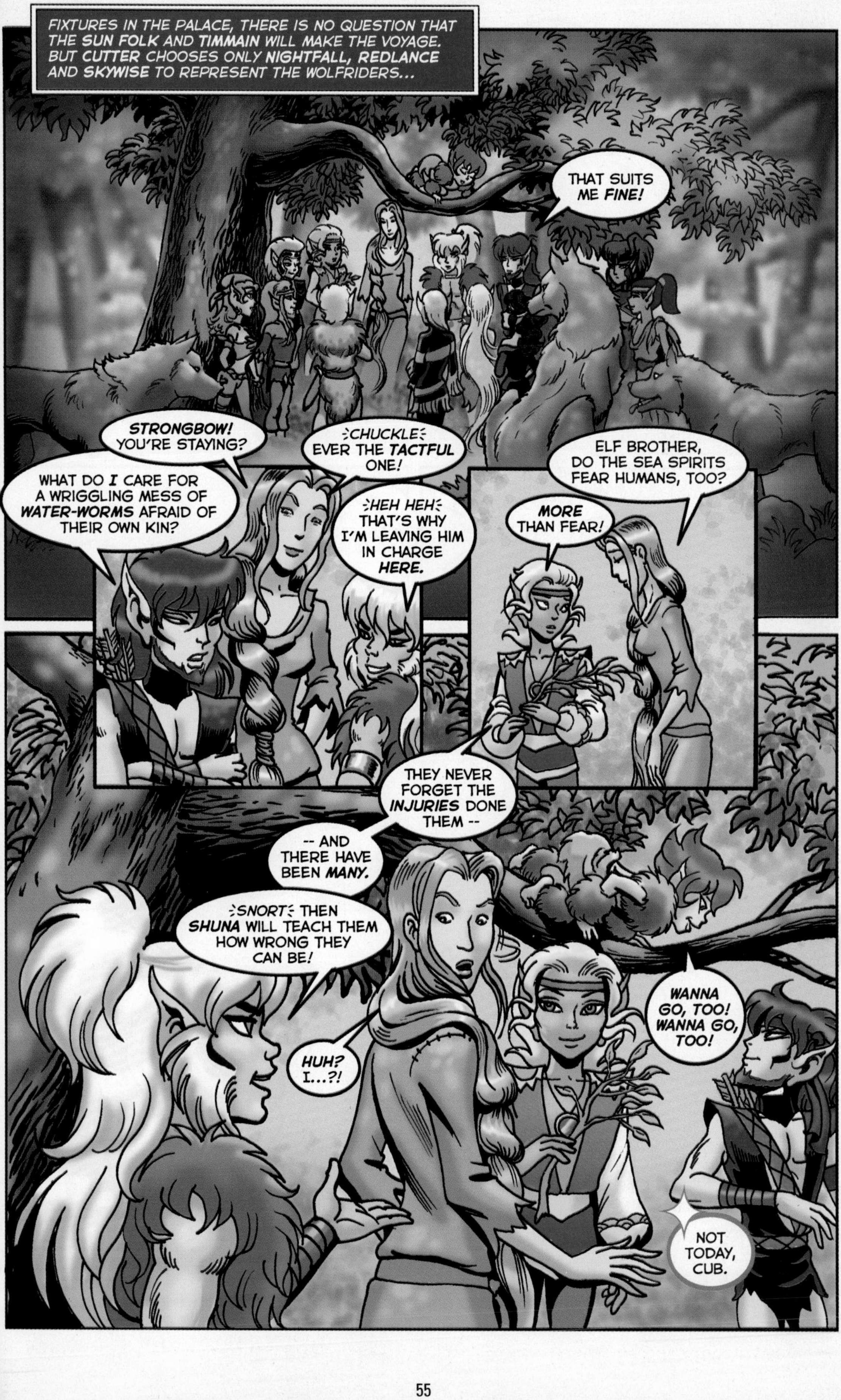
FIXTURES IN THE PALACE, THERE IS NO QUESTION THAT THE SUN FOLK AND TIMMAIN WILL MAKE THE VOYAGE. BUT CUTTER CHOOSES ONLY NIGHTFALL, REDLANCE AND SKYWISE TO REPRESENT THE WOLFRIDERS...
THAT SUITS ME FINE!
STRONGBOW! YOU'RE STAYING?
WHAT DO I CARE FOR A WRIGGLING MESS OF WATER-WORMS AFRAID OF THEIR OWN KIN?
CHUCKLE EVER THE TACTFUL ONE!
HEH HEH THAT'S WHY I'M LEAVING HIM IN CHARGE HERE.
ELF BROTHER, DO THE SEA SPIRITS FEAR HUMANS, TOO?
MORE THAN FEAR!
THEY NEVER FORGET THE INJURIES DONE THEM --
-- AND THERE HAVE BEEN MANY.
SNORT THEN SHUNA WILL TEACH THEM HOW WRONG THEY CAN BE!
HUH? I...?!
WANNA GO, TOO! WANNA GO, TOO!
NOT TODAY, CUB.

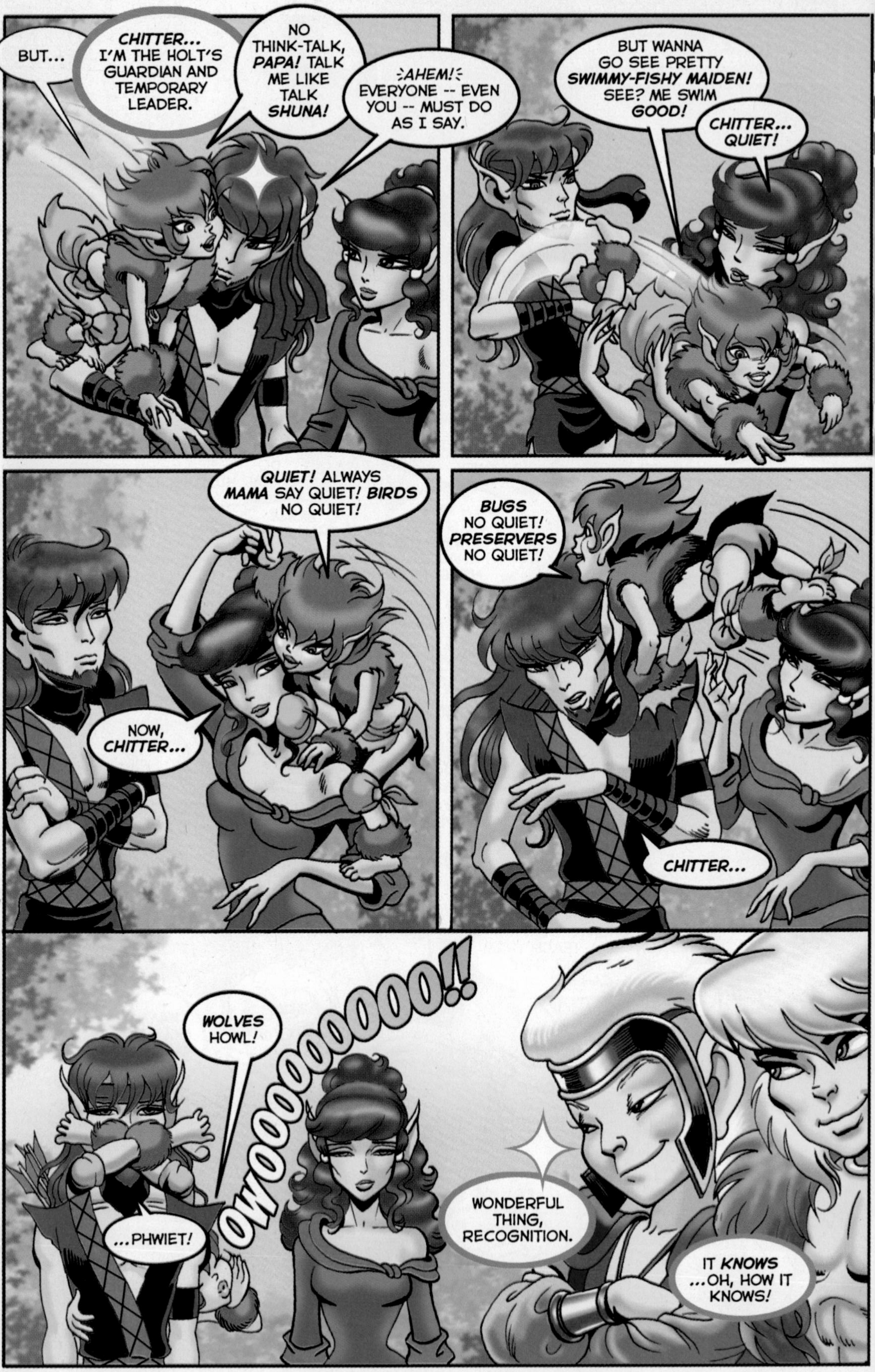
BUT...
CHITTER... I'M THE HOLT'S GUARDIAN AND TEMPORARY LEADER.
NO THINK-TALK, PAPA! TALK ME LIKE TALK SHUNA!
AHEM! EVERYONE -- EVEN YOU -- MUST DO AS I SAY.
BUT WANNA GO SEE PRETTY SWIMMY-FISHY MAIDEN! SEE? ME SWIM GOOD!
CHITTER... QUIET!
QUIET! ALWAYS MAMA SAY QUIET! BIRDS NO QUIET!
NOW, CHITTER...
BUGS NO QUIET! PRESERVERS NO QUIET!
CHITTER...
WOLVES HOWL!
OWOOOOOOOOOO!!
...PHWIET!
WONDERFUL THING, RECOGNITION.
IT KNOWS ...OH, HOW IT KNOWS!

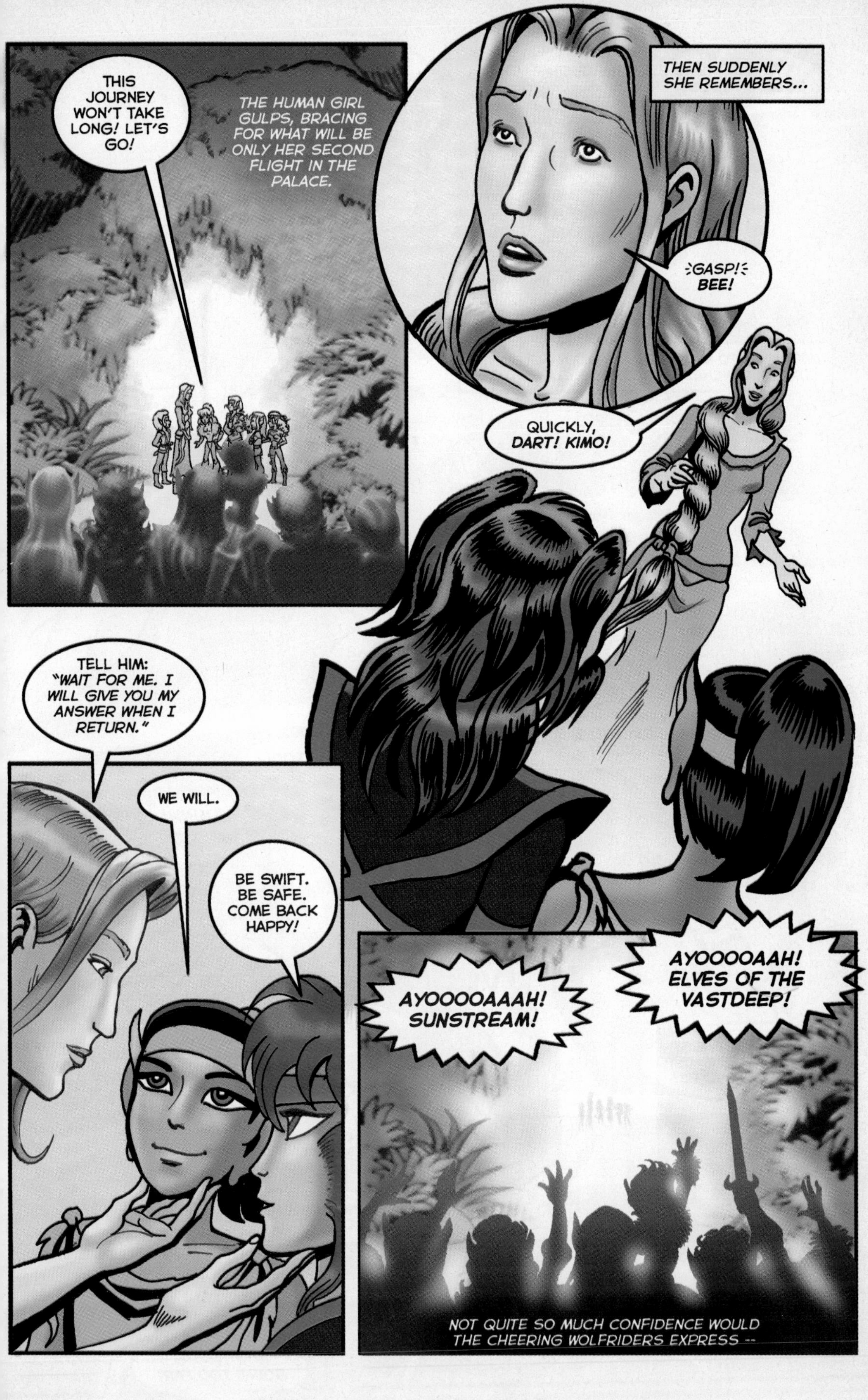

THIS JOURNEY WON'T TAKE LONG! LET'S GO!
THE HUMAN GIRL GULPS, BRACING FOR WHAT WILL BE ONLY HER SECOND FLIGHT IN THE PALACE.
THEN SUDDENLY SHE REMEMBERS...
GASP! BEE!
QUICKLY, DART! KIMO!
TELL HIM: "WAIT FOR ME. I WILL GIVE YOU MY ANSWER WHEN I RETURN."
WE WILL.
BE SWIFT. BE SAFE. COME BACK HAPPY!
AYOOOOAAAH! SUNSTREAM!
AYOOOOAAH! ELVES OF THE VASTDEEP!
NOT QUITE SO MUCH CONFIDENCE WOULD THE CHEERING WOLFRIDERS EXPRESS --

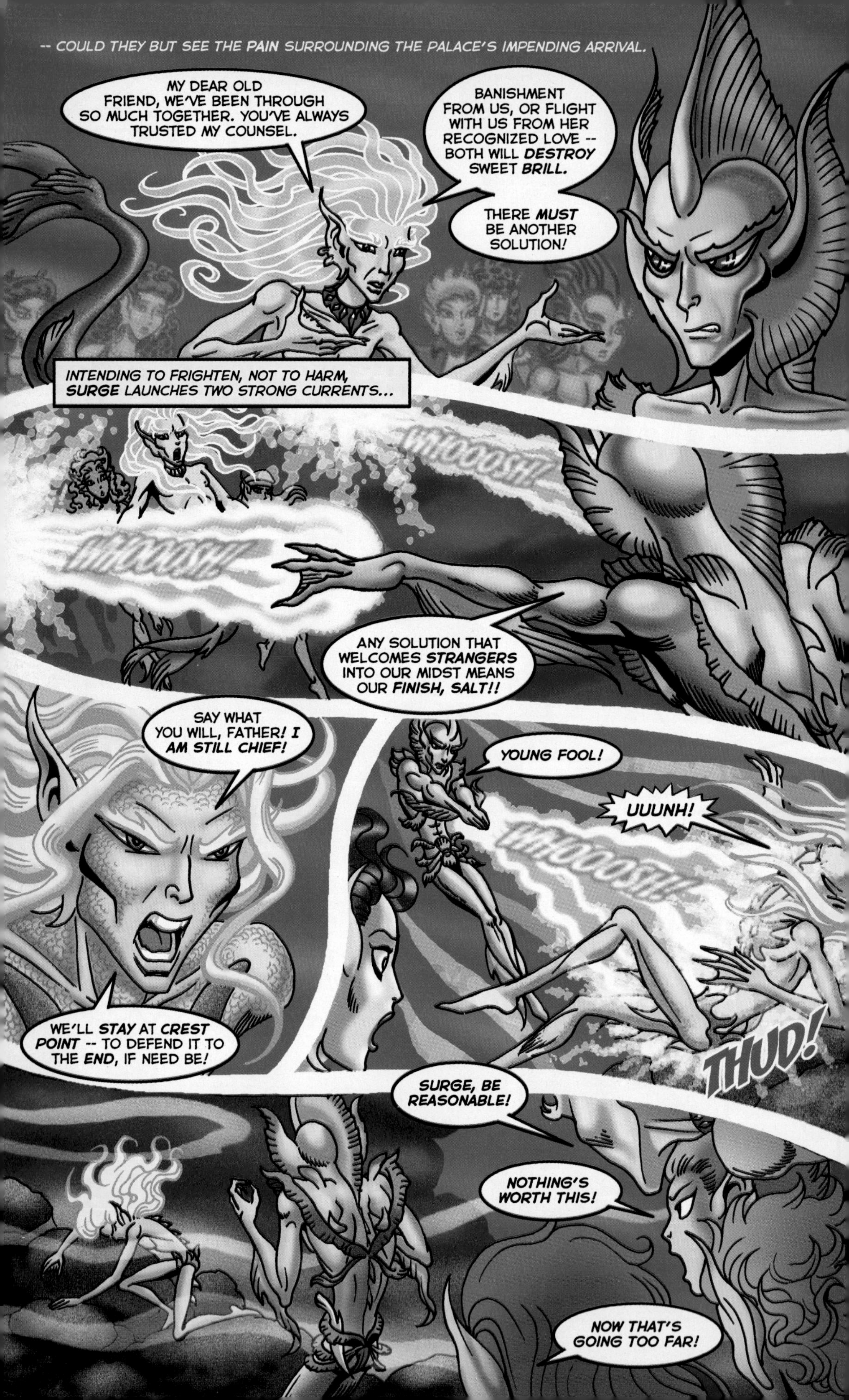
-- COULD THEY BUT SEE THE PAIN SURROUNDING THE PALACE'S IMPENDING ARRIVAL.
MY DEAR OLD FRIEND, WE'VE BEEN THROUGH SO MUCH TOGETHER. YOU'VE ALWAYS TRUSTED MY COUNSEL.
BANISHMENT FROM US, OR FLIGHT WITH US FROM HER RECOGNIZED LOVE -- BOTH WILL DESTROY SWEET BRILL.
THERE MUST BE ANOTHER SOLUTION!
INTENDING TO FRIGHTEN, NOT TO HARM, SURGE LAUNCHES TWO STRONG CURRENTS...
WHOOOSH!
WHOOOSH!
ANY SOLUTION THAT WELCOMES STRANGERS INTO OUR MIDST MEANS OUR FINISH, SALT!!
SAY WHAT YOU WILL, FATHER! I AM STILL CHIEF!
WE'LL STAY AT CREST POINT -- TO DEFEND IT TO THE END, IF NEED BE!
YOUNG FOOL!
UUUNH!
WHOOOOSH!!
THUD!
SURGE, BE REASONABLE!
NOTHING'S WORTH THIS!
NOW THAT'S GOING TOO FAR!

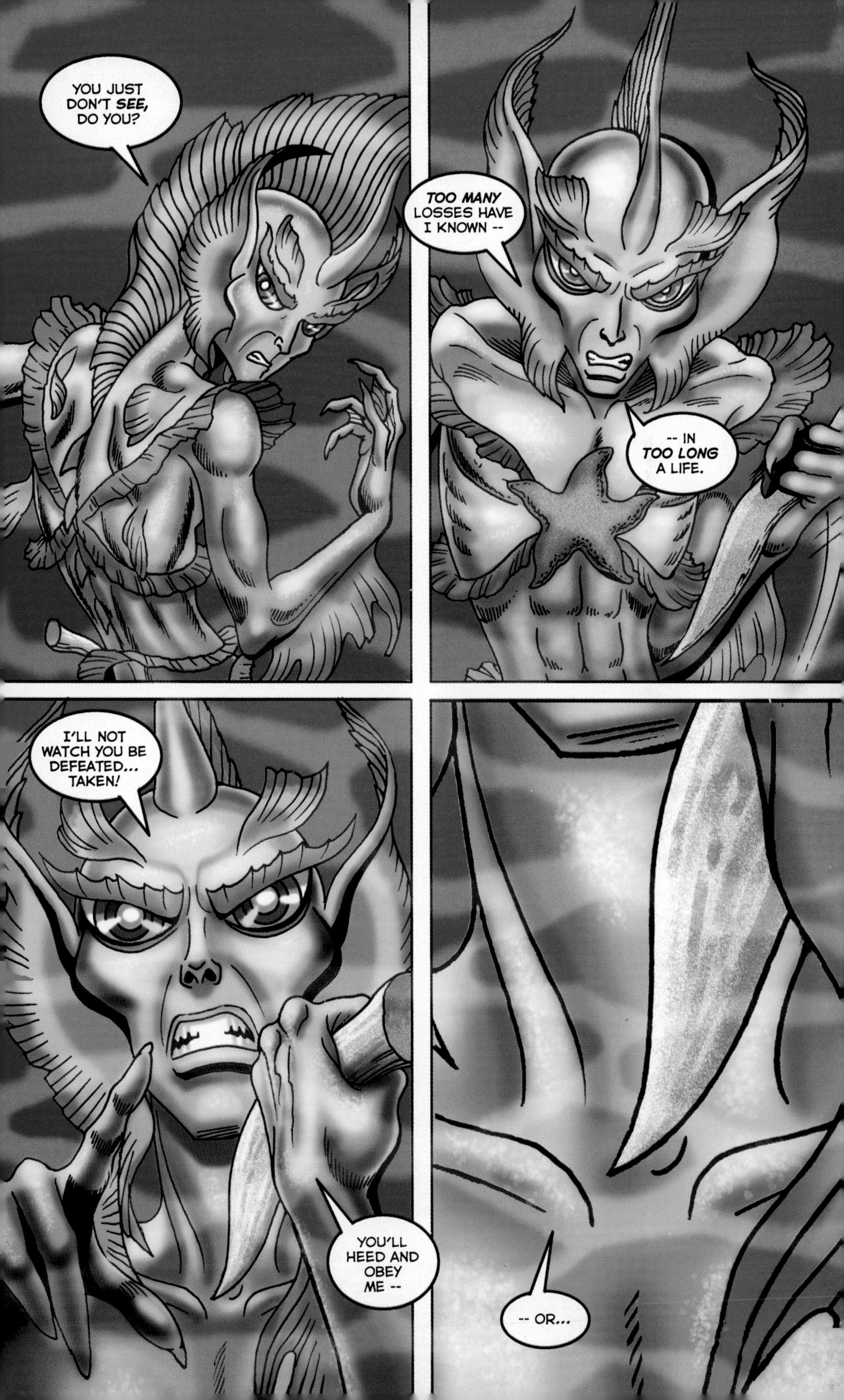
YOU JUST DON'T SEE, DO YOU?
TOO MANY LOSSES HAVE I KNOWN --
-- IN TOO LONG A LIFE.
I'LL NOT WATCH YOU BE DEFEATED... TAKEN!
YOU'LL HEED AND OBEY ME --
-- OR...

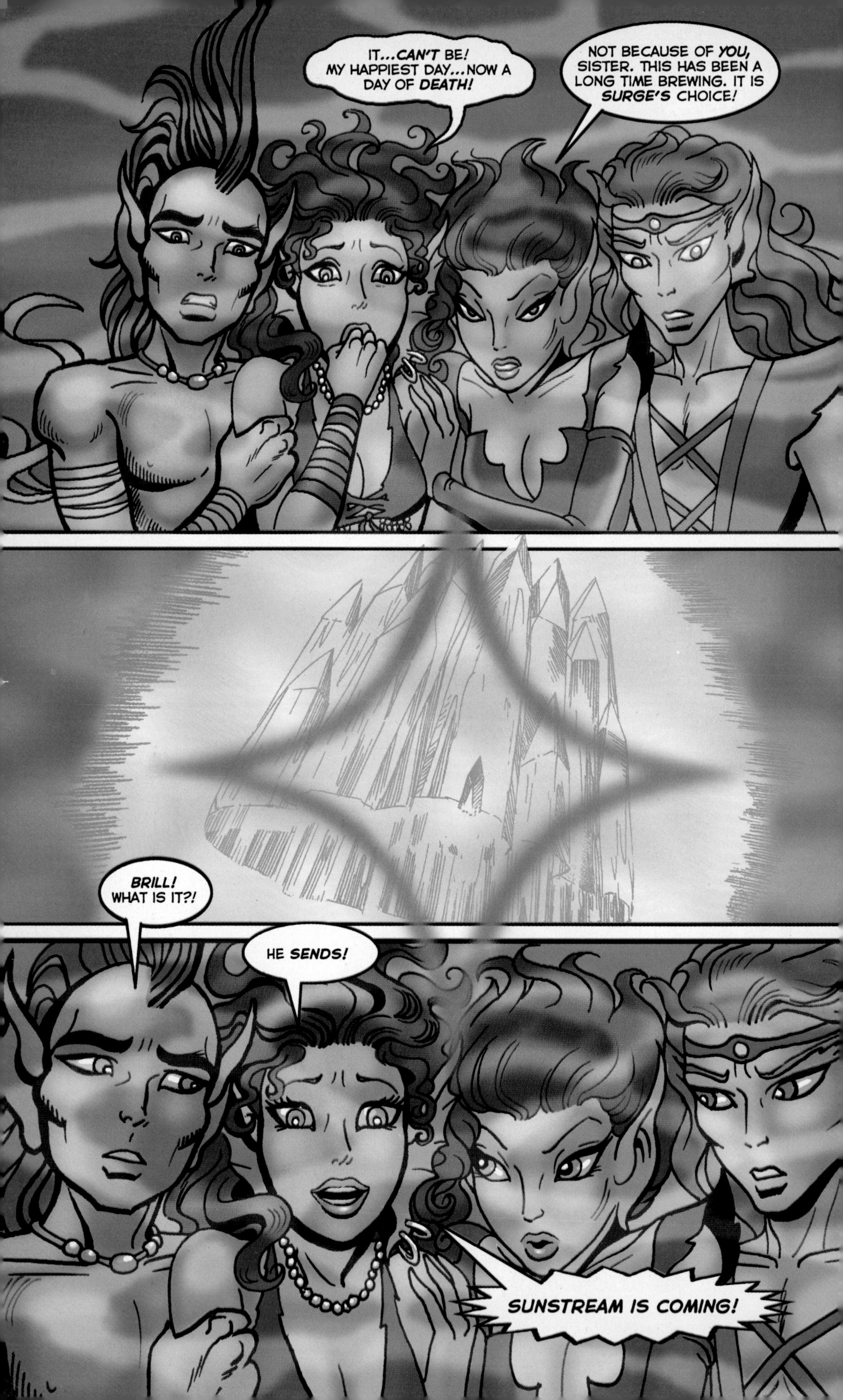
IT...CAN'T BE! MY HAPPIEST DAY...NOW A DAY OF DEATH!
NOT BECAUSE OF YOU, SISTER. THIS HAS BEEN A LONG TIME BREWING. IT IS SURGE'S CHOICE!
BRILL! WHAT IS IT?!
HE SENDS!
SUNSTREAM IS COMING!

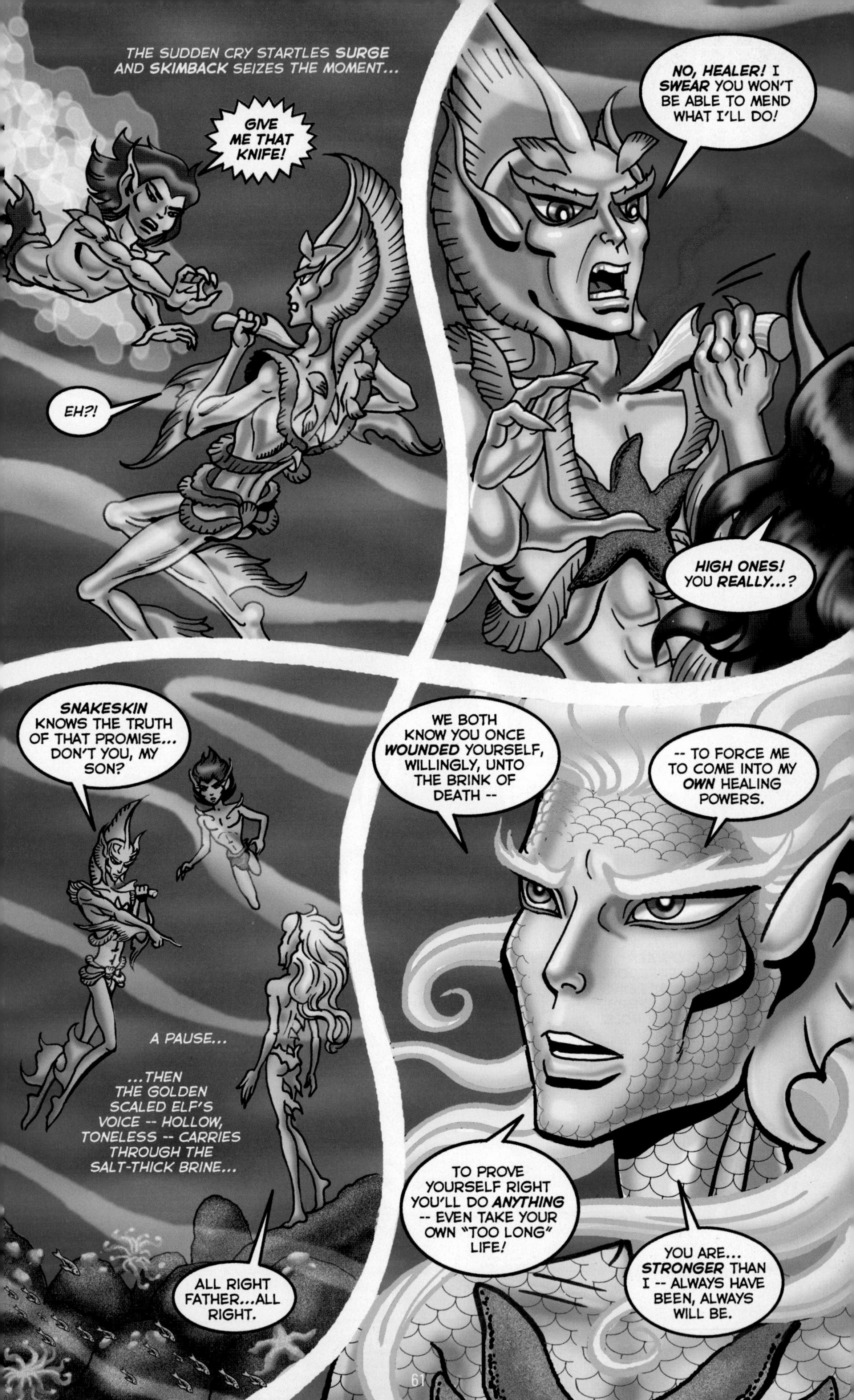
THE SUDDEN CRY STARTLES SURGE AND SKIMBACK SEIZES THE MOMENT...
GIVE ME THAT KNIFE!
EH?!
NO, HEALER! I SWEAR YOU WON'T BE ABLE TO MEND WHAT I'LL DO!
HIGH ONES! YOU REALLY...?
SNAKESKIN KNOWS THE TRUTH OF THAT PROMISE... DON'T YOU, MY SON?
A PAUSE...
...THEN THE GOLDEN SCALED ELF'S VOICE -- HOLLOW, TONELESS -- CARRIES THROUGH THE SALT-THICK BRINE...
ALL RIGHT FATHER...ALL RIGHT.
WE BOTH KNOW YOU ONCE WOUNDED YOURSELF, WILLINGLY, UNTO THE BRINK OF DEATH --
-- TO FORCE ME TO COME INTO MY OWN HEALING POWERS.
TO PROVE YOURSELF RIGHT YOU'LL DO ANYTHING -- EVEN TAKE YOUR OWN "TOO LONG" LIFE!
YOU ARE... STRONGER THAN I -- ALWAYS HAVE BEEN, ALWAYS WILL BE.

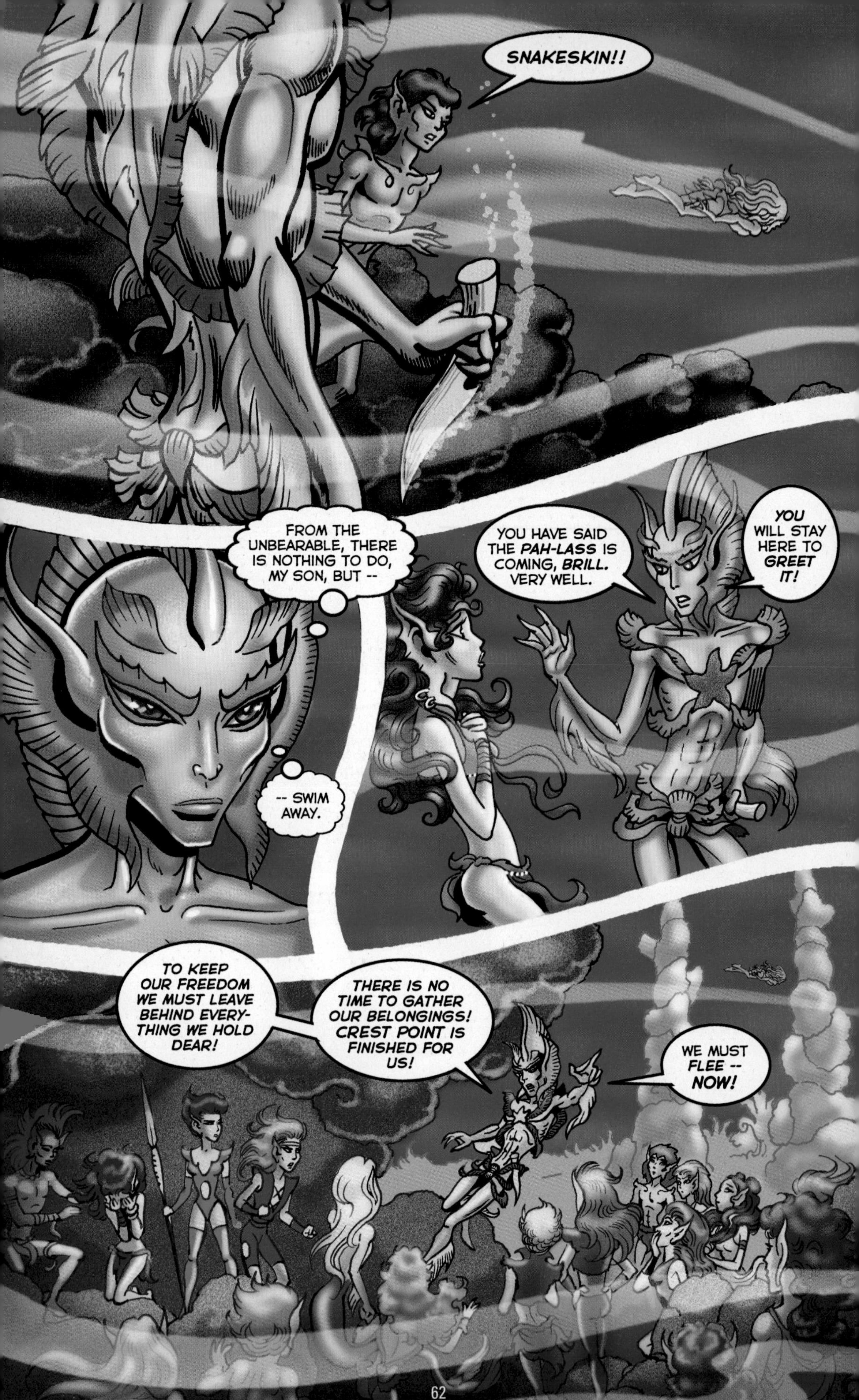
SNAKESKIN!!
FROM THE UNBEARABLE, THERE IS NOTHING TO DO, MY SON, BUT --
-- SWIM AWAY.
YOU HAVE SAID THE PAH-LASS IS COMING, BRILL. VERY WELL.
YOU WILL STAY HERE TO GREET IT!
TO KEEP OUR FREEDOM WE MUST LEAVE BEHIND EVERY-THING WE HOLD DEAR!
THERE IS NO TIME TO GATHER OUR BELONGINGS! CREST POINT IS FINISHED FOR US!
WE MUST FLEE -- NOW!

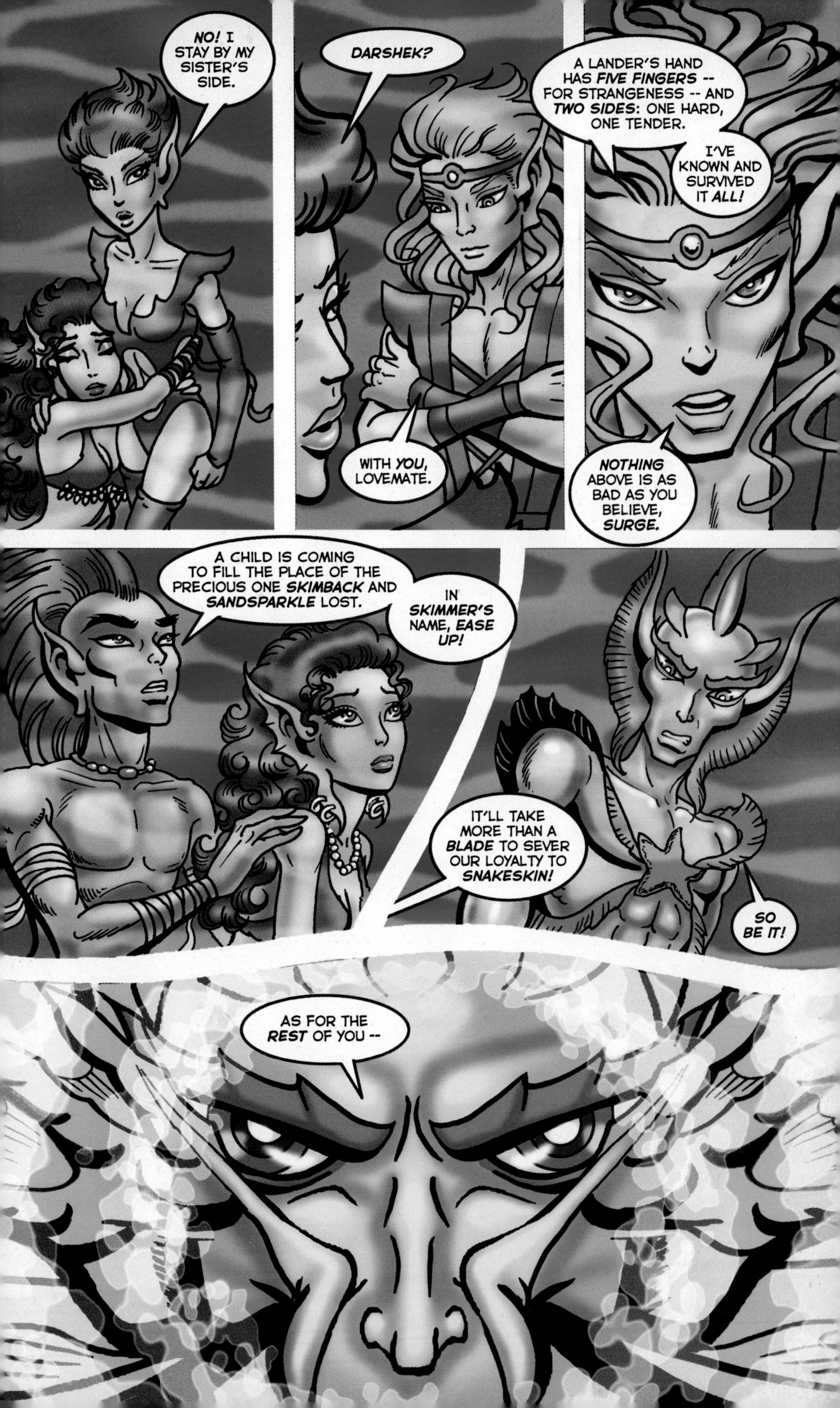

NO! I STAY BY MY SISTER'S SIDE.
DARSHEK?
WITH YOU, LOVEMATE.
A LANDER'S HAND HAS FIVE FINGERS -- FOR STRANGENESS -- AND TWO SIDES: ONE HARD, ONE TENDER.
I'VE KNOWN AND SURVIVED IT ALL!
NOTHING ABOVE IS AS BAD AS YOU BELIEVE, SURGE.
A CHILD IS COMING TO FILL THE PLACE OF THE PRECIOUS ONE SKIMBACK AND SANDSPARKLE LOST.
IN SKIMMER'S NAME, EASE UP!
IT'LL TAKE MORE THAN A BLADE TO SEVER OUR LOYALTY TO SNAKESKIN!
SO BE IT!
AS FOR THE REST OF YOU --

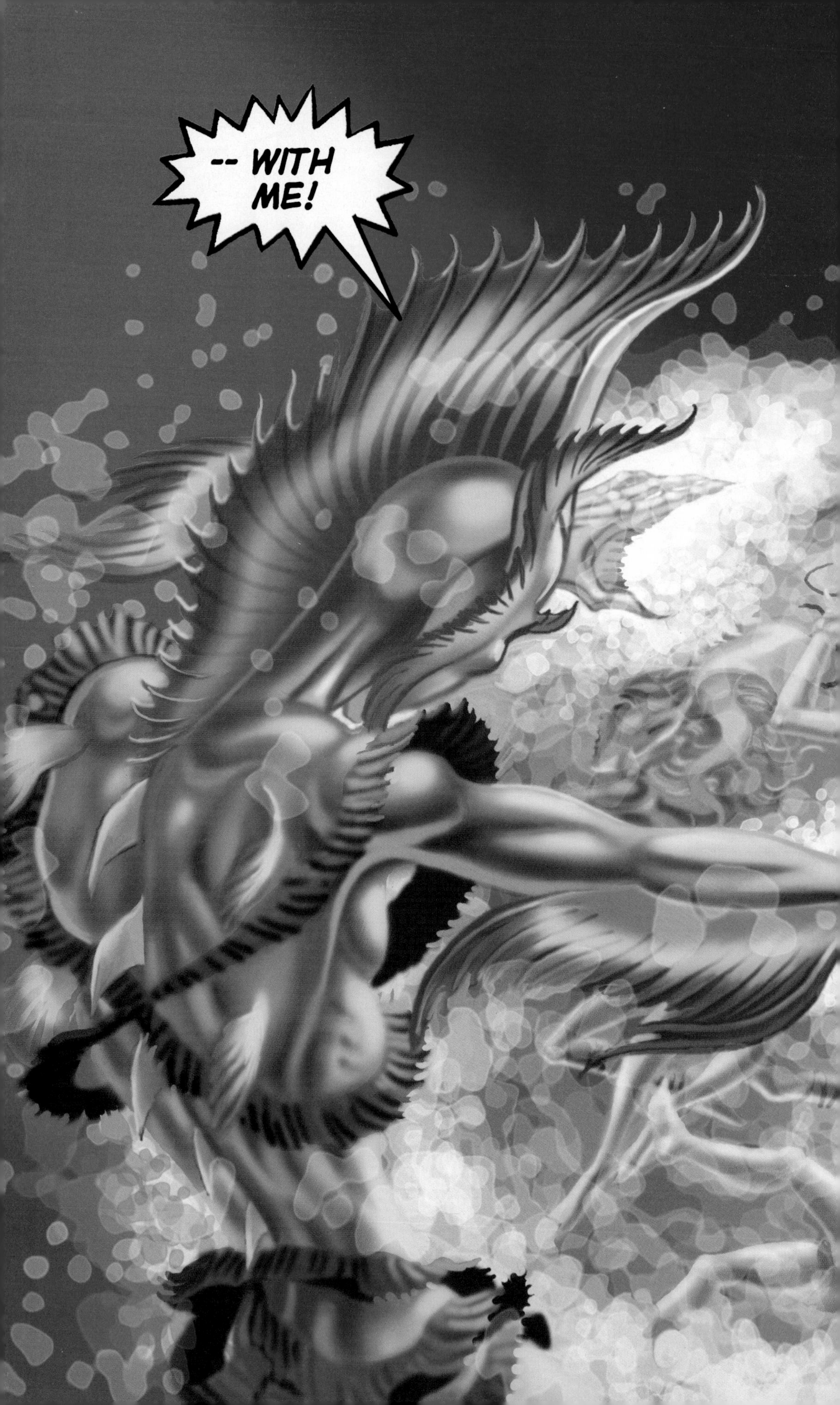
-- WITH ME!

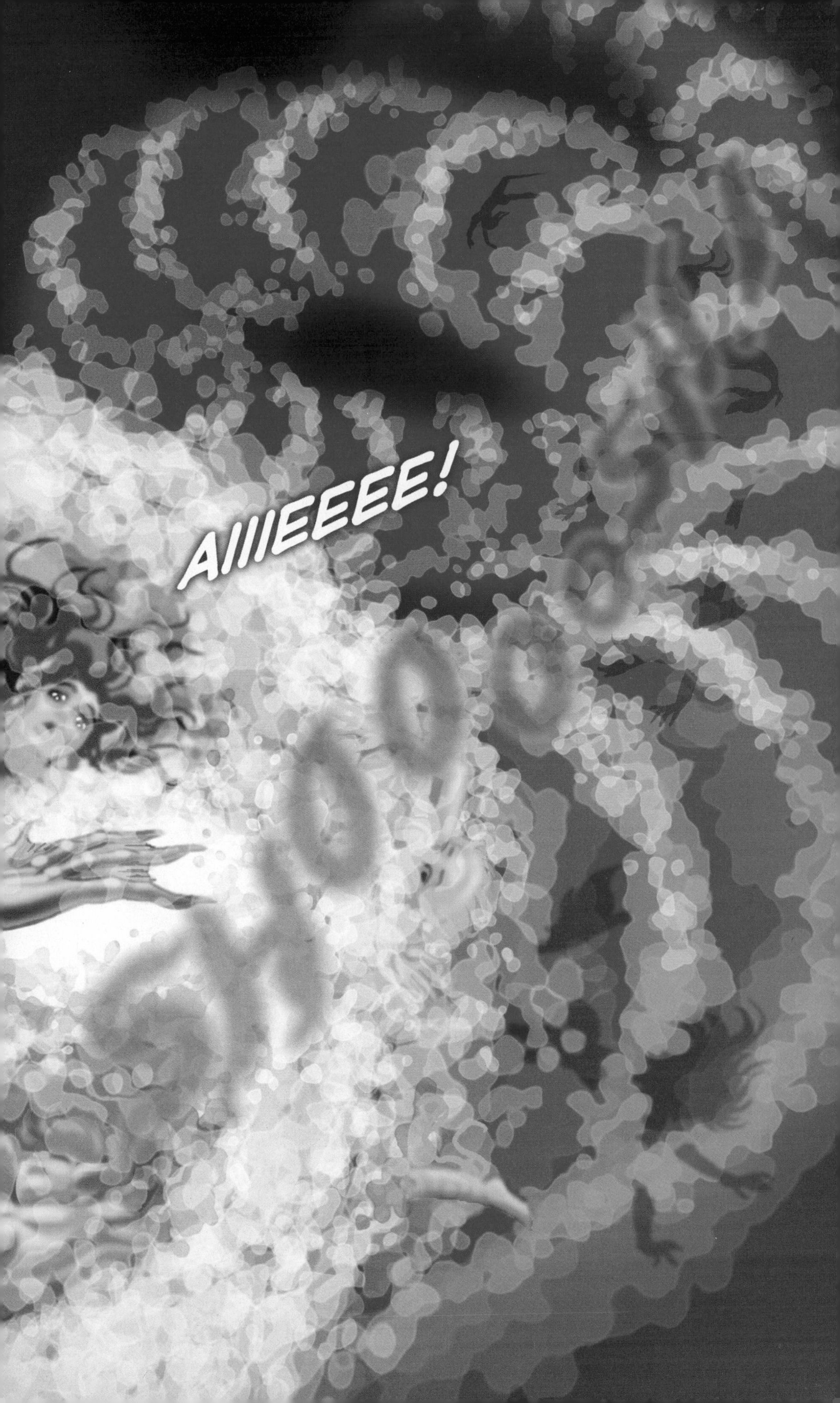
AIIIEEEE!

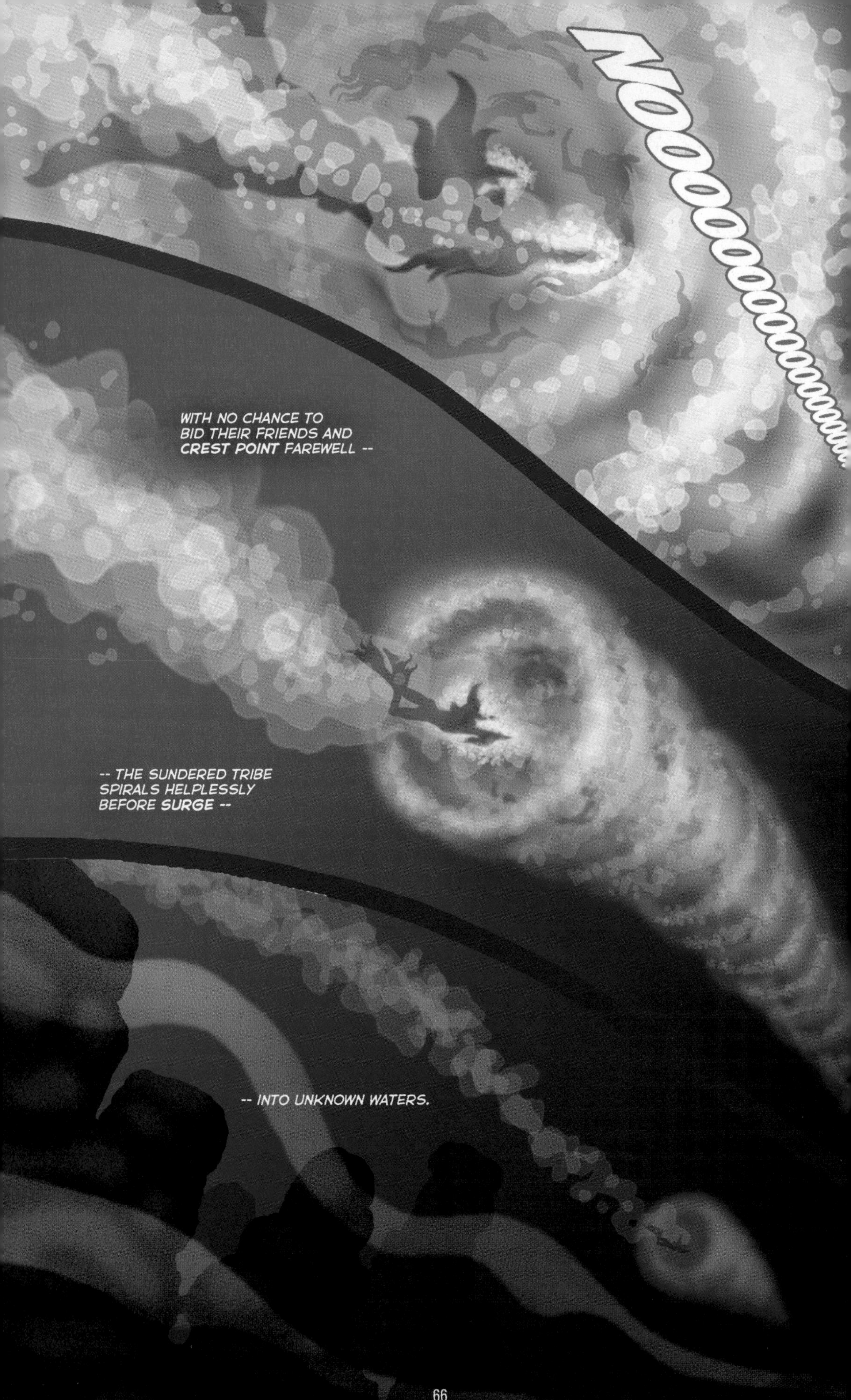
NOOOOOOOOOOOOOOOOOOOO
WITH NO CHANCE TO BID THEIR FRIENDS AND **CREST POINT** FAREWELL --
-- THE SUNDERED TRIBE SPIRALS HELPLESSLY BEFORE **SURGE** --
-- INTO UNKNOWN WATERS.

CHAPTER THREE

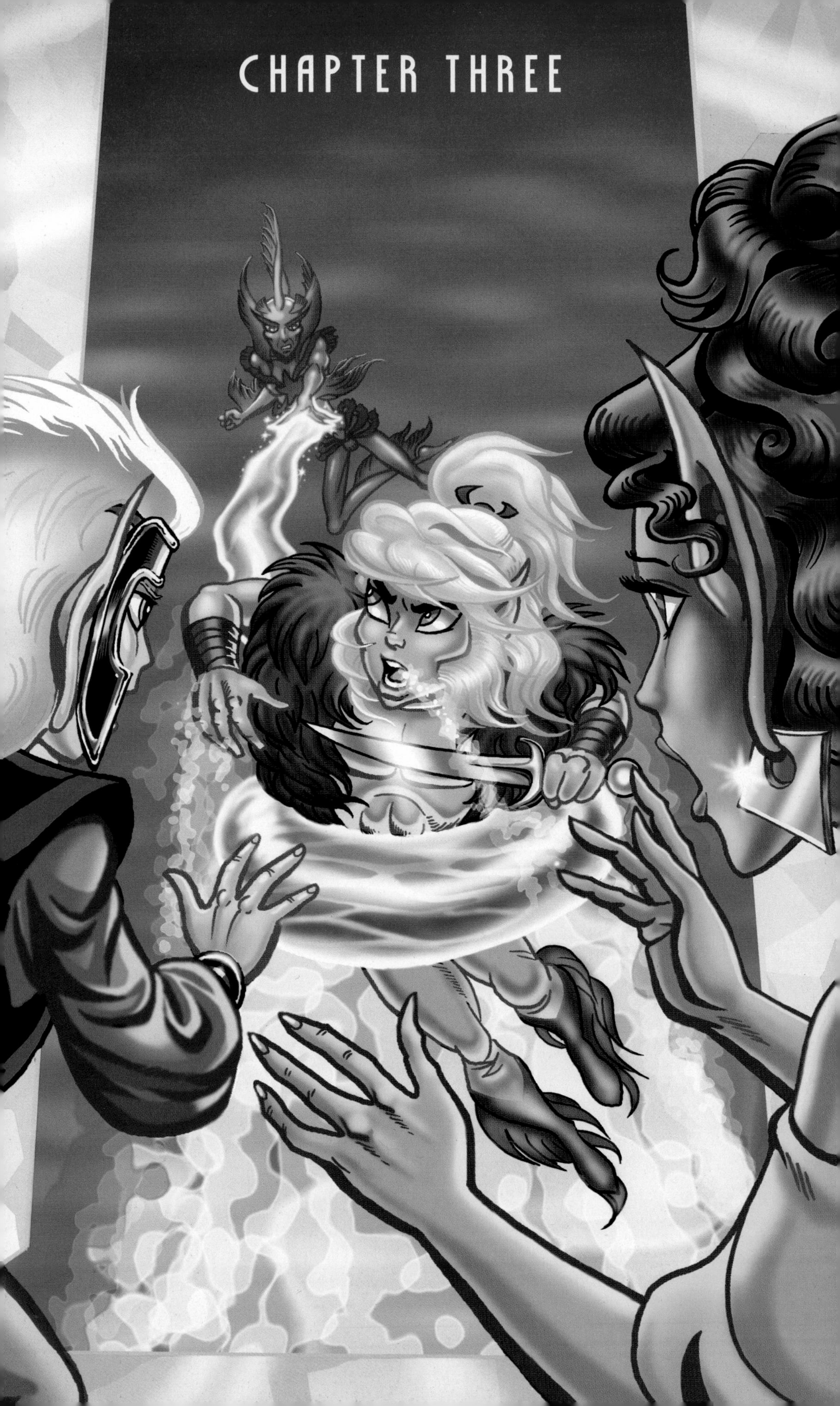

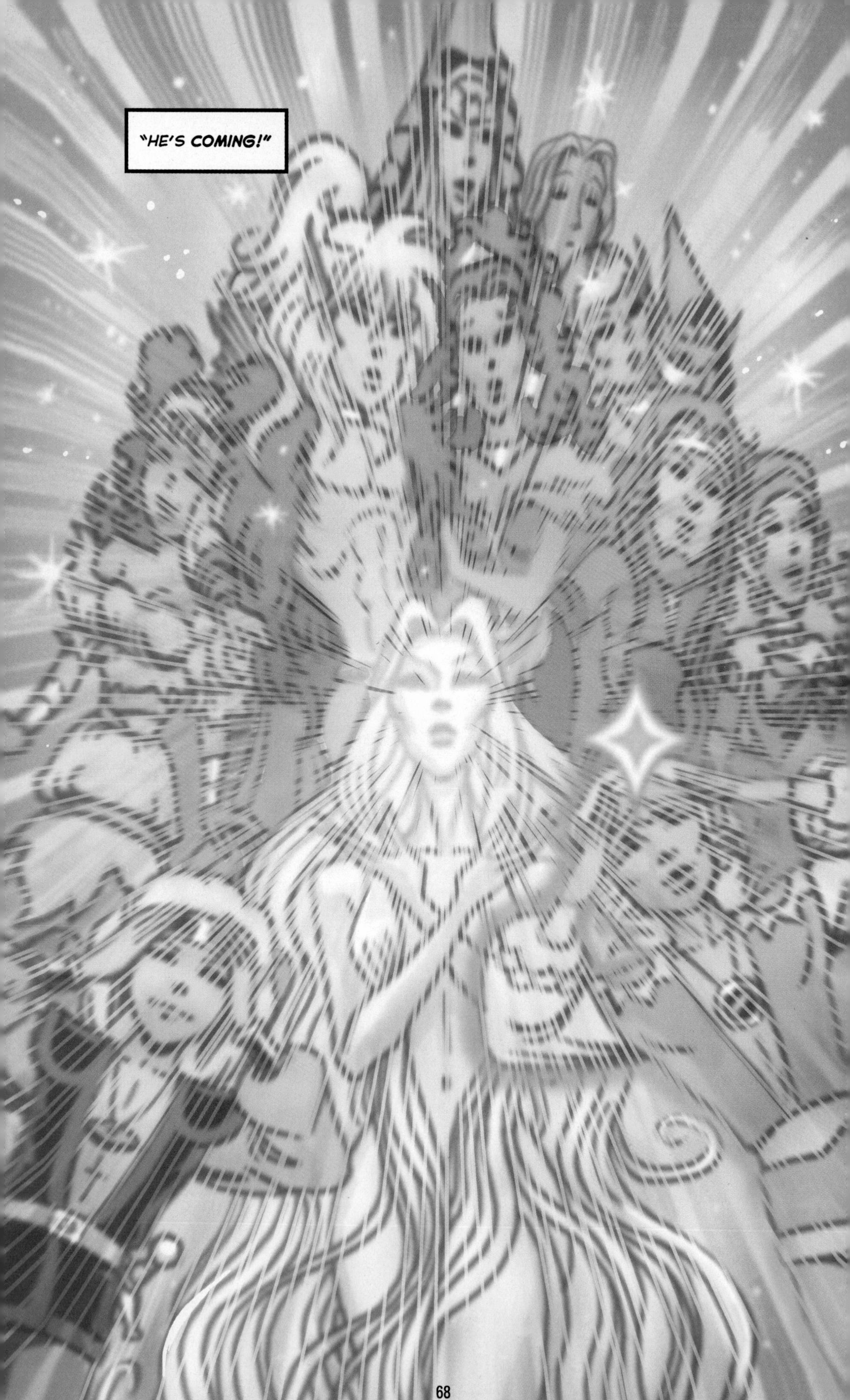
"HE'S COMING!"

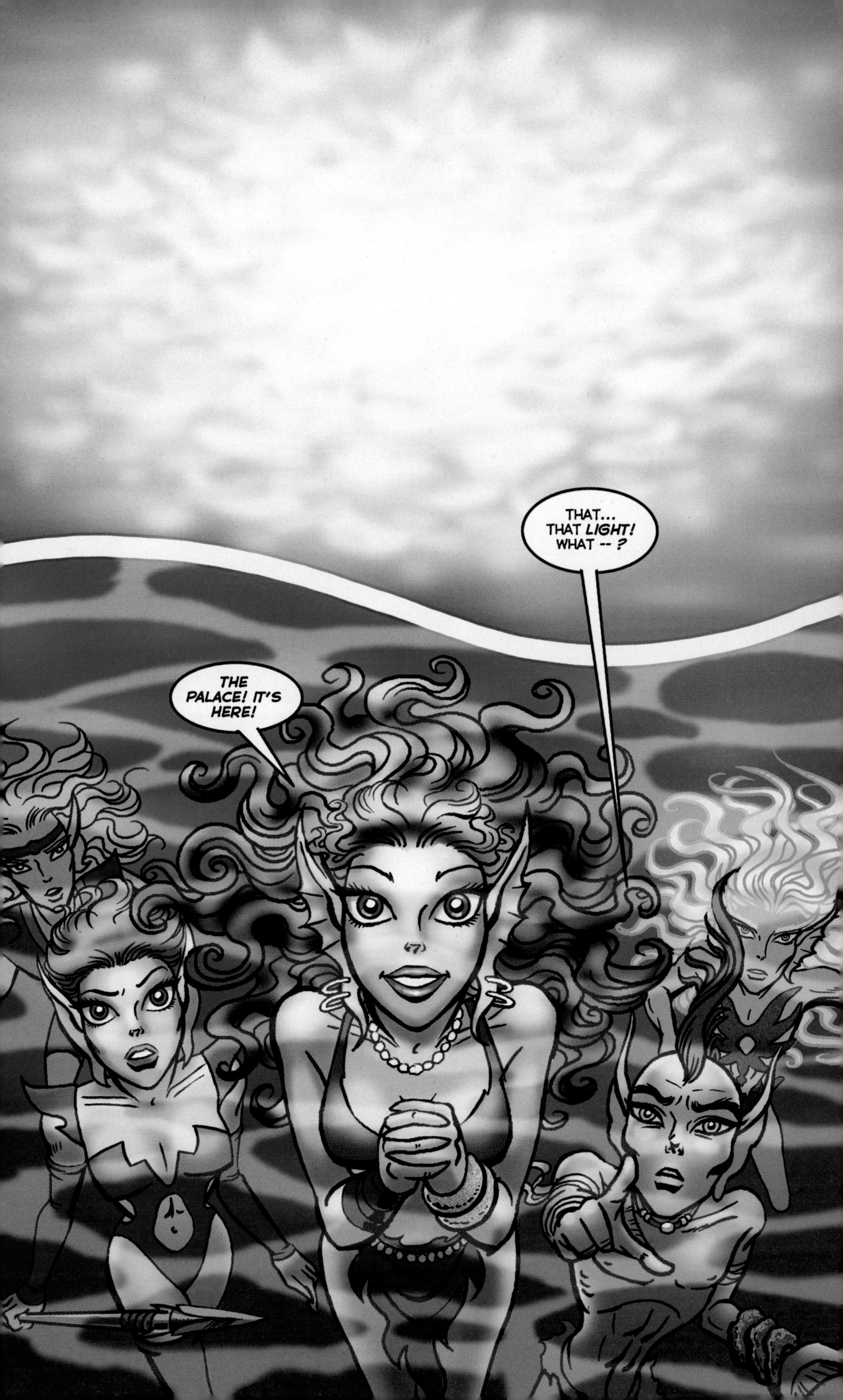
THE PALACE! IT'S HERE!
THAT... THAT LIGHT! WHAT -- ?

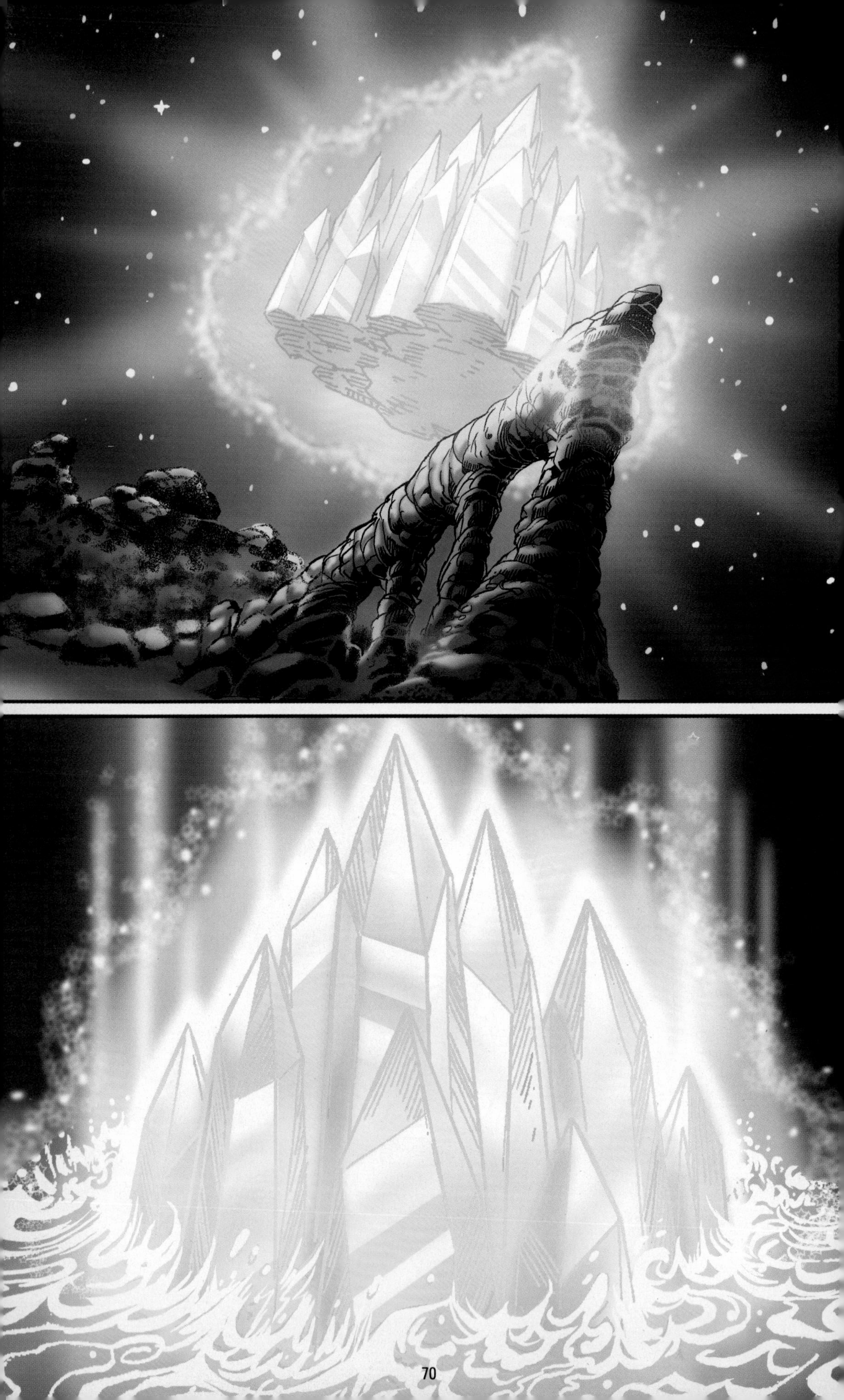

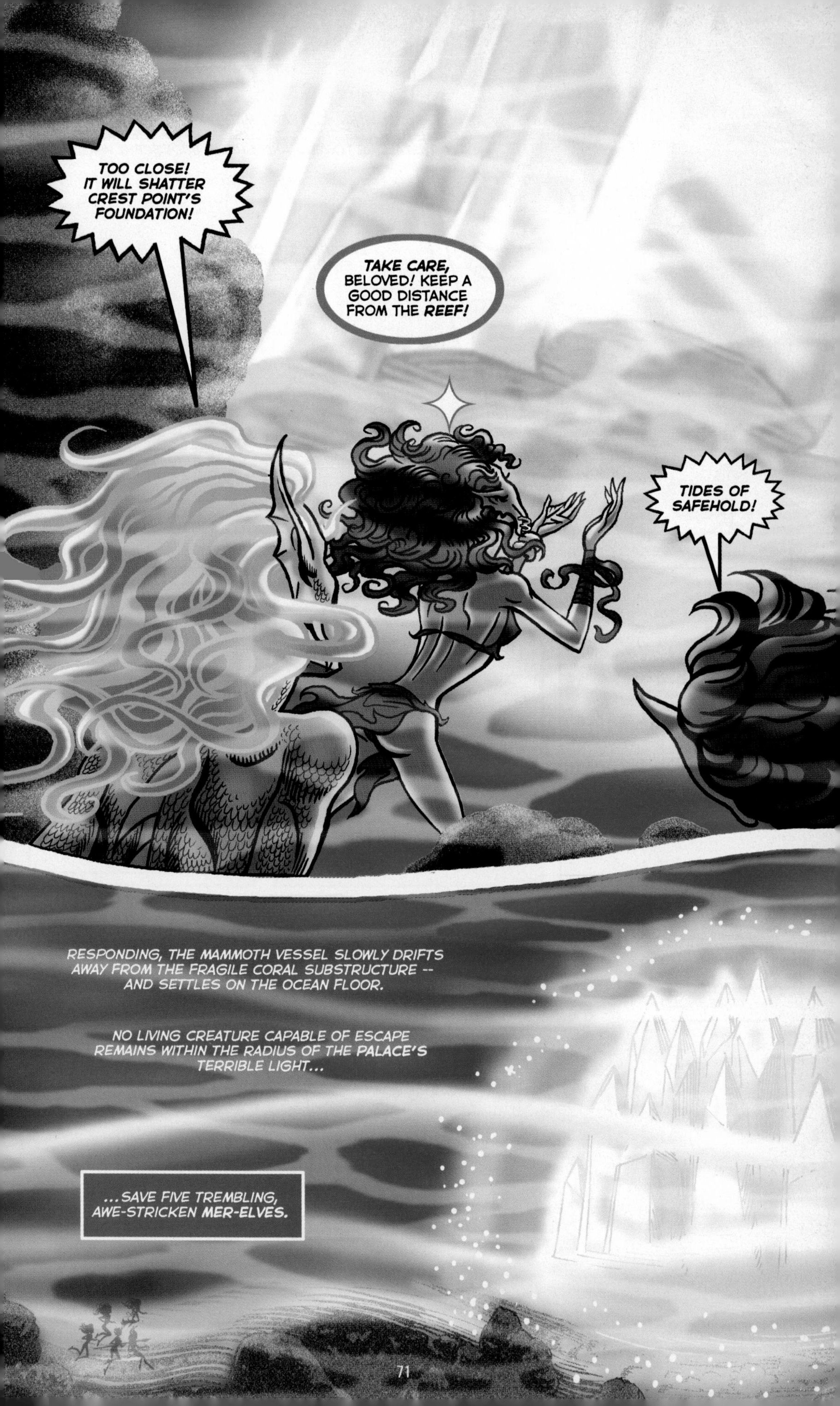
TOO CLOSE! IT WILL SHATTER CREST POINT'S FOUNDATION!
TAKE CARE, BELOVED! KEEP A GOOD DISTANCE FROM THE REEF!
TIDES OF SAFEHOLD!
RESPONDING, THE MAMMOTH VESSEL SLOWLY DRIFTS AWAY FROM THE FRAGILE CORAL SUBSTRUCTURE -- AND SETTLES ON THE OCEAN FLOOR.
NO LIVING CREATURE CAPABLE OF ESCAPE REMAINS WITHIN THE RADIUS OF THE PALACE'S TERRIBLE LIGHT...
...SAVE FIVE TREMBLING, AWE-STRICKEN MER-ELVES.

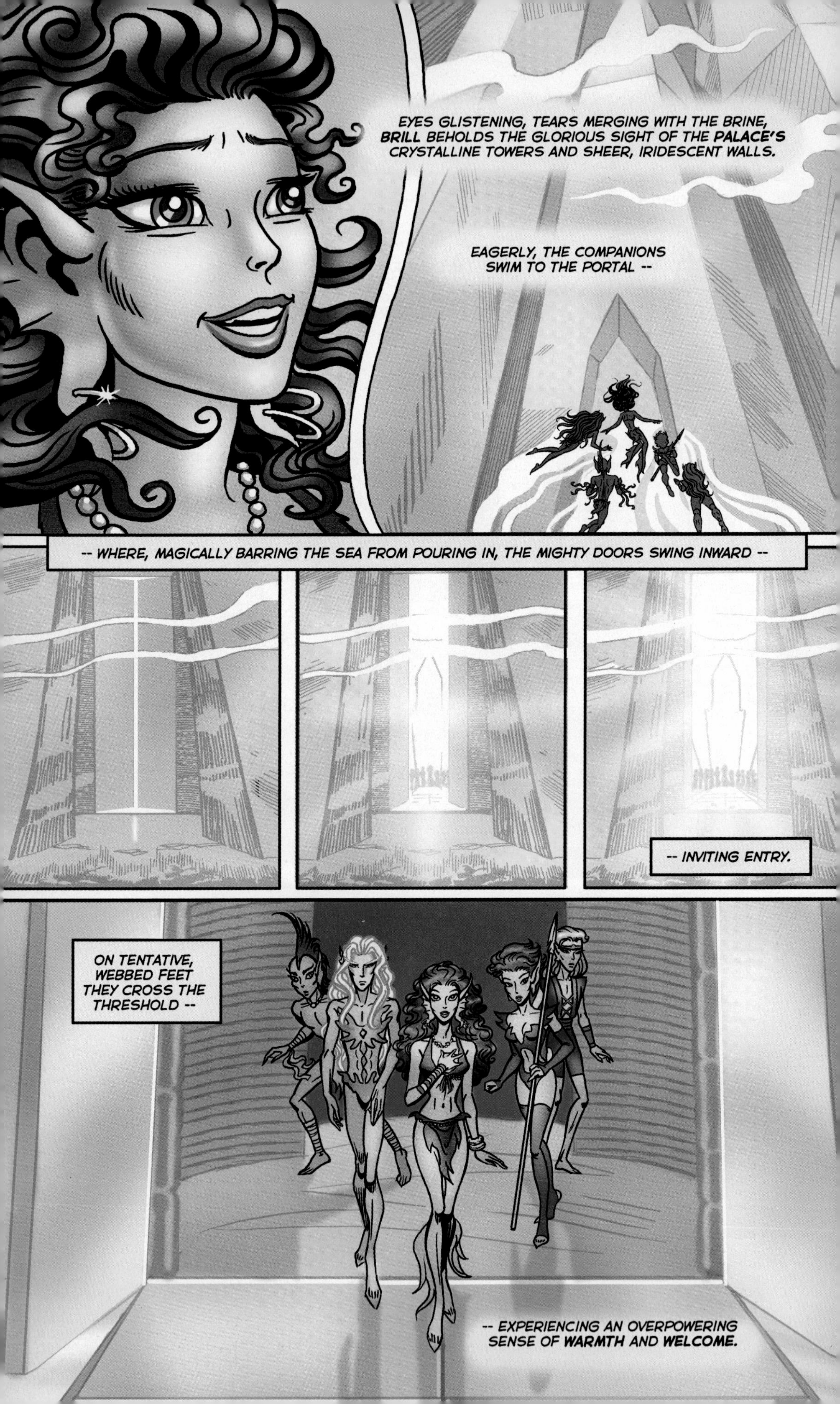
EYES GLISTENING, TEARS MERGING WITH THE BRINE, BRILL BEHOLDS THE GLORIOUS SIGHT OF THE PALACE'S CRYSTALLINE TOWERS AND SHEER, IRIDESCENT WALLS.
EAGERLY, THE COMPANIONS SWIM TO THE PORTAL --
-- WHERE, MAGICALLY BARRING THE SEA FROM POURING IN, THE MIGHTY DOORS SWING INWARD --
-- INVITING ENTRY.
ON TENTATIVE, WEBBED FEET THEY CROSS THE THRESHOLD --
-- EXPERIENCING AN OVERPOWERING SENSE OF WARMTH AND WELCOME.

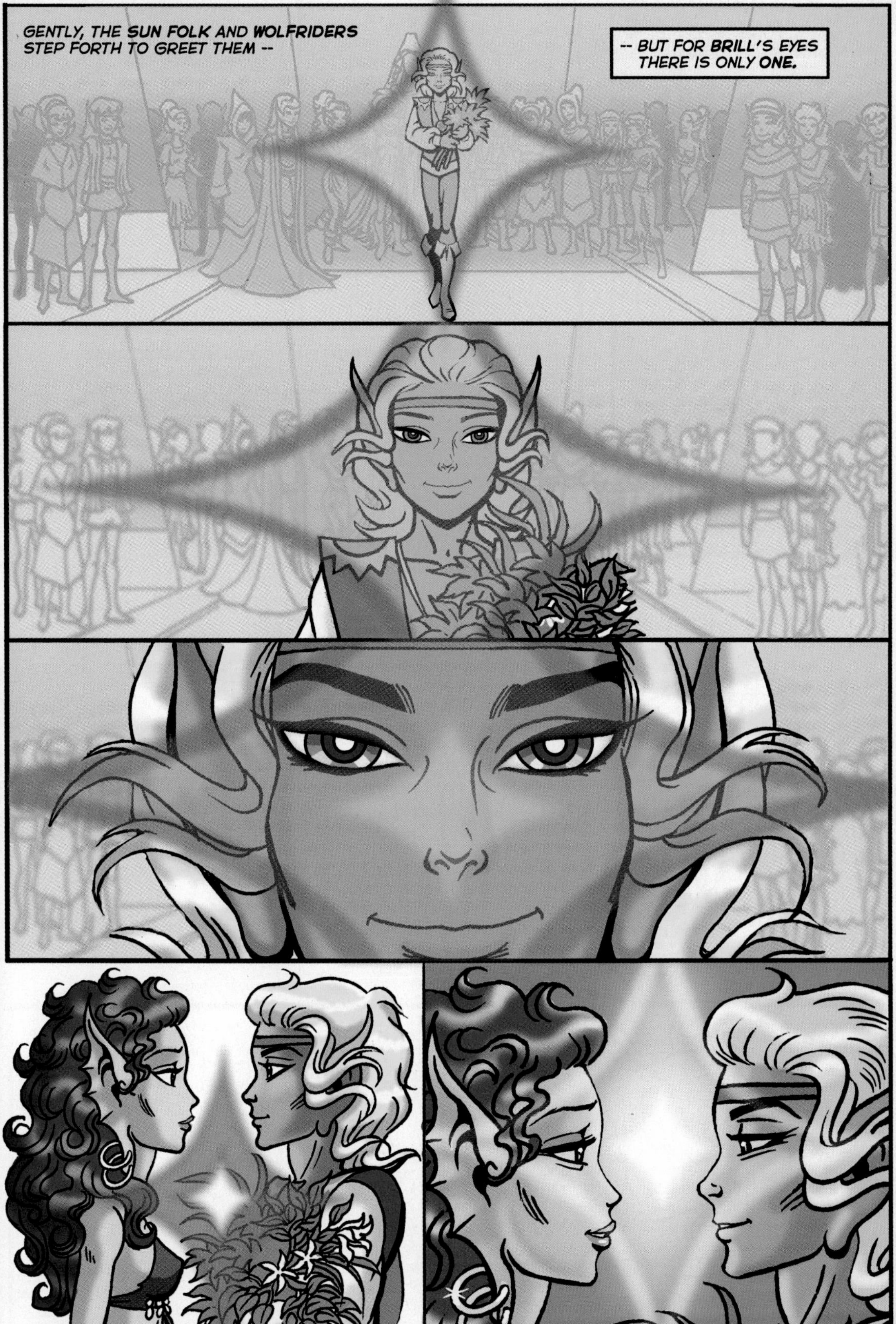
GENTLY, THE SUN FOLK AND WOLFRIDERS STEP FORTH TO GREET THEM --
-- BUT FOR BRILL'S EYES THERE IS ONLY ONE.

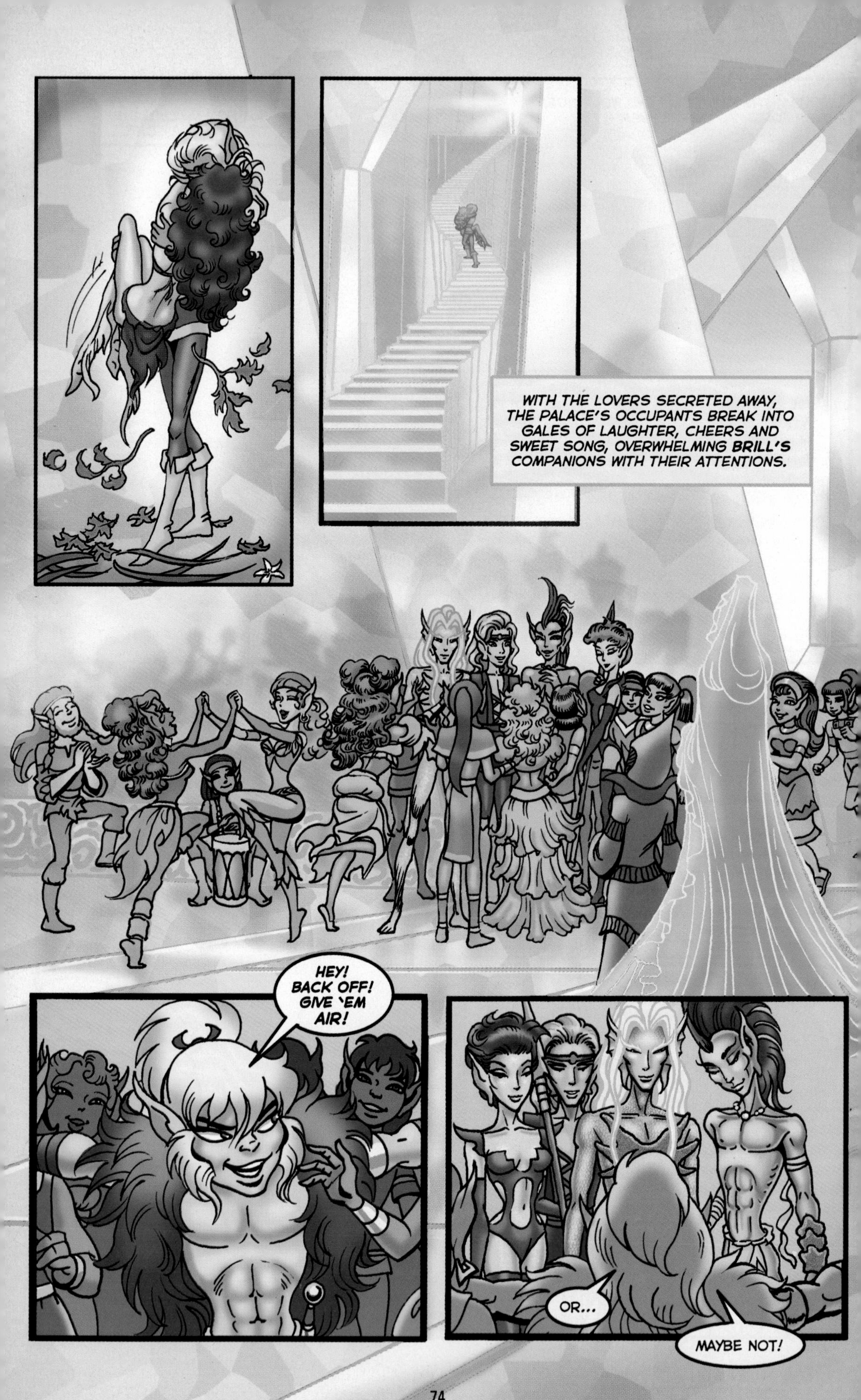
WITH THE LOVERS SECRETED AWAY, THE PALACE'S OCCUPANTS BREAK INTO GALES OF LAUGHTER, CHEERS AND SWEET SONG, OVERWHELMING BRILL'S COMPANIONS WITH THEIR ATTENTIONS.
HEY! BACK OFF! GIVE 'EM AIR!
OR...
MAYBE NOT!

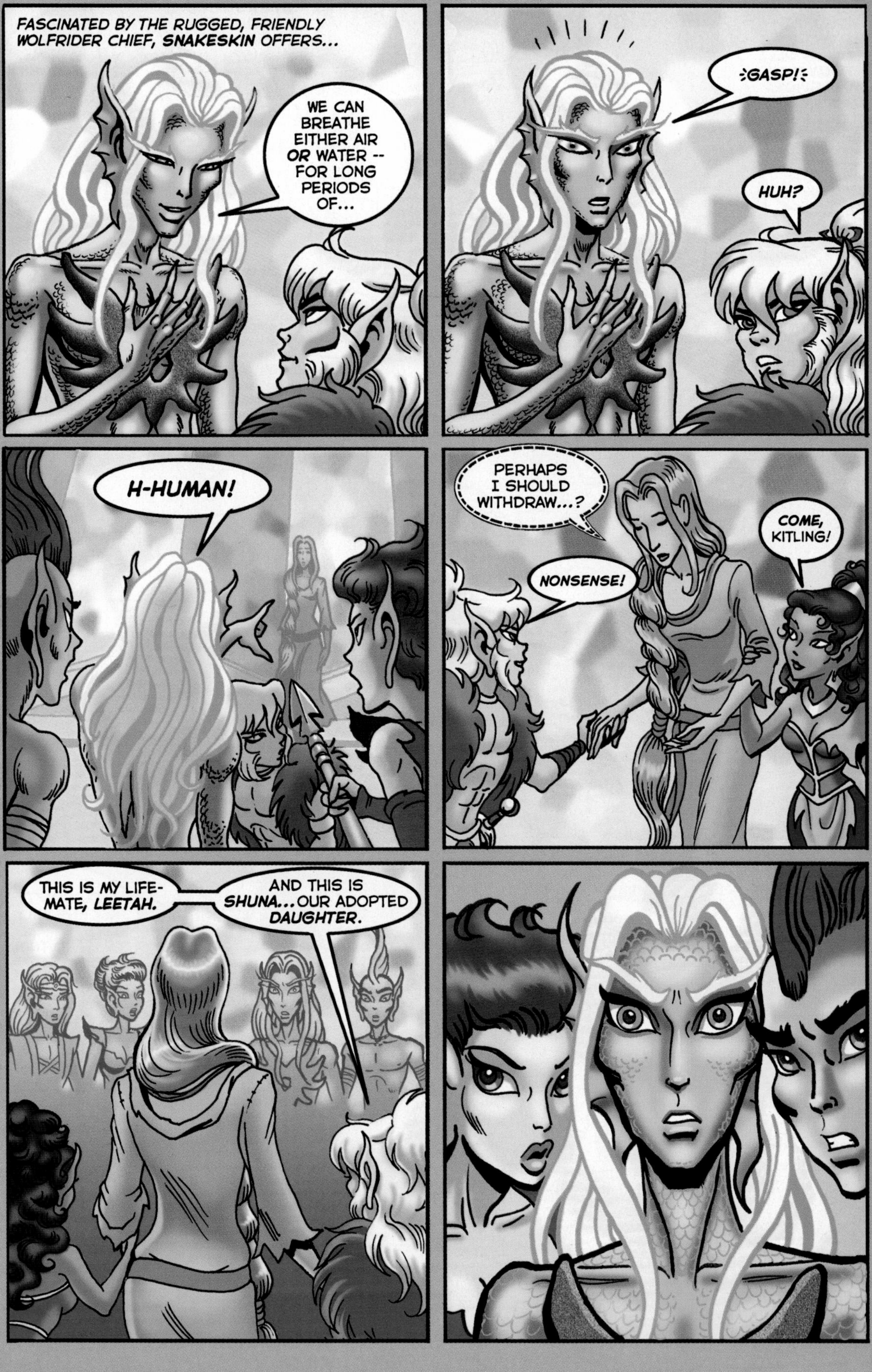
FASCINATED BY THE RUGGED, FRIENDLY WOLFRIDER CHIEF, SNAKESKIN OFFERS...
WE CAN BREATHE EITHER AIR OR WATER -- FOR LONG PERIODS OF...
:GASP!:
HUH?
H-HUMAN!
PERHAPS I SHOULD WITHDRAW...?
COME, KITLING!
NONSENSE!
THIS IS MY LIFE-MATE, LEETAH.
AND THIS IS SHUNA...OUR ADOPTED DAUGHTER.

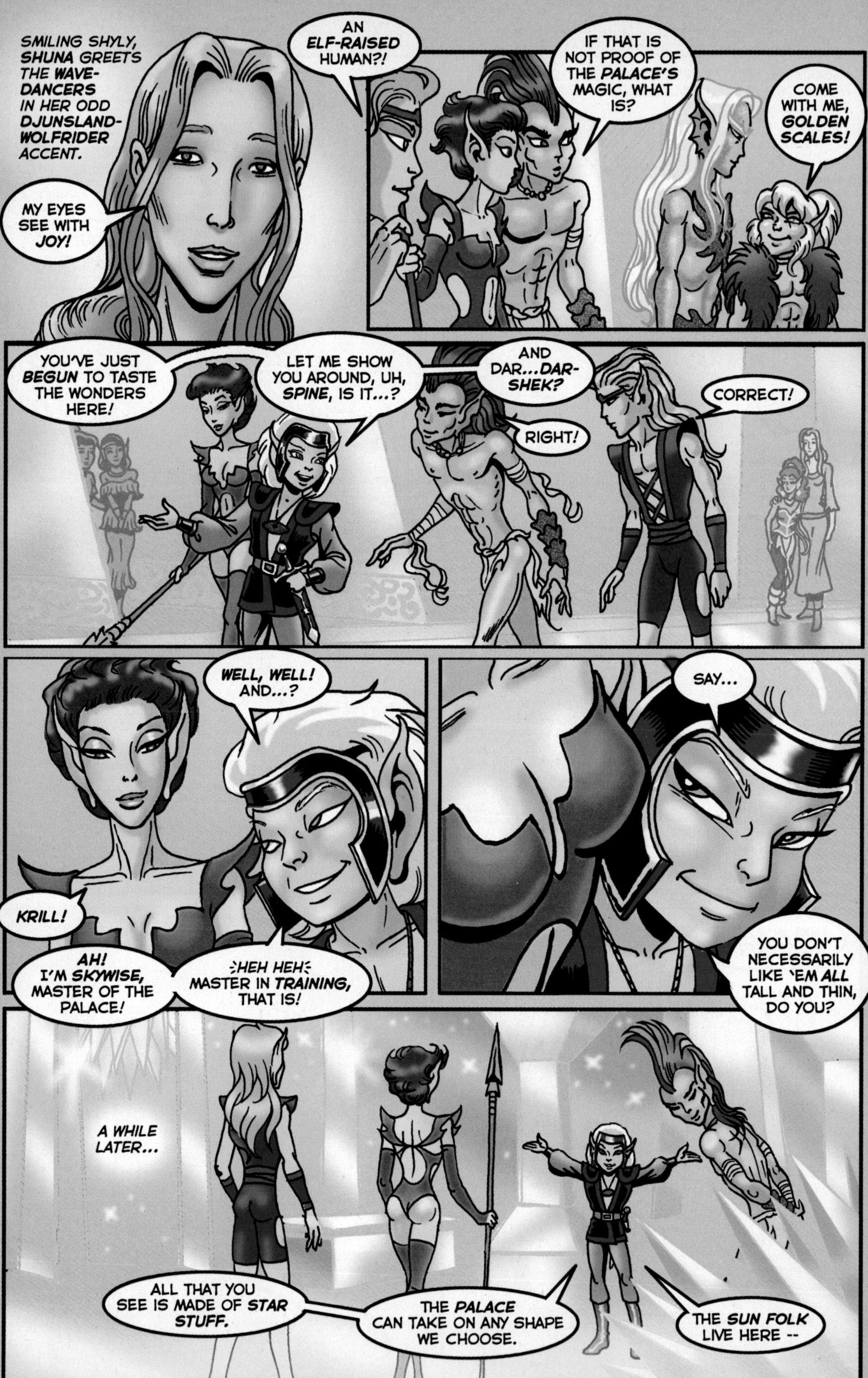
SMILING SHYLY, SHUNA GREETS THE WAVE-DANCERS IN HER ODD DJUNSLAND-WOLFRIDER ACCENT.
MY EYES SEE WITH JOY!
AN ELF-RAISED HUMAN?!
IF THAT IS NOT PROOF OF THE PALACE'S MAGIC, WHAT IS?
COME WITH ME, GOLDEN SCALES!
YOU'VE JUST BEGUN TO TASTE THE WONDERS HERE!
LET ME SHOW YOU AROUND, UH, SPINE, IS IT...?
AND DAR...DAR-SHEK?
RIGHT!
CORRECT!
WELL, WELL! AND...?
KRILL!
AH! I'M SKYWISE, MASTER OF THE PALACE!
HEH HEH MASTER IN TRAINING, THAT IS!
SAY...
YOU DON'T NECESSARILY LIKE 'EM ALL TALL AND THIN, DO YOU?
A WHILE LATER...
ALL THAT YOU SEE IS MADE OF STAR STUFF.
THE PALACE CAN TAKE ON ANY SHAPE WE CHOOSE.
THE SUN FOLK LIVE HERE --

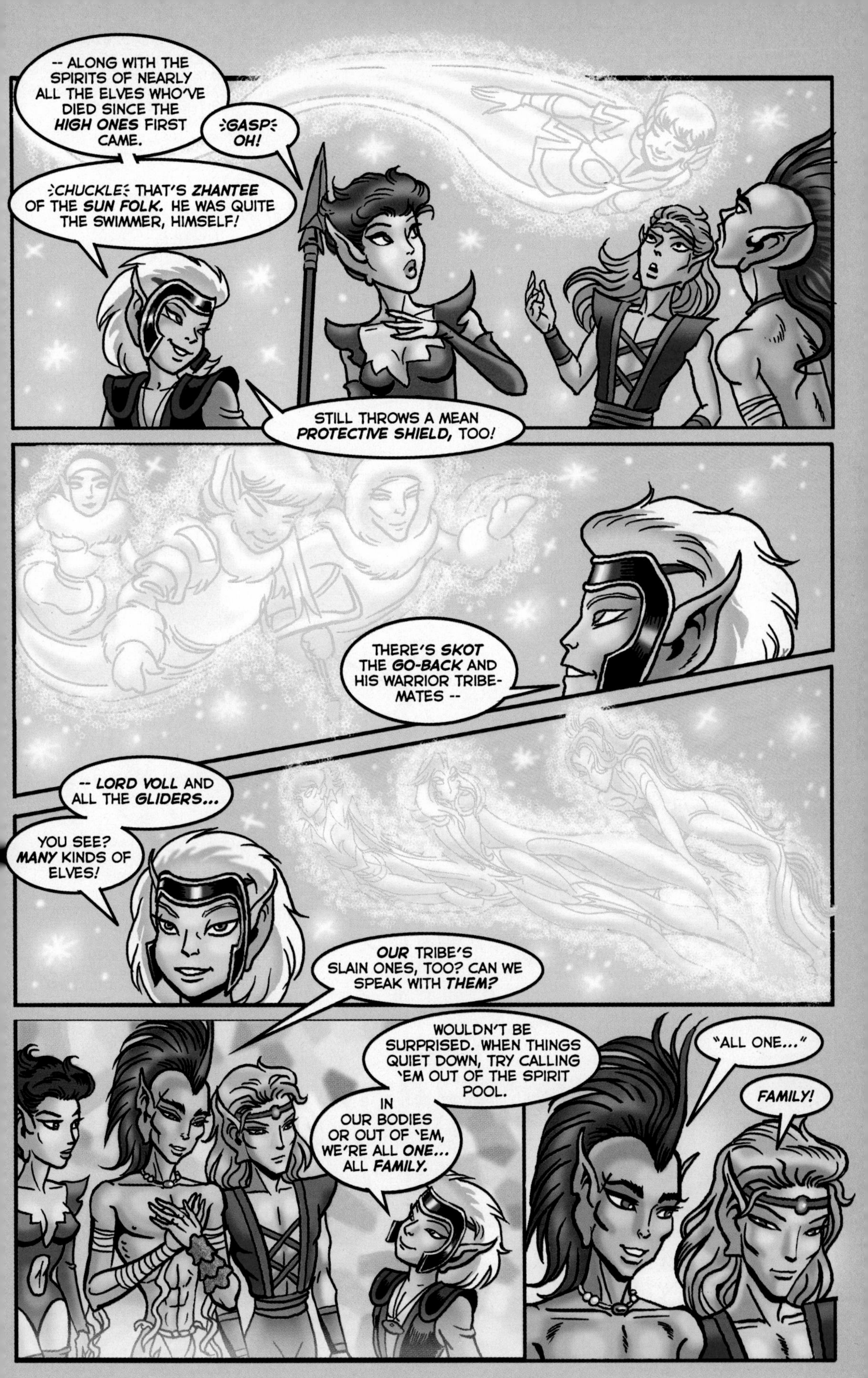

-- ALONG WITH THE SPIRITS OF NEARLY ALL THE ELVES WHO'VE DIED SINCE THE HIGH ONES FIRST CAME.
:GASP: OH!
:CHUCKLE: THAT'S ZHANTEE OF THE SUN FOLK. HE WAS QUITE THE SWIMMER, HIMSELF!
STILL THROWS A MEAN PROTECTIVE SHIELD, TOO!
THERE'S SKOT THE GO-BACK AND HIS WARRIOR TRIBE-MATES --
-- LORD VOLL AND ALL THE GLIDERS...
YOU SEE? MANY KINDS OF ELVES!
OUR TRIBE'S SLAIN ONES, TOO? CAN WE SPEAK WITH THEM?
WOULDN'T BE SURPRISED. WHEN THINGS QUIET DOWN, TRY CALLING 'EM OUT OF THE SPIRIT POOL.
IN OUR BODIES OR OUT OF 'EM, WE'RE ALL ONE... ALL FAMILY.
"ALL ONE..."
FAMILY!

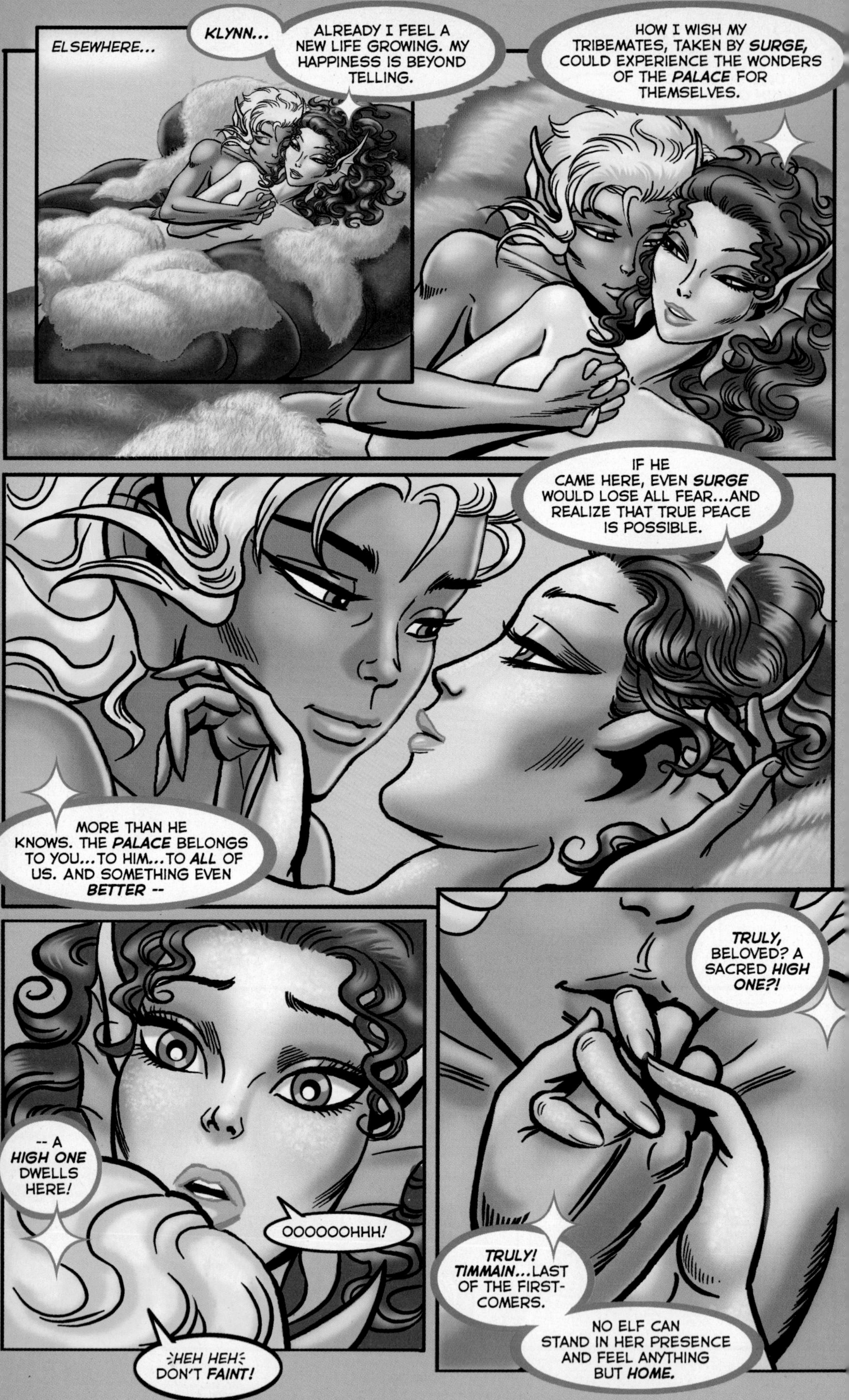

ELSEWHERE...
KLYNN...
ALREADY I FEEL A NEW LIFE GROWING. MY HAPPINESS IS BEYOND TELLING.
HOW I WISH MY TRIBEMATES, TAKEN BY SURGE, COULD EXPERIENCE THE WONDERS OF THE PALACE FOR THEMSELVES.
IF HE CAME HERE, EVEN SURGE WOULD LOSE ALL FEAR...AND REALIZE THAT TRUE PEACE IS POSSIBLE.
MORE THAN HE KNOWS. THE PALACE BELONGS TO YOU...TO HIM...TO ALL OF US. AND SOMETHING EVEN BETTER --
-- A HIGH ONE DWELLS HERE!
OOOOOOHHH!
HEH HEH DON'T FAINT!
TRULY, BELOVED? A SACRED HIGH ONE?!
TRULY! TIMMAIN...LAST OF THE FIRST-COMERS.
NO ELF CAN STAND IN HER PRESENCE AND FEEL ANYTHING BUT HOME.

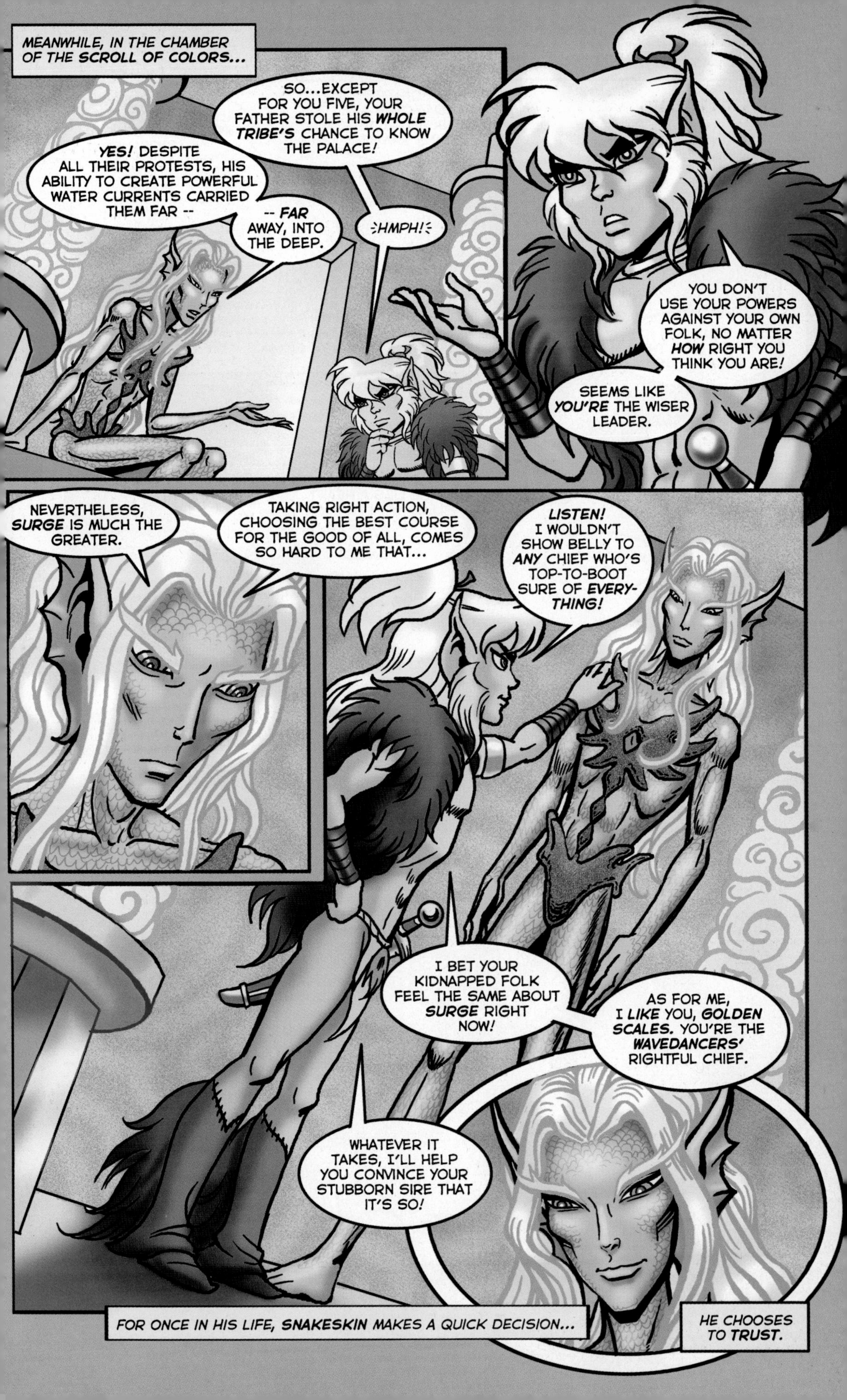
MEANWHILE, IN THE CHAMBER OF THE SCROLL OF COLORS...
SO...EXCEPT FOR YOU FIVE, YOUR FATHER STOLE HIS WHOLE TRIBE'S CHANCE TO KNOW THE PALACE!
YES! DESPITE ALL THEIR PROTESTS, HIS ABILITY TO CREATE POWERFUL WATER CURRENTS CARRIED THEM FAR --
-- FAR AWAY, INTO THE DEEP.
HMPH!
YOU DON'T USE YOUR POWERS AGAINST YOUR OWN FOLK, NO MATTER HOW RIGHT YOU THINK YOU ARE!
SEEMS LIKE YOU'RE THE WISER LEADER.
NEVERTHELESS, SURGE IS MUCH THE GREATER.
TAKING RIGHT ACTION, CHOOSING THE BEST COURSE FOR THE GOOD OF ALL, COMES SO HARD TO ME THAT...
LISTEN! I WOULDN'T SHOW BELLY TO ANY CHIEF WHO'S TOP-TO-BOOT SURE OF EVERY-THING!
I BET YOUR KIDNAPPED FOLK FEEL THE SAME ABOUT SURGE RIGHT NOW!
AS FOR ME, I LIKE YOU, GOLDEN SCALES. YOU'RE THE WAVEDANCERS' RIGHTFUL CHIEF.
WHATEVER IT TAKES, I'LL HELP YOU CONVINCE YOUR STUBBORN SIRE THAT IT'S SO!
FOR ONCE IN HIS LIFE, SNAKESKIN MAKES A QUICK DECISION...
HE CHOOSES TO TRUST.

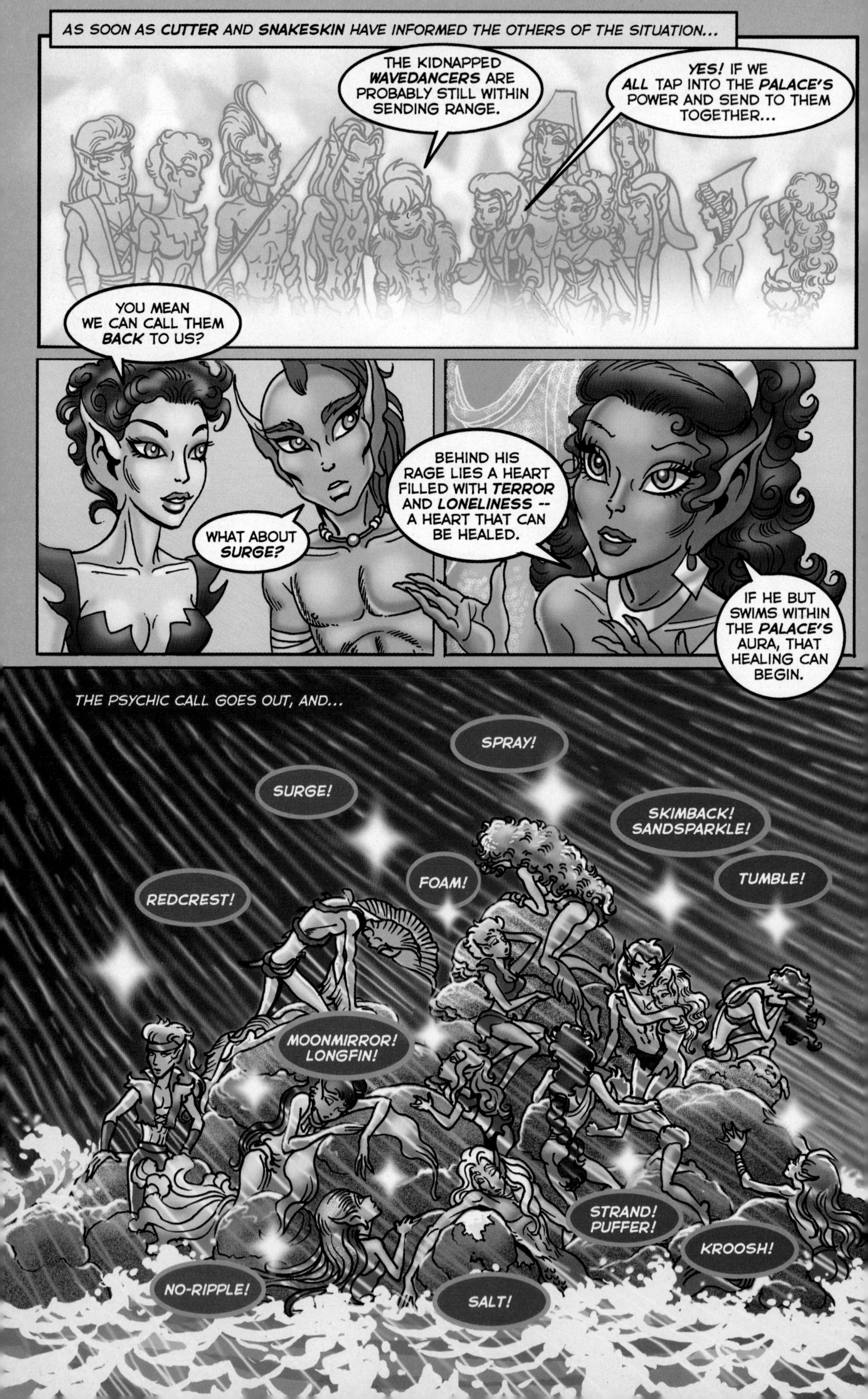
AS SOON AS CUTTER AND SNAKESKIN HAVE INFORMED THE OTHERS OF THE SITUATION...
THE KIDNAPPED WAVEDANCERS ARE PROBABLY STILL WITHIN SENDING RANGE.
YES! IF WE ALL TAP INTO THE PALACE'S POWER AND SEND TO THEM TOGETHER...
YOU MEAN WE CAN CALL THEM BACK TO US?
WHAT ABOUT SURGE?
BEHIND HIS RAGE LIES A HEART FILLED WITH TERROR AND LONELINESS -- A HEART THAT CAN BE HEALED.
IF HE BUT SWIMS WITHIN THE PALACE'S AURA, THAT HEALING CAN BEGIN.
THE PSYCHIC CALL GOES OUT, AND...
SPRAY!
SURGE!
SKIMBACK! SANDSPARKLE!
FOAM!
TUMBLE!
REDCREST!
MOONMIRROR! LONGFIN!
STRAND! PUFFER!
KROOSH!
NO-RIPPLE!
SALT!

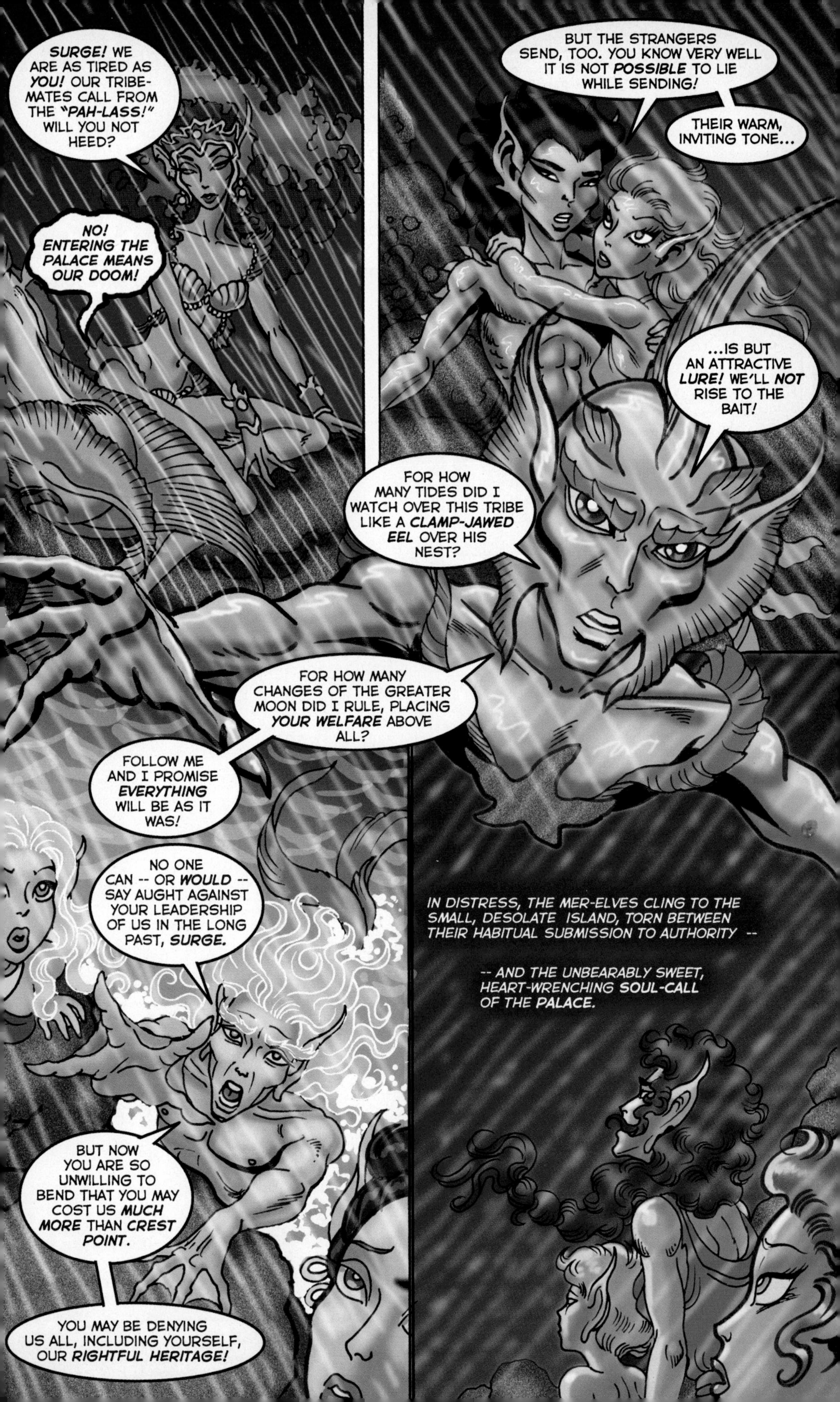
SURGE! WE ARE AS TIRED AS YOU! OUR TRIBE-MATES CALL FROM THE "PAH-LASS!" WILL YOU NOT HEED?
NO! ENTERING THE PALACE MEANS OUR DOOM!
BUT THE STRANGERS SEND, TOO. YOU KNOW VERY WELL IT IS NOT POSSIBLE TO LIE WHILE SENDING!
THEIR WARM, INVITING TONE...
...IS BUT AN ATTRACTIVE LURE! WE'LL NOT RISE TO THE BAIT!
FOR HOW MANY TIDES DID I WATCH OVER THIS TRIBE LIKE A CLAMP-JAWED EEL OVER HIS NEST?
FOR HOW MANY CHANGES OF THE GREATER MOON DID I RULE, PLACING YOUR WELFARE ABOVE ALL?
FOLLOW ME AND I PROMISE EVERYTHING WILL BE AS IT WAS!
NO ONE CAN -- OR WOULD -- SAY AUGHT AGAINST YOUR LEADERSHIP OF US IN THE LONG PAST, SURGE.
BUT NOW YOU ARE SO UNWILLING TO BEND THAT YOU MAY COST US MUCH MORE THAN CREST POINT.
YOU MAY BE DENYING US ALL, INCLUDING YOURSELF, OUR RIGHTFUL HERITAGE!
IN DISTRESS, THE MER-ELVES CLING TO THE SMALL, DESOLATE ISLAND, TORN BETWEEN THEIR HABITUAL SUBMISSION TO AUTHORITY --
-- AND THE UNBEARABLY SWEET, HEART-WRENCHING SOUL-CALL OF THE PALACE.

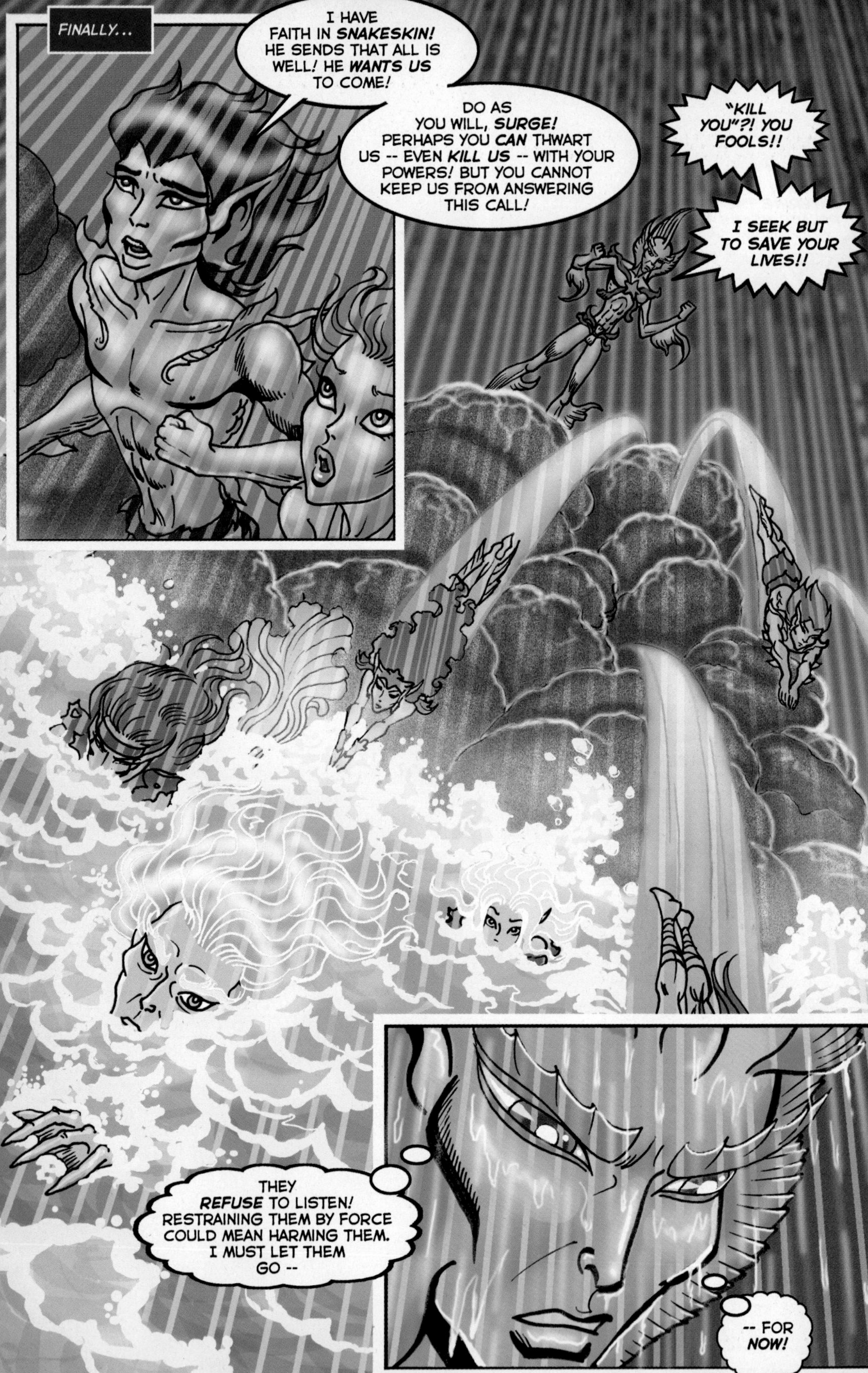
FINALLY...
I HAVE FAITH IN SNAKESKIN! HE SENDS THAT ALL IS WELL! HE WANTS US TO COME!
DO AS YOU WILL, SURGE! PERHAPS YOU CAN THWART US -- EVEN KILL US -- WITH YOUR POWERS! BUT YOU CANNOT KEEP US FROM ANSWERING THIS CALL!
"KILL YOU"?! YOU FOOLS!!
I SEEK BUT TO SAVE YOUR LIVES!!
THEY REFUSE TO LISTEN! RESTRAINING THEM BY FORCE COULD MEAN HARMING THEM. I MUST LET THEM GO --
-- FOR NOW!

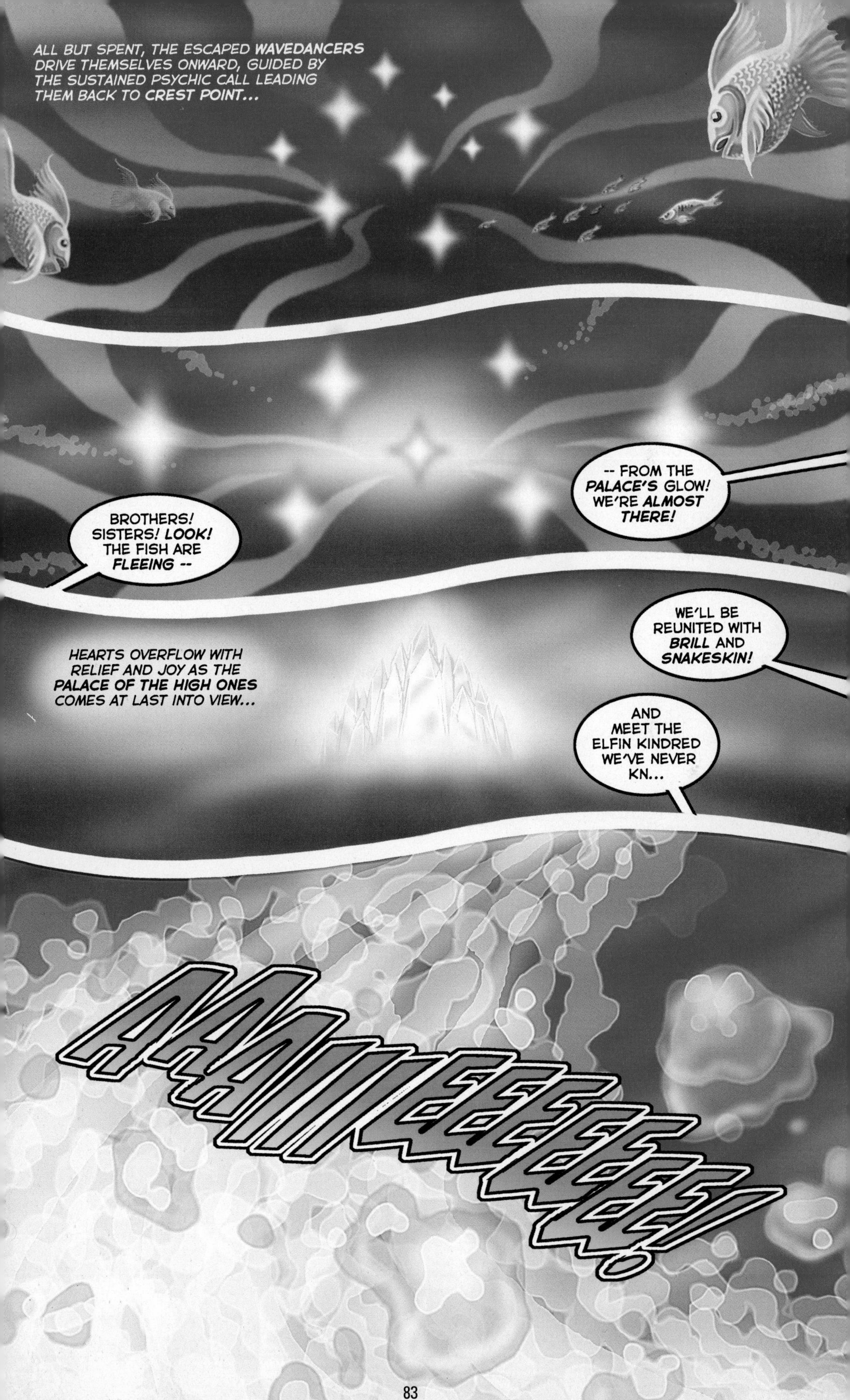

ALL BUT SPENT, THE ESCAPED WAVEDANCERS DRIVE THEMSELVES ONWARD, GUIDED BY THE SUSTAINED PSYCHIC CALL LEADING THEM BACK TO CREST POINT...
BROTHERS! SISTERS! LOOK! THE FISH ARE FLEEING --
-- FROM THE PALACE'S GLOW! WE'RE ALMOST THERE!
HEARTS OVERFLOW WITH RELIEF AND JOY AS THE PALACE OF THE HIGH ONES COMES AT LAST INTO VIEW...
WE'LL BE REUNITED WITH BRILL AND SNAKESKIN!
AND MEET THE ELFIN KINDRED WE'VE NEVER KN...
AAAIIEEEEEE!

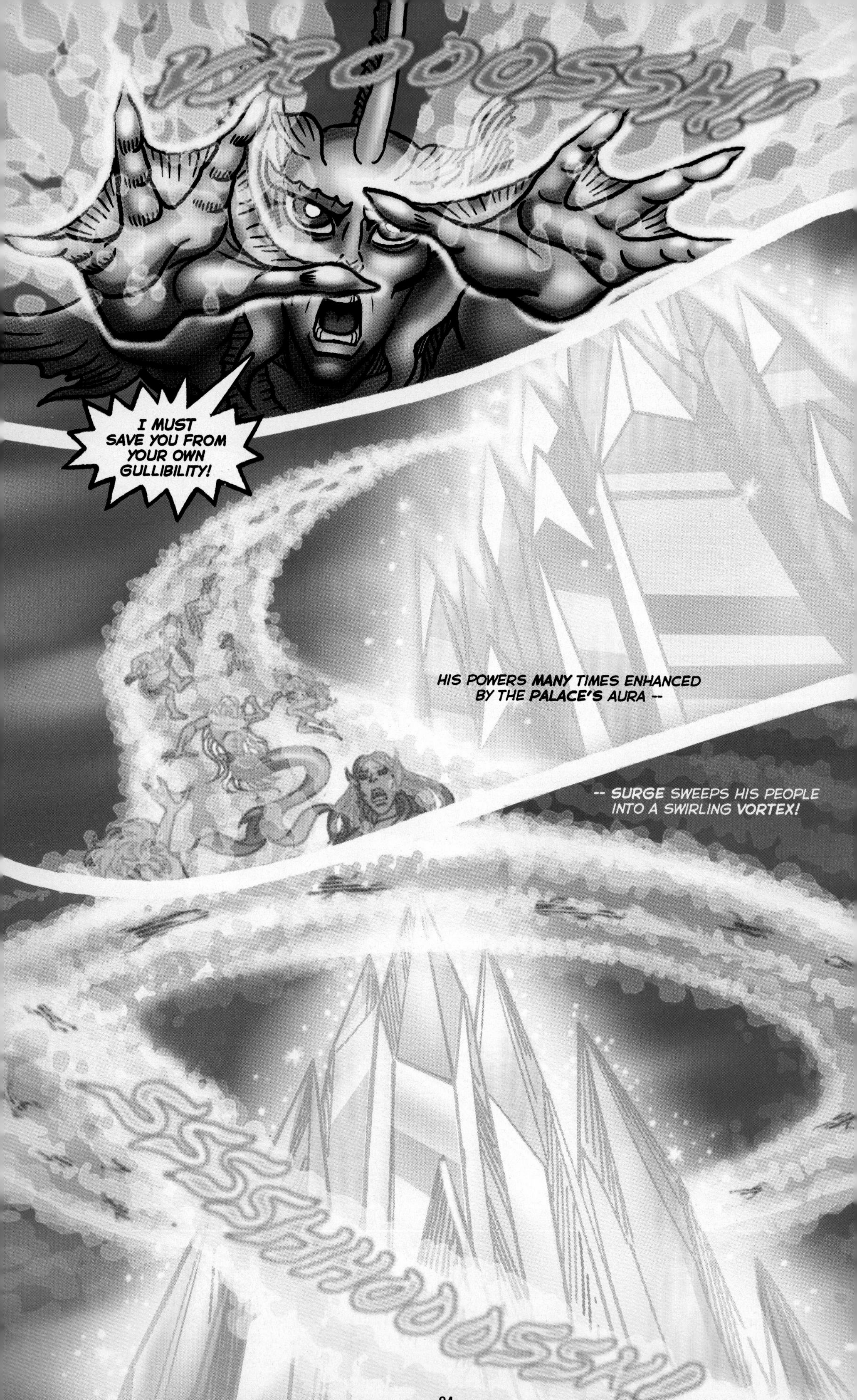
VRROOOSSH!!
I MUST SAVE YOU FROM YOUR OWN GULLIBILITY!
HIS POWERS MANY TIMES ENHANCED BY THE PALACE'S AURA --
-- SURGE SWEEPS HIS PEOPLE INTO A SWIRLING VORTEX!
SSSSHHOOOSSH!

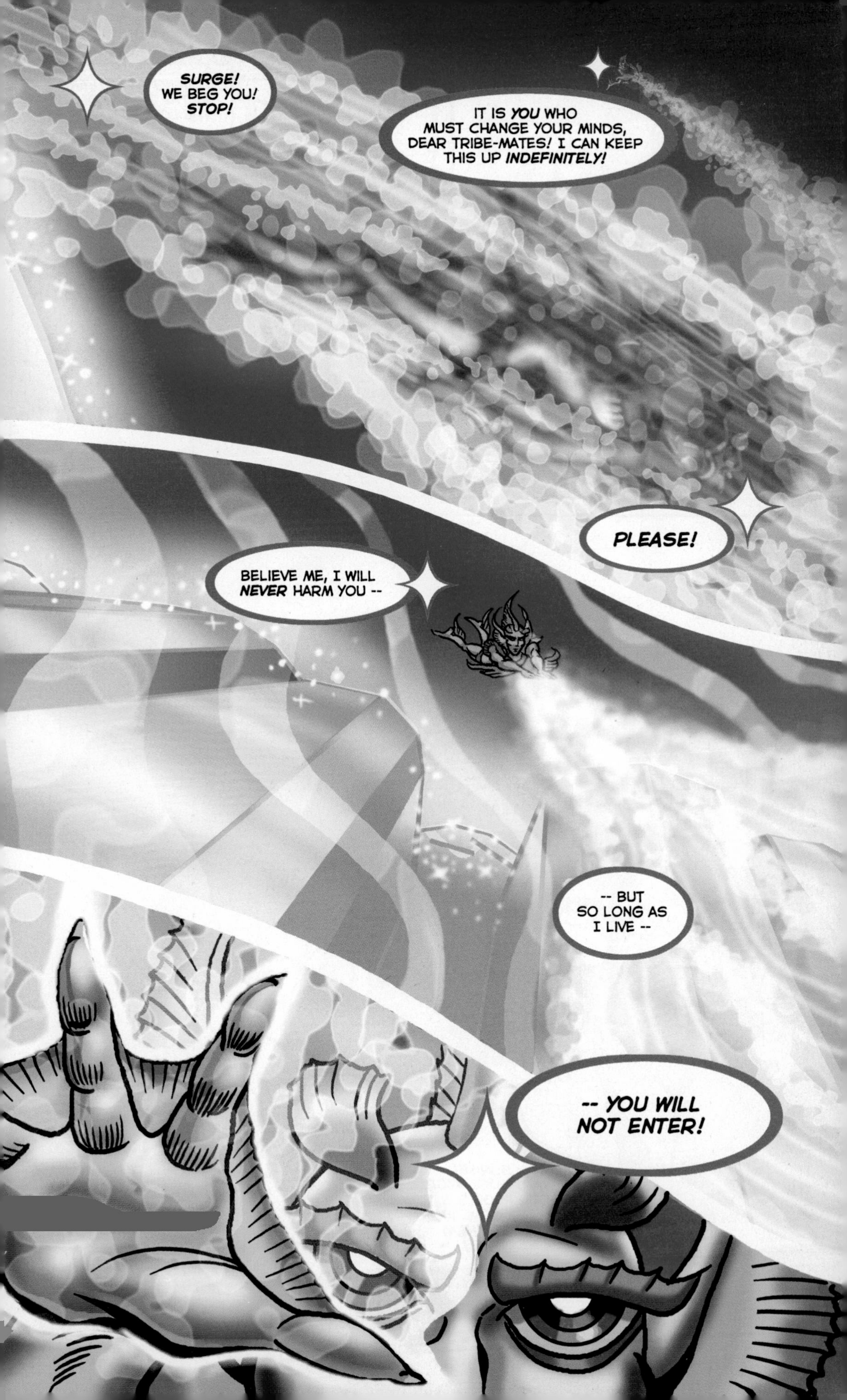
SURGE! WE BEG YOU! STOP!
IT IS YOU WHO MUST CHANGE YOUR MINDS, DEAR TRIBE-MATES! I CAN KEEP THIS UP INDEFINITELY!
PLEASE!
BELIEVE ME, I WILL NEVER HARM YOU --
-- BUT SO LONG AS I LIVE --
-- YOU WILL NOT ENTER!

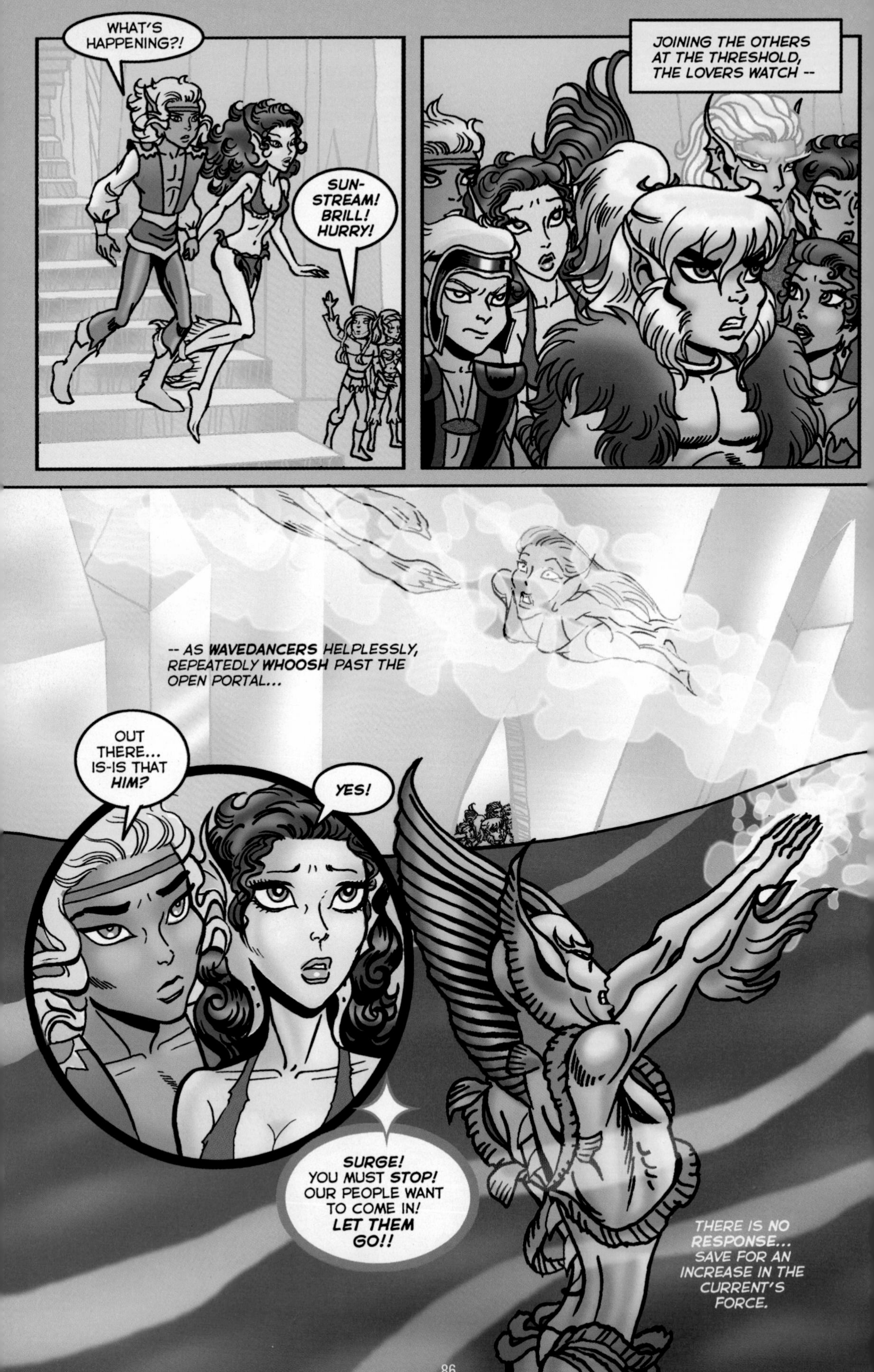
WHAT'S HAPPENING?!
SUN-STREAM! BRILL! HURRY!
JOINING THE OTHERS AT THE THRESHOLD, THE LOVERS WATCH --
-- AS WAVEDANCERS HELPLESSLY, REPEATEDLY WHOOSH PAST THE OPEN PORTAL...
OUT THERE... IS-IS THAT HIM?
YES!
SURGE! YOU MUST STOP! OUR PEOPLE WANT TO COME IN! LET THEM GO!!
THERE IS NO RESPONSE... SAVE FOR AN INCREASE IN THE CURRENT'S FORCE.

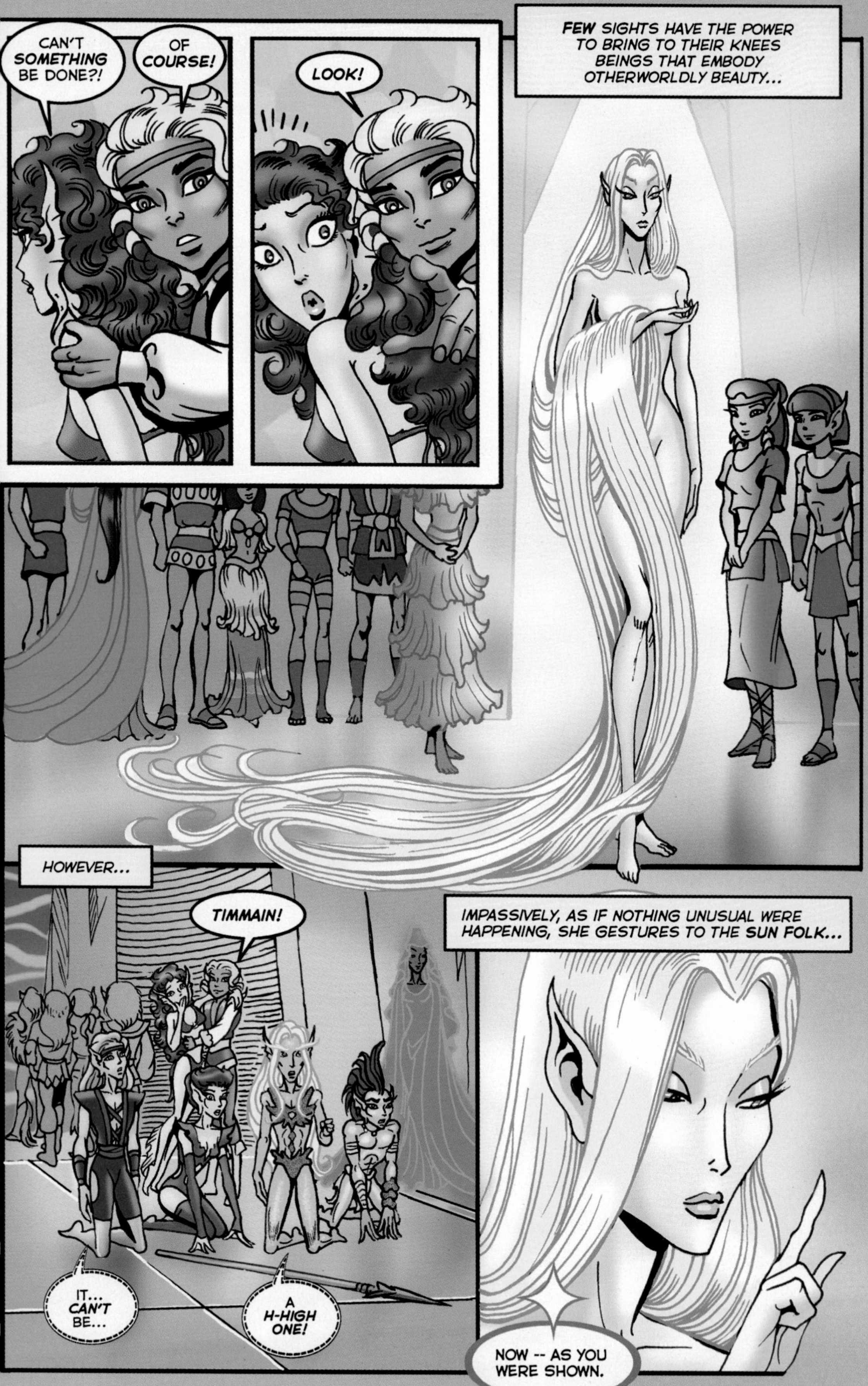
CAN'T SOMETHING BE DONE?!
OF COURSE!
LOOK!
FEW SIGHTS HAVE THE POWER TO BRING TO THEIR KNEES BEINGS THAT EMBODY OTHERWORLDLY BEAUTY...
HOWEVER...
TIMMAIN!
IT... CAN'T BE...
A H-HIGH ONE!
IMPASSIVELY, AS IF NOTHING UNUSUAL WERE HAPPENING, SHE GESTURES TO THE SUN FOLK...
NOW -- AS YOU WERE SHOWN.

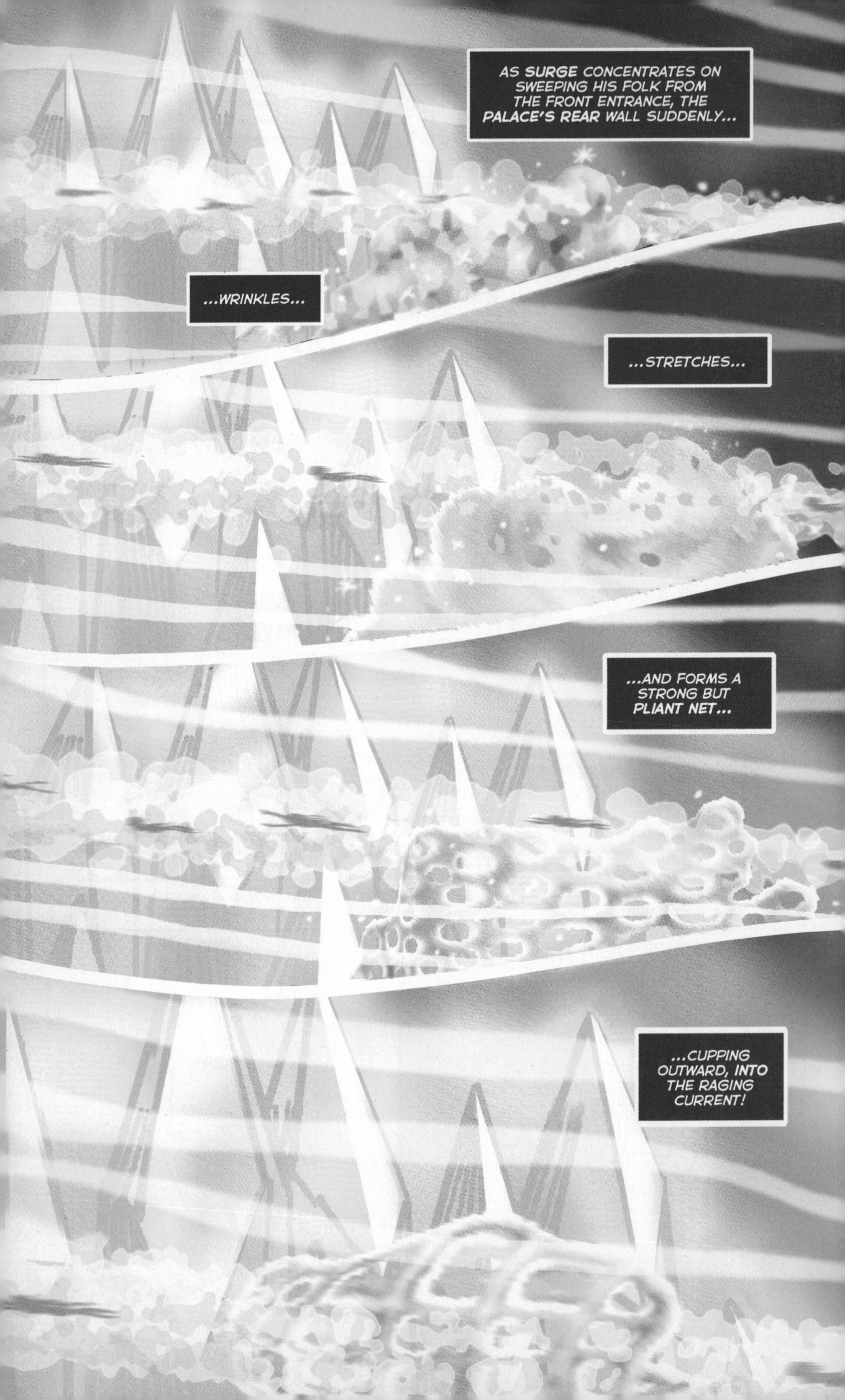
AS SURGE CONCENTRATES ON SWEEPING HIS FOLK FROM THE FRONT ENTRANCE, THE PALACE'S REAR WALL SUDDENLY...
...WRINKLES...
...STRETCHES...
...AND FORMS A STRONG BUT PLIANT NET...
...CUPPING OUTWARD, INTO THE RAGING CURRENT!

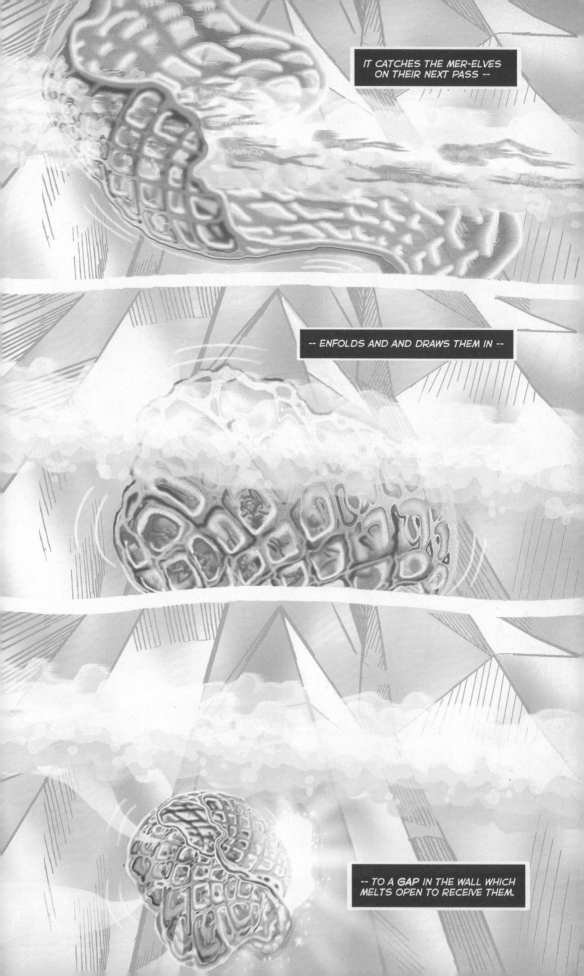

IT CATCHES THE MER-ELVES ON THEIR NEXT PASS --

-- ENFOLDS AND AND DRAWS THEM IN --

-- TO A GAP IN THE WALL WHICH MELTS OPEN TO RECEIVE THEM.

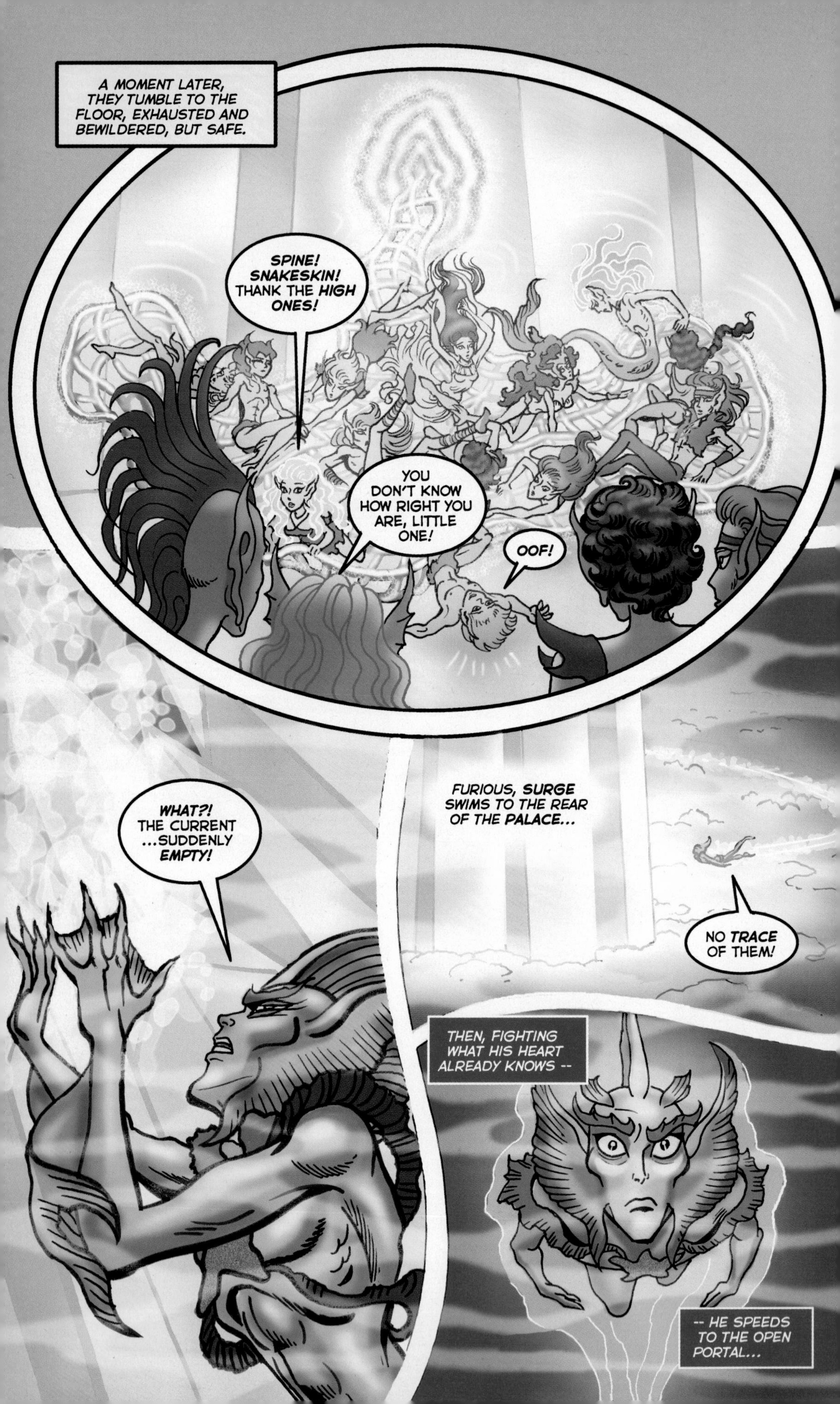
A MOMENT LATER, THEY TUMBLE TO THE FLOOR, EXHAUSTED AND BEWILDERED, BUT SAFE.
SPINE! SNAKESKIN! THANK THE HIGH ONES!
YOU DON'T KNOW HOW RIGHT YOU ARE, LITTLE ONE!
OOF!
WHAT?! THE CURRENT ...SUDDENLY EMPTY!
FURIOUS, SURGE SWIMS TO THE REAR OF THE PALACE...
NO TRACE OF THEM!
THEN, FIGHTING WHAT HIS HEART ALREADY KNOWS --
-- HE SPEEDS TO THE OPEN PORTAL...

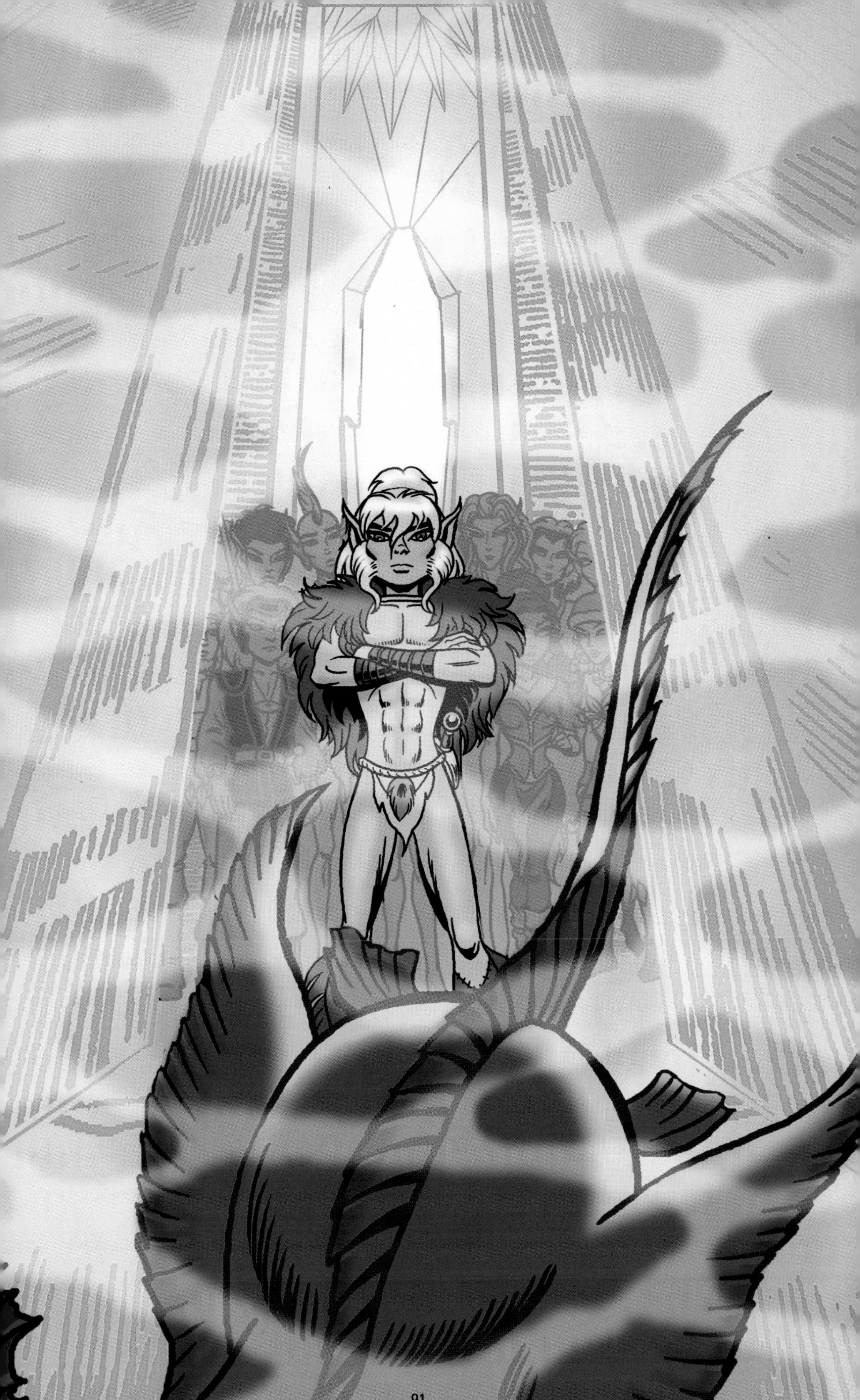

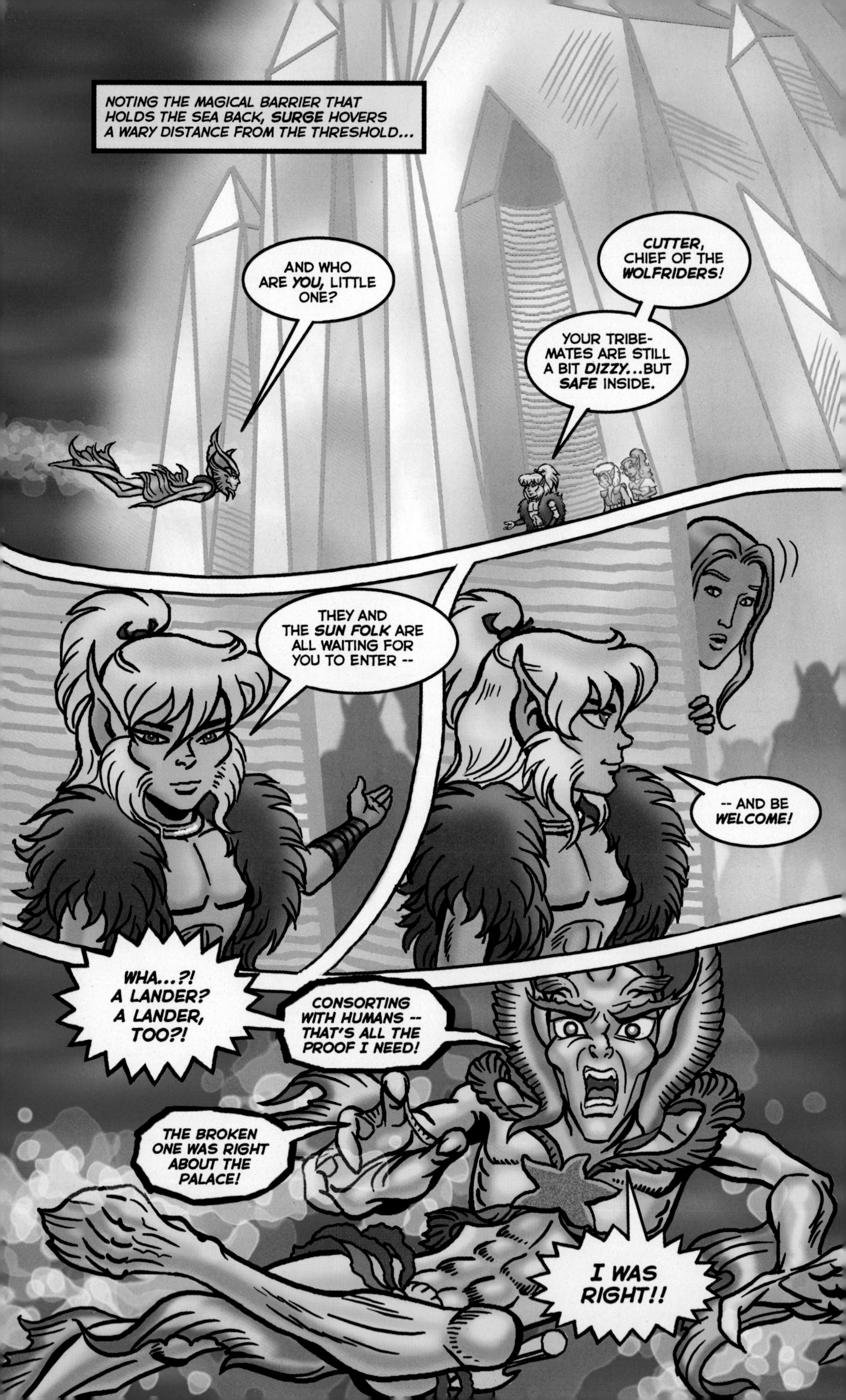
NOTING THE MAGICAL BARRIER THAT HOLDS THE SEA BACK, SURGE HOVERS A WARY DISTANCE FROM THE THRESHOLD...
AND WHO ARE YOU, LITTLE ONE?
CUTTER, CHIEF OF THE WOLFRIDERS!
YOUR TRIBE-MATES ARE STILL A BIT DIZZY...BUT SAFE INSIDE.
THEY AND THE SUN FOLK ARE ALL WAITING FOR YOU TO ENTER --
-- AND BE WELCOME!
WHA...?! A LANDER? A LANDER, TOO?!
CONSORTING WITH HUMANS -- THAT'S ALL THE PROOF I NEED!
THE BROKEN ONE WAS RIGHT ABOUT THE PALACE!
I WAS RIGHT!!

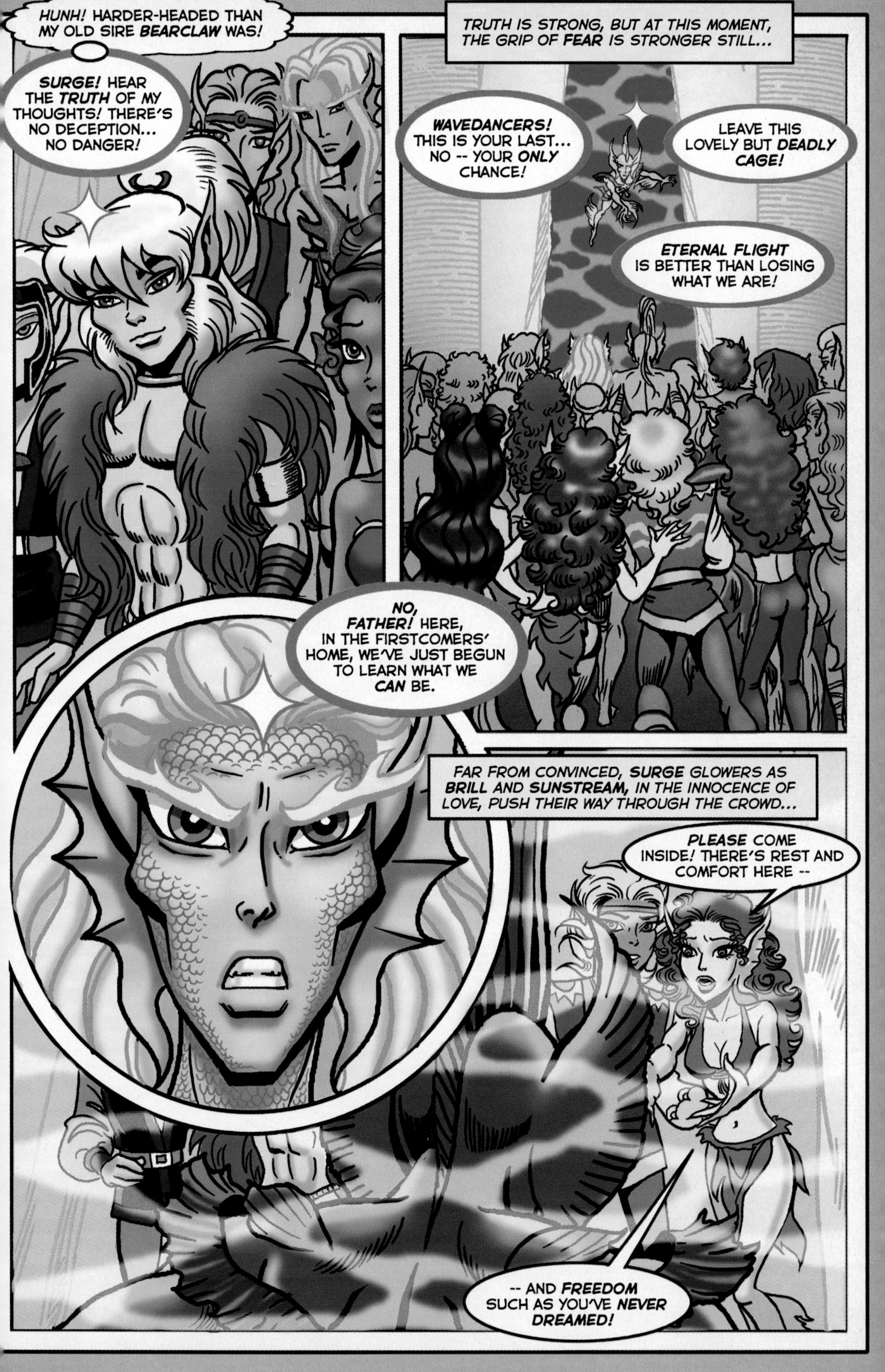

HUNH! HARDER-HEADED THAN MY OLD SIRE BEARCLAW WAS!
SURGE! HEAR THE TRUTH OF MY THOUGHTS! THERE'S NO DECEPTION... NO DANGER!
TRUTH IS STRONG, BUT AT THIS MOMENT, THE GRIP OF FEAR IS STRONGER STILL...
WAVEDANCERS! THIS IS YOUR LAST... NO -- YOUR ONLY CHANCE!
LEAVE THIS LOVELY BUT DEADLY CAGE!
ETERNAL FLIGHT IS BETTER THAN LOSING WHAT WE ARE!
NO, FATHER! HERE, IN THE FIRSTCOMERS' HOME, WE'VE JUST BEGUN TO LEARN WHAT WE CAN BE.
FAR FROM CONVINCED, SURGE GLOWERS AS BRILL AND SUNSTREAM, IN THE INNOCENCE OF LOVE, PUSH THEIR WAY THROUGH THE CROWD...
PLEASE COME INSIDE! THERE'S REST AND COMFORT HERE --
-- AND FREEDOM SUCH AS YOU'VE NEVER DREAMED!

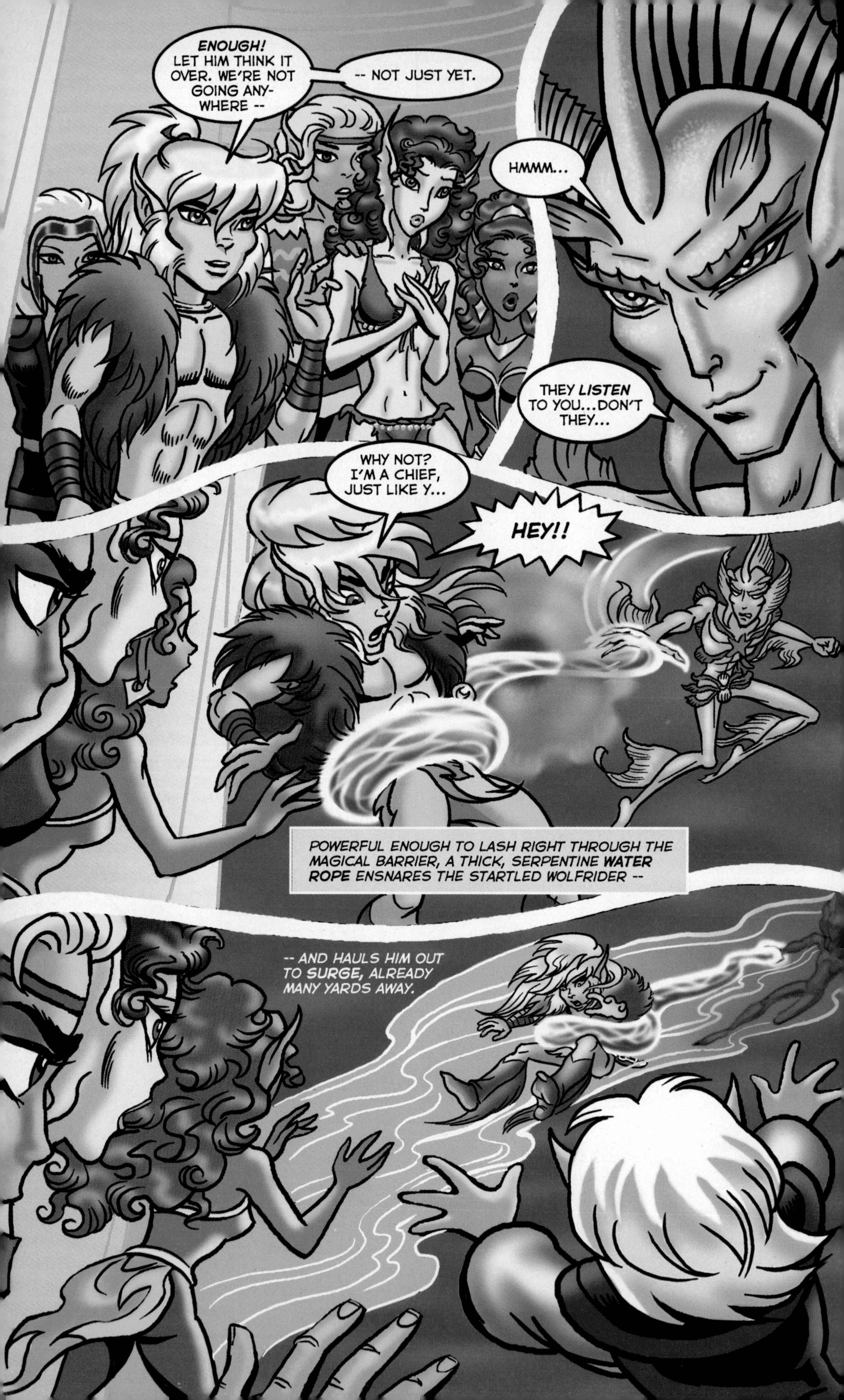
ENOUGH! LET HIM THINK IT OVER. WE'RE NOT GOING ANY-WHERE --
-- NOT JUST YET.
HMMM...
THEY LISTEN TO YOU...DON'T THEY...
WHY NOT? I'M A CHIEF, JUST LIKE Y...
HEY!!
POWERFUL ENOUGH TO LASH RIGHT THROUGH THE MAGICAL BARRIER, A THICK, SERPENTINE WATER ROPE ENSNARES THE STARTLED WOLFRIDER --
-- AND HAULS HIM OUT TO SURGE, ALREADY MANY YARDS AWAY.

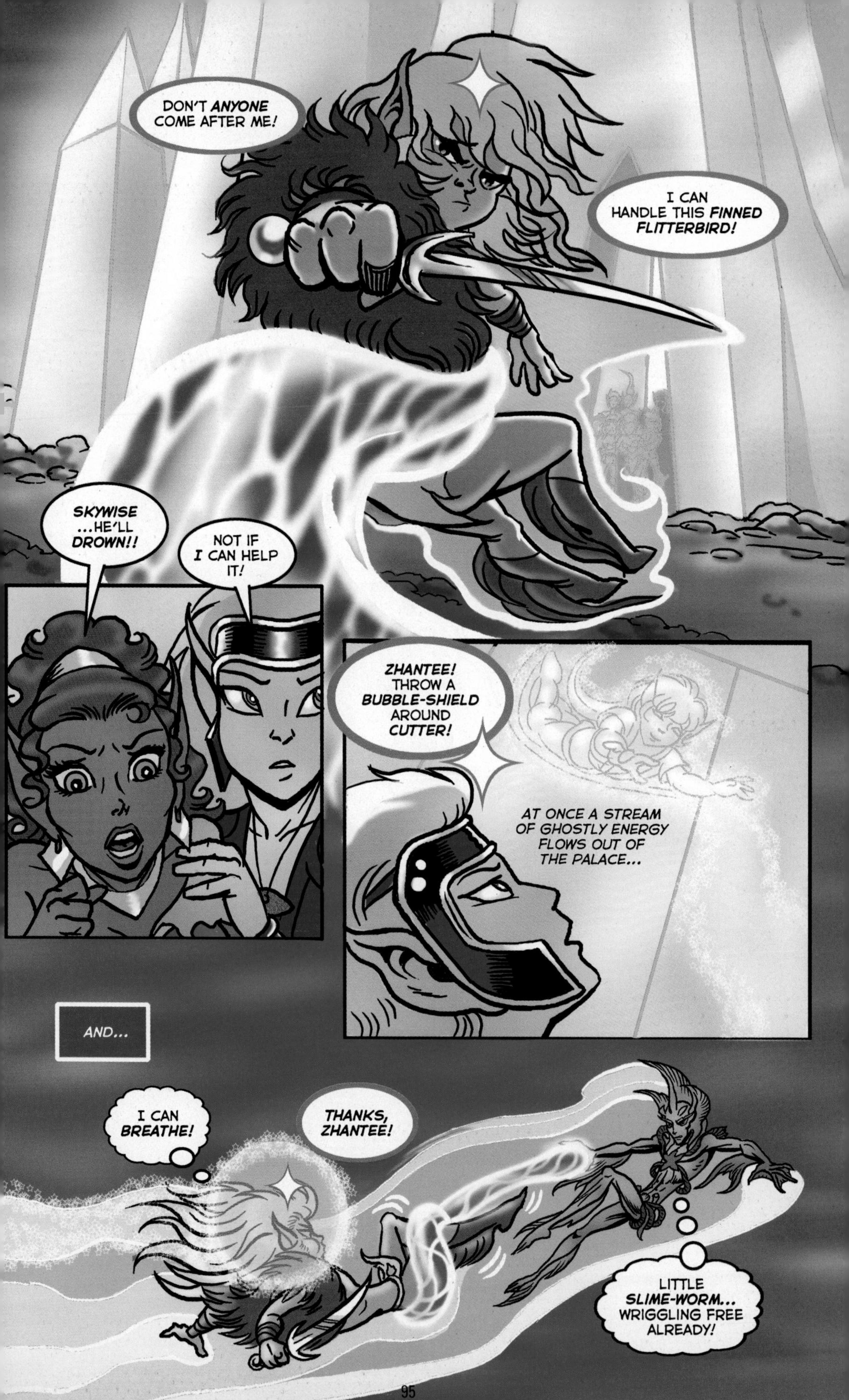
DON'T ANYONE COME AFTER ME!
I CAN HANDLE THIS FINNED FLITTERBIRD!
SKYWISE ...HE'LL DROWN!!
NOT IF I CAN HELP IT!
ZHANTEE! THROW A BUBBLE-SHIELD AROUND CUTTER!
AT ONCE A STREAM OF GHOSTLY ENERGY FLOWS OUT OF THE PALACE...
AND...
I CAN BREATHE!
THANKS, ZHANTEE!
LITTLE SLIME-WORM... WRIGGLING FREE ALREADY!

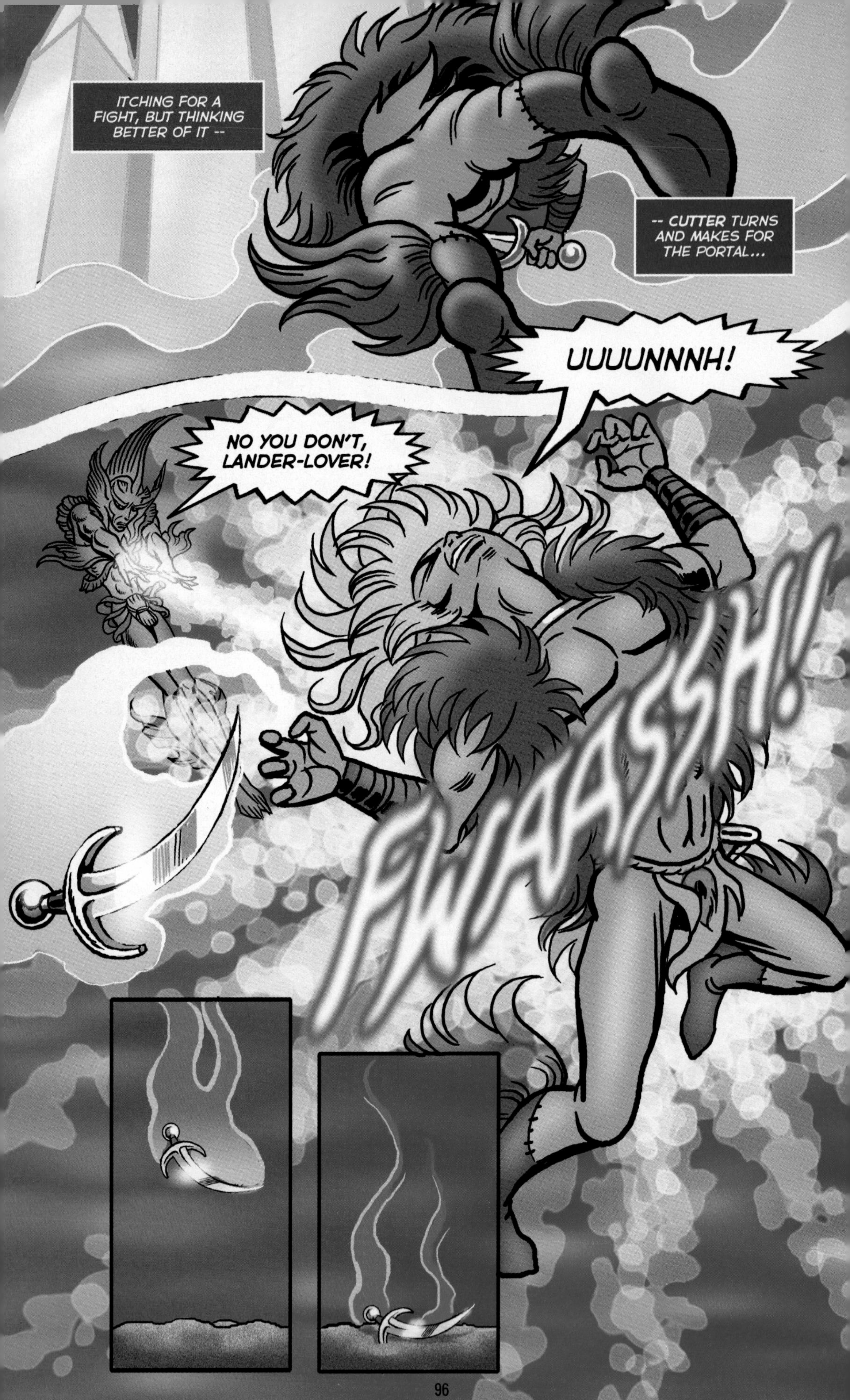
ITCHING FOR A FIGHT, BUT THINKING BETTER OF IT --
-- CUTTER TURNS AND MAKES FOR THE PORTAL...
UUUUNNNH!
NO YOU DON'T, LANDER-LOVER!
FWAASSH!!

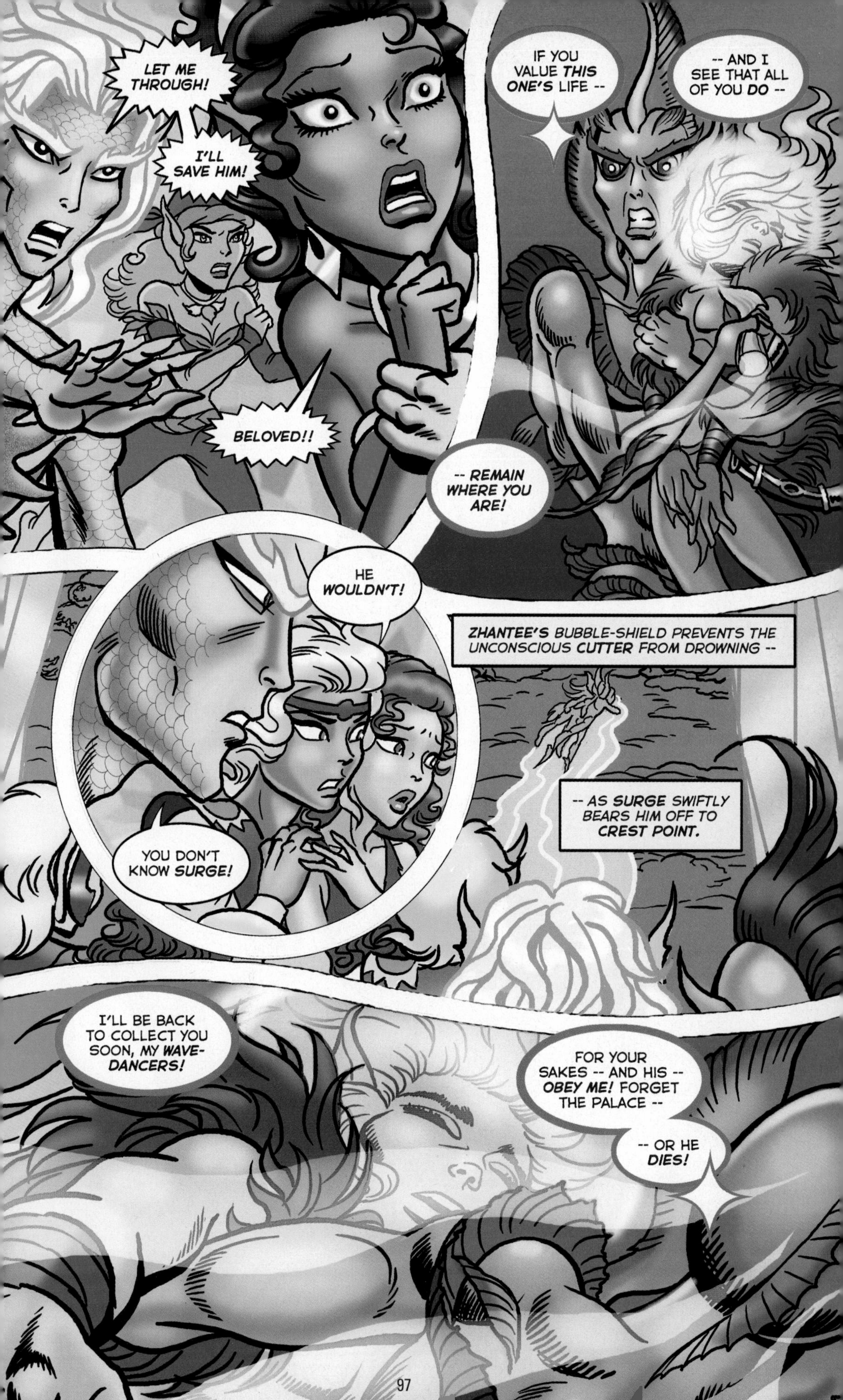

LET ME THROUGH!
I'LL SAVE HIM!
BELOVED!!
IF YOU VALUE THIS ONE'S LIFE --
-- AND I SEE THAT ALL OF YOU DO --
-- REMAIN WHERE YOU ARE!
HE WOULDN'T!
YOU DON'T KNOW SURGE!
ZHANTEE'S BUBBLE-SHIELD PREVENTS THE UNCONSCIOUS CUTTER FROM DROWNING --
-- AS SURGE SWIFTLY BEARS HIM OFF TO CREST POINT.
I'LL BE BACK TO COLLECT YOU SOON, MY WAVE-DANCERS!
FOR YOUR SAKES -- AND HIS -- OBEY ME! FORGET THE PALACE --
-- OR HE DIES!

CHAPTER FOUR

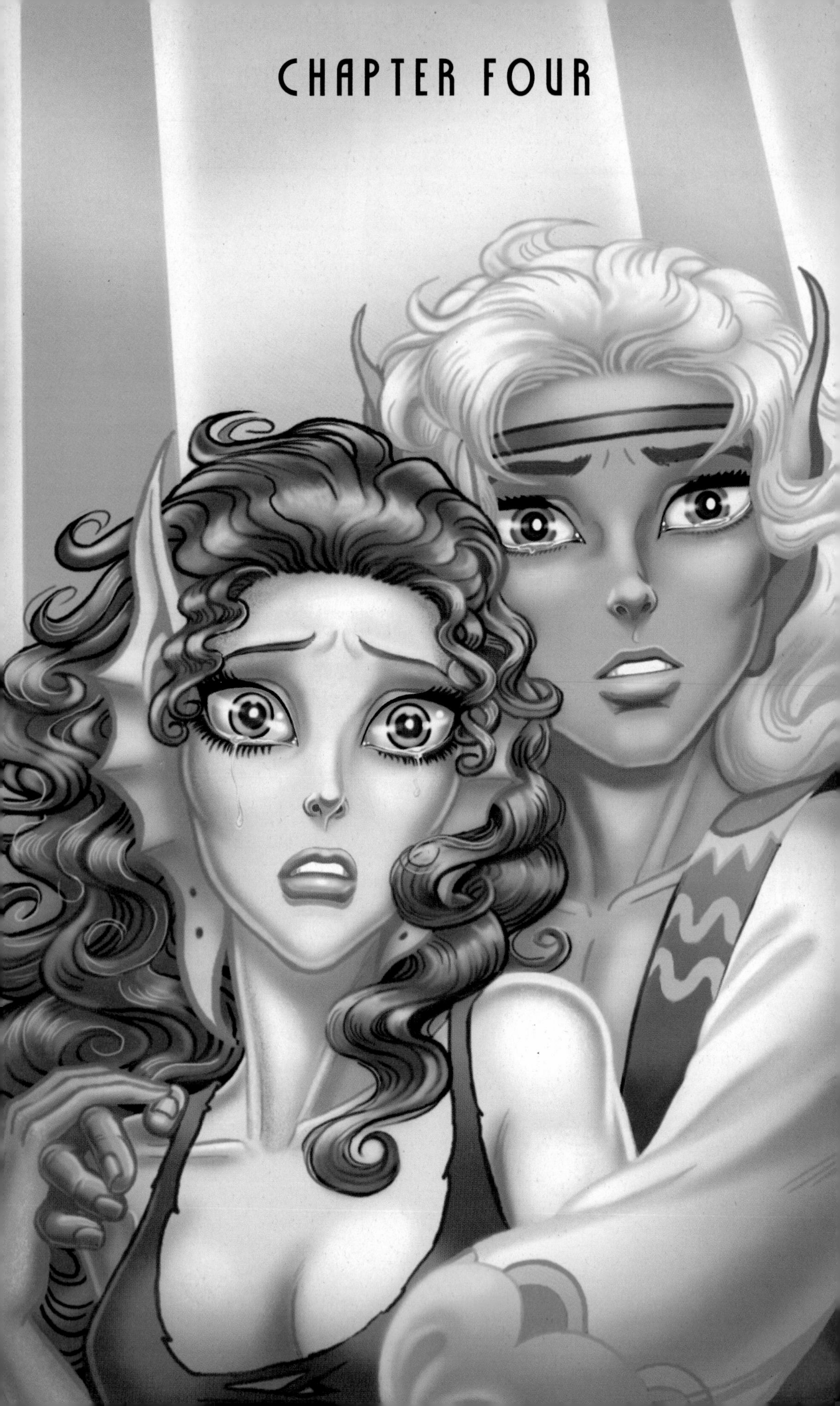

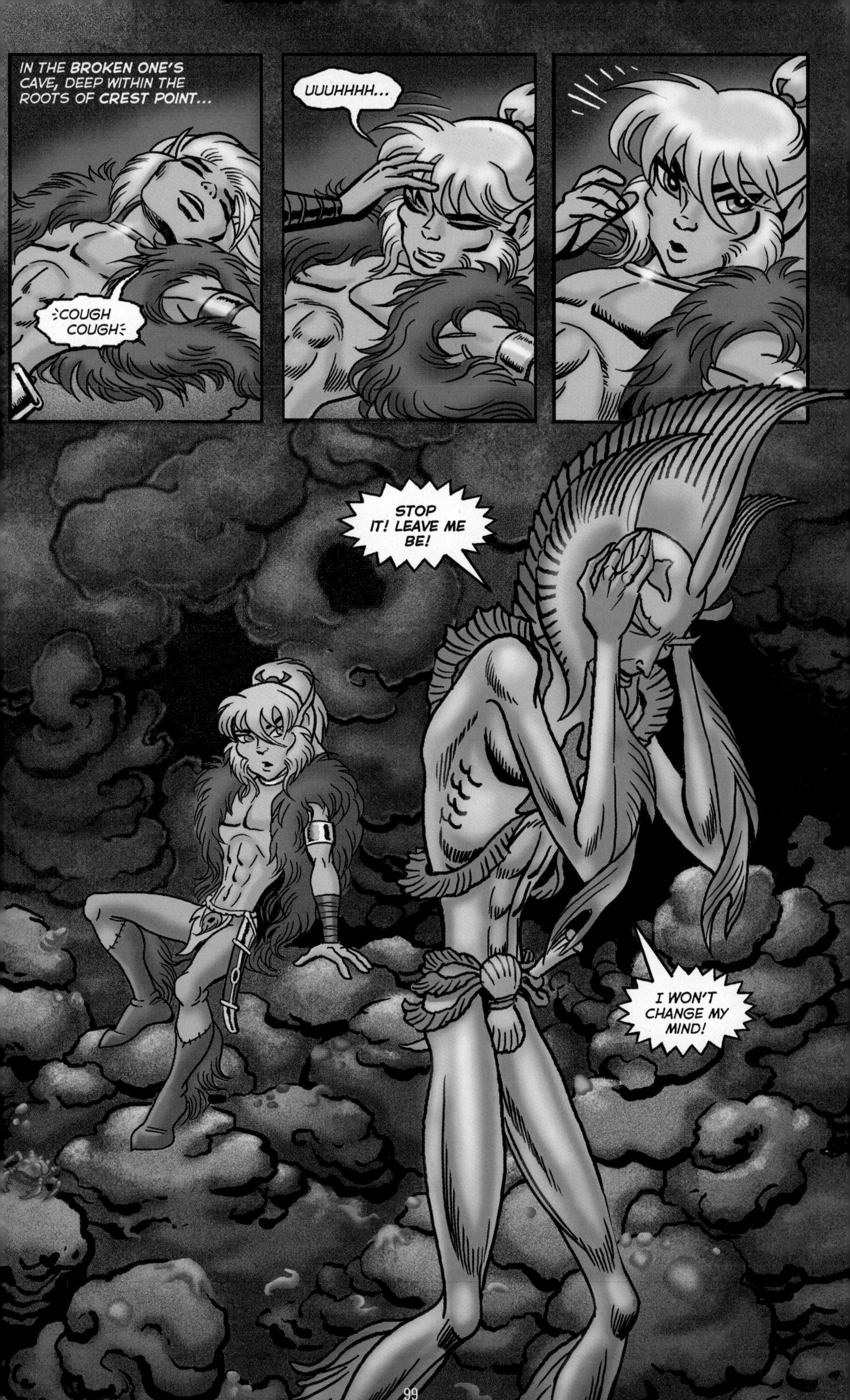
IN THE BROKEN ONE'S CAVE, DEEP WITHIN THE ROOTS OF CREST POINT...
COUGH COUGH
UUUHHHH...
STOP IT! LEAVE ME BE!
I WON'T CHANGE MY MIND!

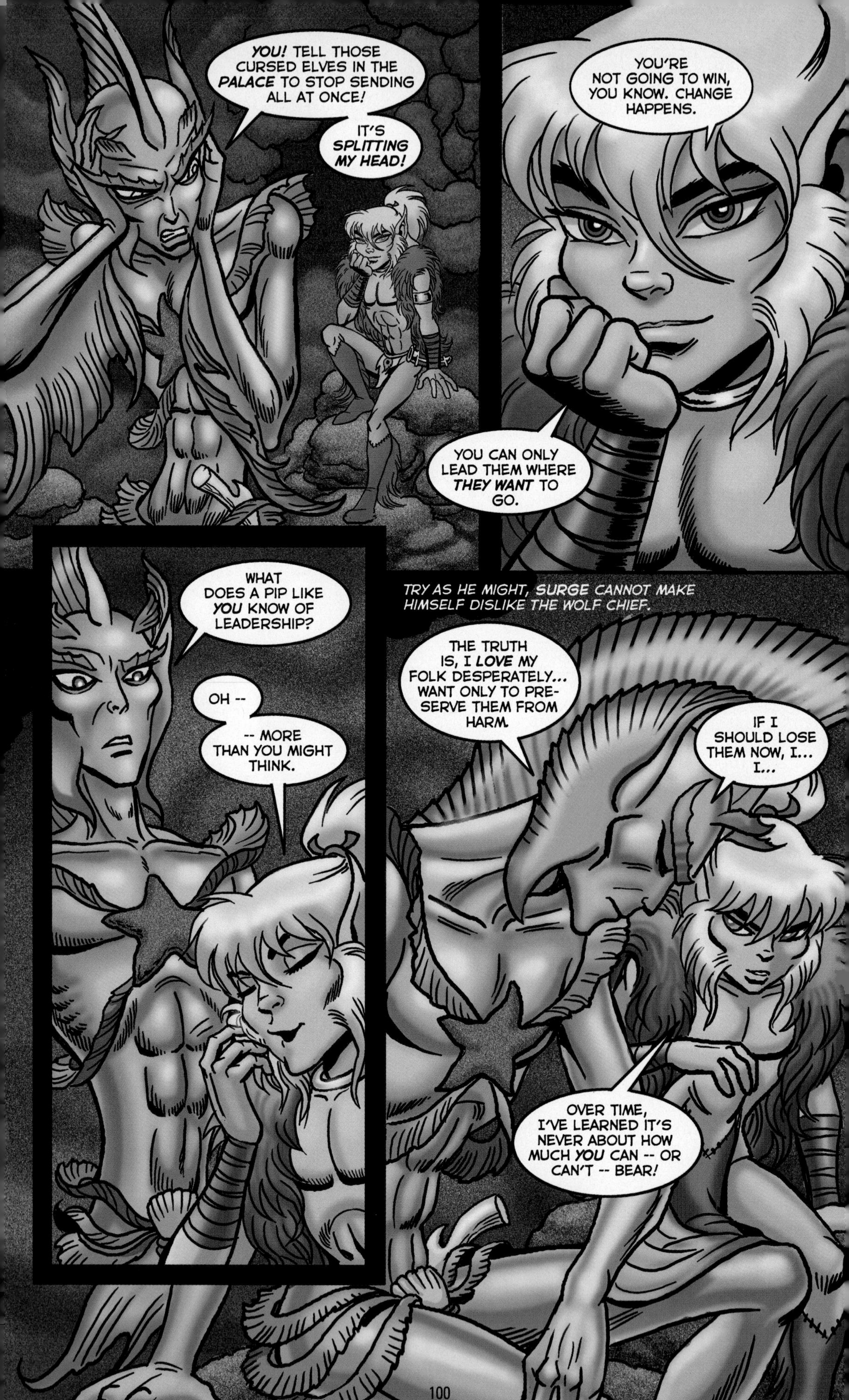
YOU! TELL THOSE CURSED ELVES IN THE PALACE TO STOP SENDING ALL AT ONCE!
IT'S SPLITTING MY HEAD!
YOU'RE NOT GOING TO WIN, YOU KNOW. CHANGE HAPPENS.
YOU CAN ONLY LEAD THEM WHERE THEY WANT TO GO.
WHAT DOES A PIP LIKE YOU KNOW OF LEADERSHIP?
OH --
-- MORE THAN YOU MIGHT THINK.
TRY AS HE MIGHT, SURGE CANNOT MAKE HIMSELF DISLIKE THE WOLF CHIEF.
THE TRUTH IS, I LOVE MY FOLK DESPERATELY... WANT ONLY TO PRESERVE THEM FROM HARM.
IF I SHOULD LOSE THEM NOW, I... I...
OVER TIME, I'VE LEARNED IT'S NEVER ABOUT HOW MUCH YOU CAN -- OR CAN'T -- BEAR!

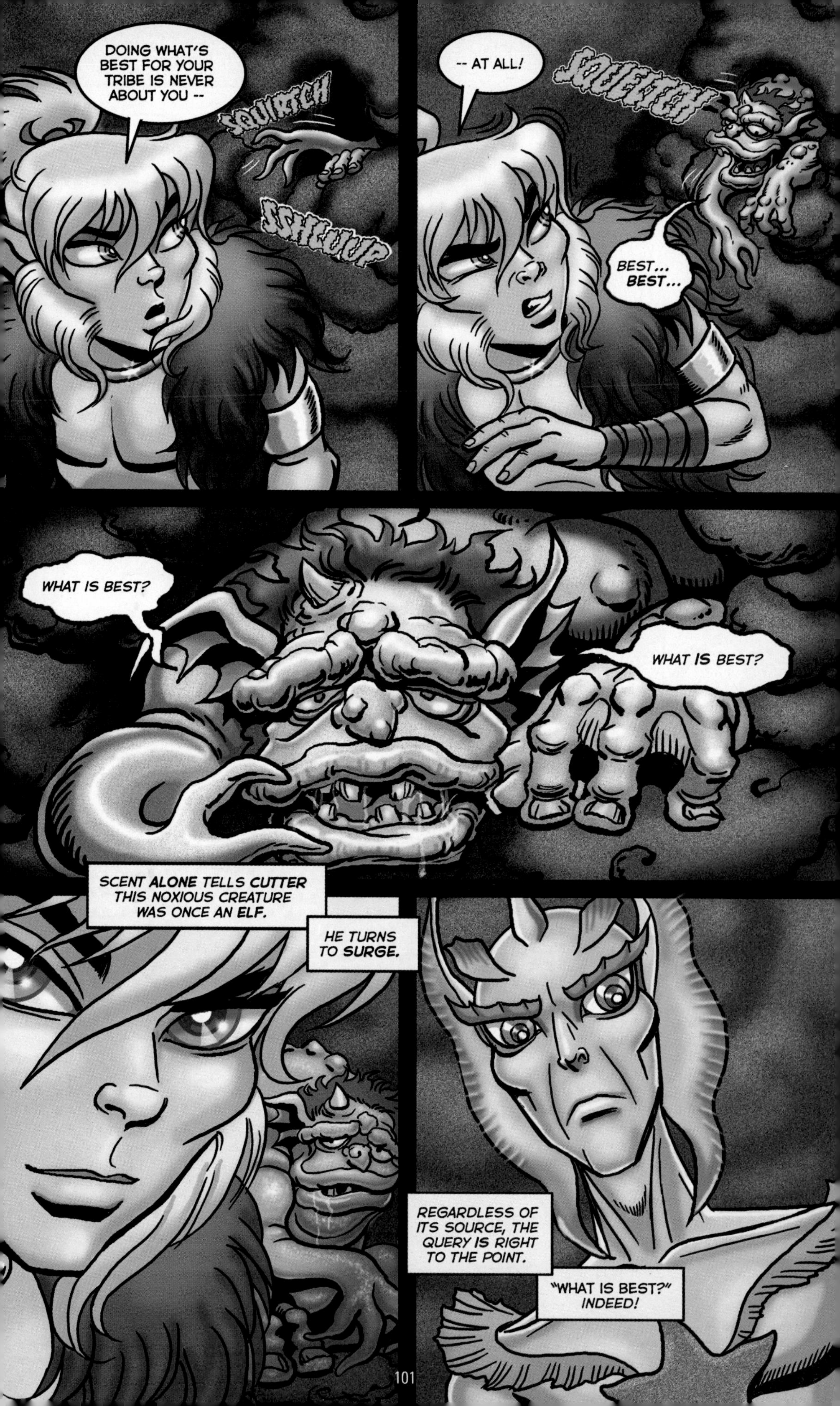
DOING WHAT'S BEST FOR YOUR TRIBE IS NEVER ABOUT YOU --
SQUIRTCH
SSHCUUP
-- AT ALL!
SQUEETCH
BEST... BEST...
WHAT IS BEST?
WHAT IS BEST?
SCENT ALONE TELLS CUTTER THIS NOXIOUS CREATURE WAS ONCE AN ELF.
HE TURNS TO SURGE.
REGARDLESS OF ITS SOURCE, THE QUERY IS RIGHT TO THE POINT.
"WHAT IS BEST?" INDEED!

AT THE SAME TIME, IN THE PALACE...

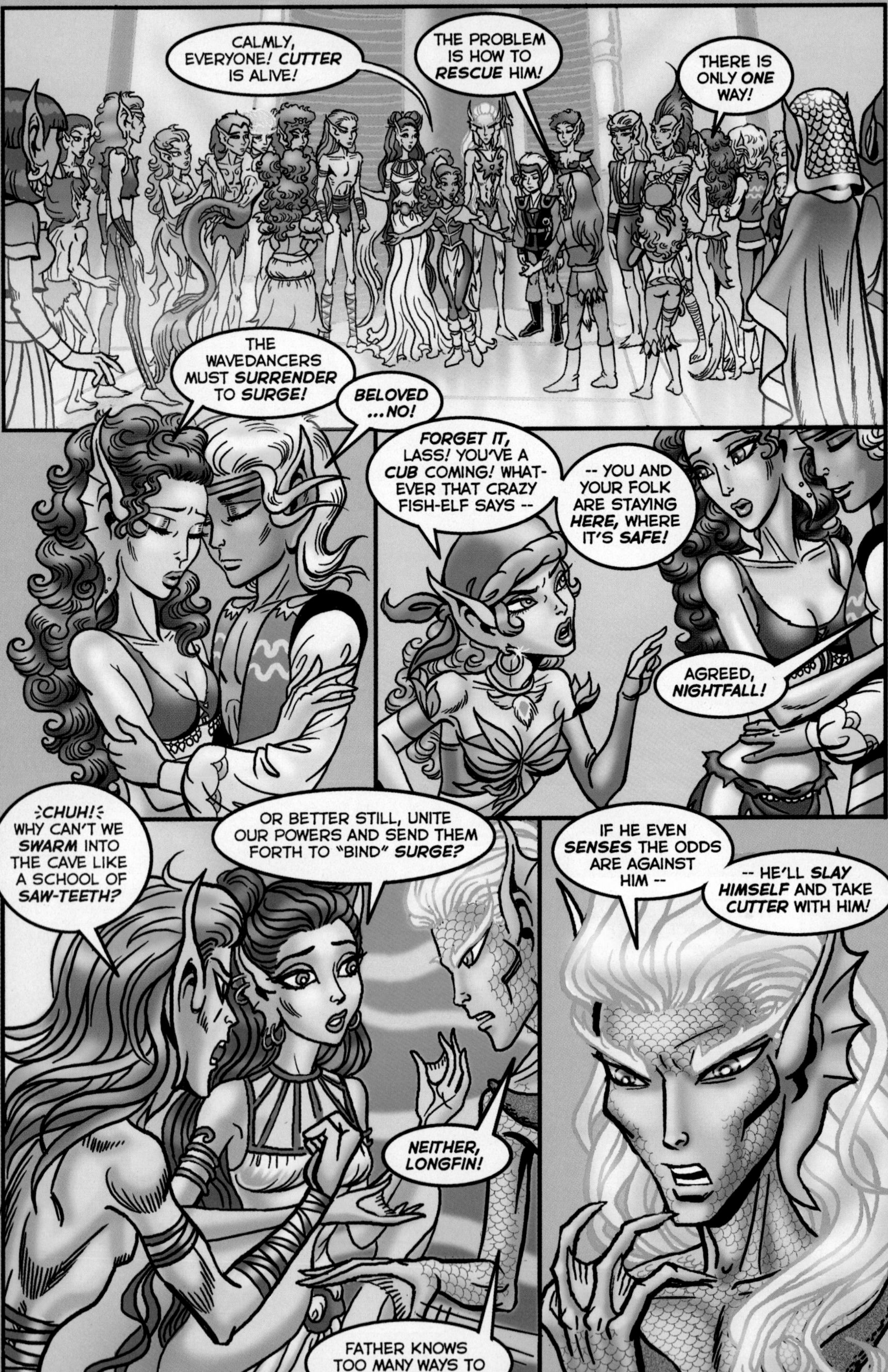
CALMLY, EVERYONE! CUTTER IS ALIVE!
THE PROBLEM IS HOW TO RESCUE HIM!
THERE IS ONLY ONE WAY!
THE WAVEDANCERS MUST SURRENDER TO SURGE!
BELOVED ...NO!
FORGET IT, LASS! YOU'VE A CUB COMING! WHATEVER THAT CRAZY FISH-ELF SAYS --
-- YOU AND YOUR FOLK ARE STAYING HERE, WHERE IT'S SAFE!
AGREED, NIGHTFALL!
CHUH!
WHY CAN'T WE SWARM INTO THE CAVE LIKE A SCHOOL OF SAW-TEETH?
OR BETTER STILL, UNITE OUR POWERS AND SEND THEM FORTH TO "BIND" SURGE?
NEITHER, LONGFIN!
FATHER KNOWS TOO MANY WAYS TO KILL QUICKLY!
IF HE EVEN SENSES THE ODDS ARE AGAINST HIM --
-- HE'LL SLAY HIMSELF AND TAKE CUTTER WITH HIM!

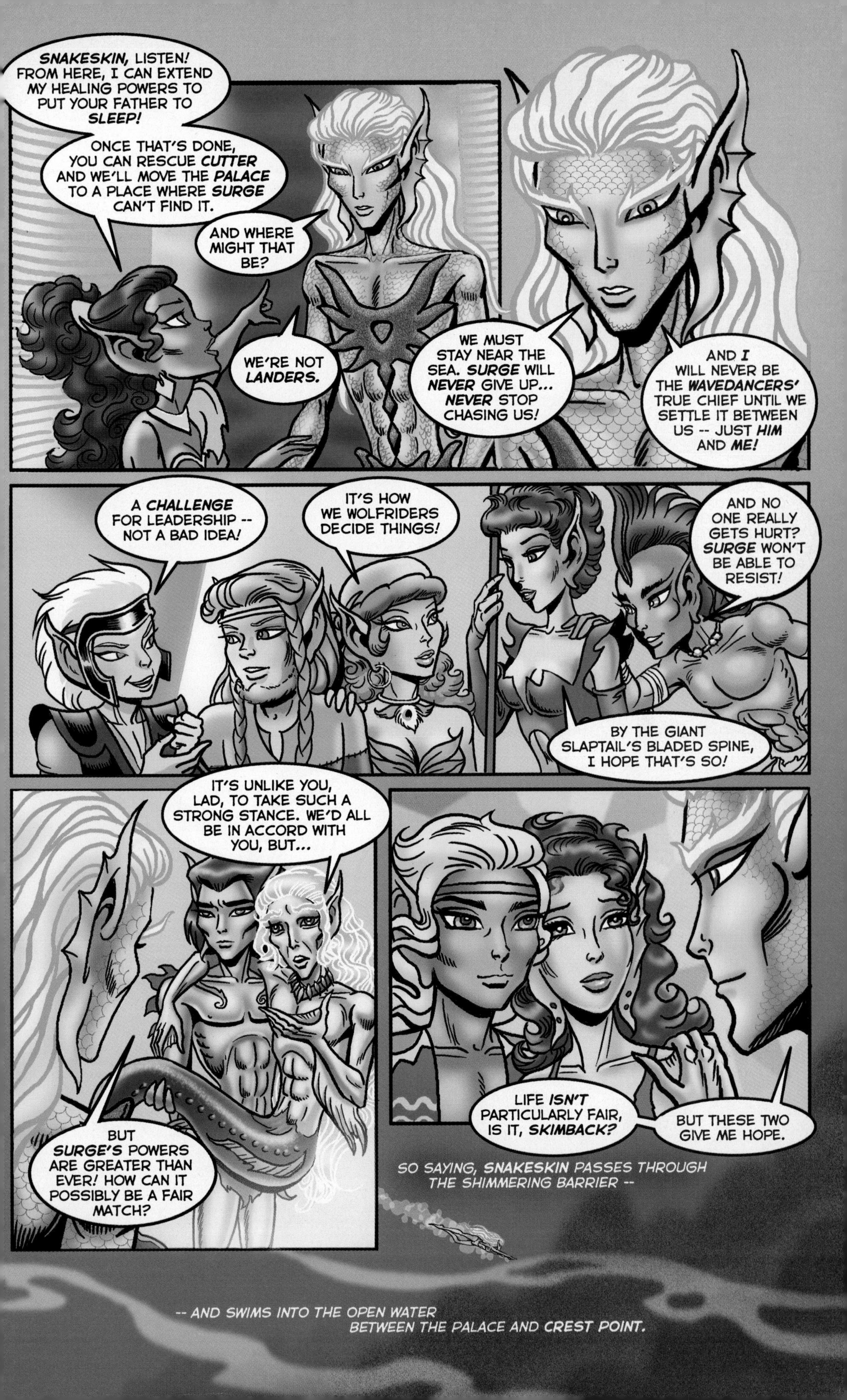
SNAKESKIN, LISTEN! FROM HERE, I CAN EXTEND MY HEALING POWERS TO PUT YOUR FATHER TO SLEEP!
ONCE THAT'S DONE, YOU CAN RESCUE CUTTER AND WE'LL MOVE THE PALACE TO A PLACE WHERE SURGE CAN'T FIND IT.
AND WHERE MIGHT THAT BE?
WE'RE NOT LANDERS.
WE MUST STAY NEAR THE SEA. SURGE WILL NEVER GIVE UP... NEVER STOP CHASING US!
AND I WILL NEVER BE THE WAVEDANCERS' TRUE CHIEF UNTIL WE SETTLE IT BETWEEN US -- JUST HIM AND ME!
A CHALLENGE FOR LEADERSHIP -- NOT A BAD IDEA!
IT'S HOW WE WOLFRIDERS DECIDE THINGS!
AND NO ONE REALLY GETS HURT? SURGE WON'T BE ABLE TO RESIST!
BY THE GIANT SLAPTAIL'S BLADED SPINE, I HOPE THAT'S SO!
IT'S UNLIKE YOU, LAD, TO TAKE SUCH A STRONG STANCE. WE'D ALL BE IN ACCORD WITH YOU, BUT...
BUT SURGE'S POWERS ARE GREATER THAN EVER! HOW CAN IT POSSIBLY BE A FAIR MATCH?
LIFE ISN'T PARTICULARLY FAIR, IS IT, SKIMBACK?
BUT THESE TWO GIVE ME HOPE.
SO SAYING, SNAKESKIN PASSES THROUGH THE SHIMMERING BARRIER --
-- AND SWIMS INTO THE OPEN WATER BETWEEN THE PALACE AND CREST POINT.

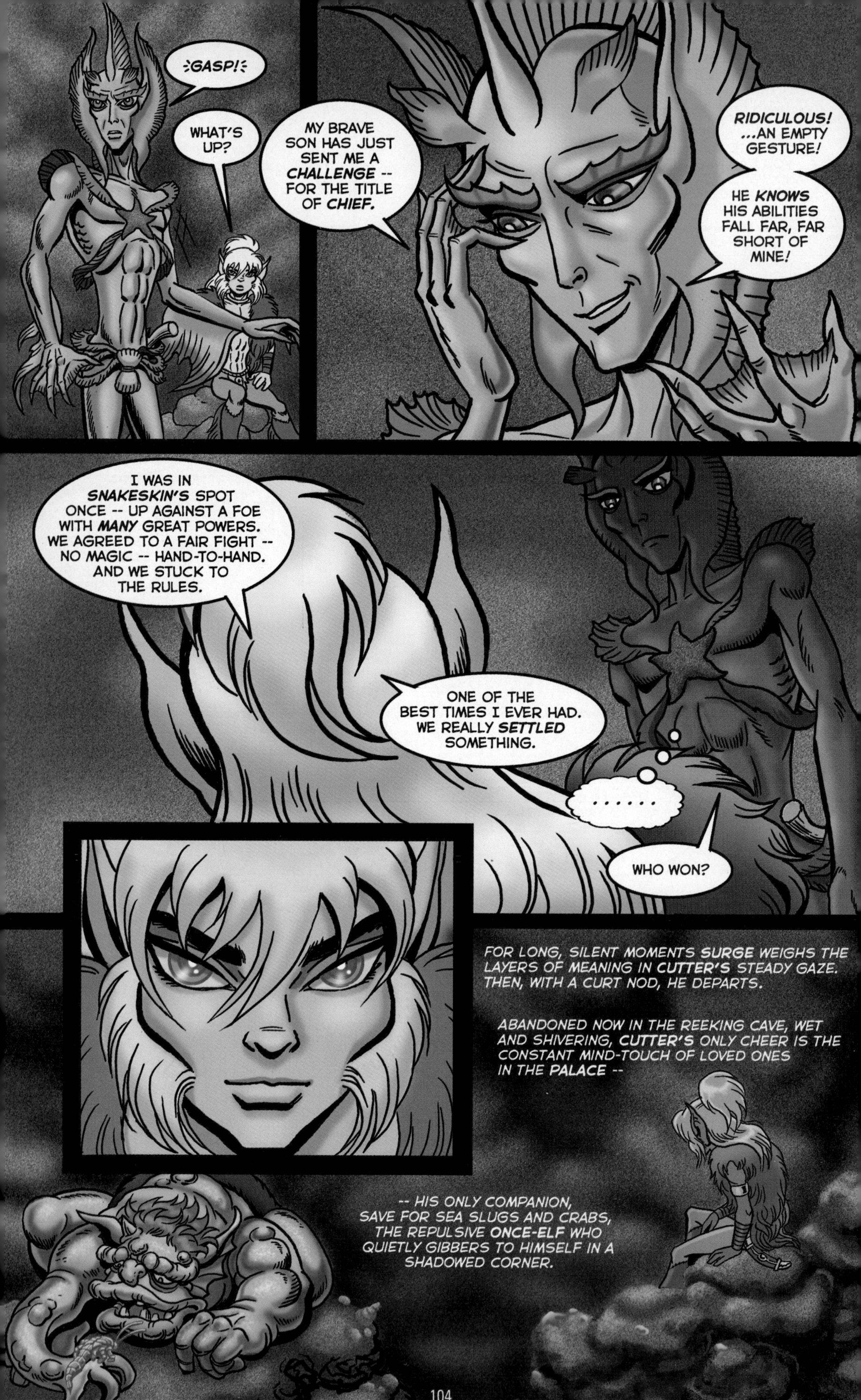

GASP!
WHAT'S UP?
MY BRAVE SON HAS JUST SENT ME A CHALLENGE -- FOR THE TITLE OF CHIEF.
RIDICULOUS! ...AN EMPTY GESTURE!
HE KNOWS HIS ABILITIES FALL FAR, FAR SHORT OF MINE!
I WAS IN SNAKESKIN'S SPOT ONCE -- UP AGAINST A FOE WITH MANY GREAT POWERS. WE AGREED TO A FAIR FIGHT -- NO MAGIC -- HAND-TO-HAND. AND WE STUCK TO THE RULES.
ONE OF THE BEST TIMES I EVER HAD. WE REALLY SETTLED SOMETHING.
......
WHO WON?
FOR LONG, SILENT MOMENTS SURGE WEIGHS THE LAYERS OF MEANING IN CUTTER'S STEADY GAZE. THEN, WITH A CURT NOD, HE DEPARTS.
ABANDONED NOW IN THE REEKING CAVE, WET AND SHIVERING, CUTTER'S ONLY CHEER IS THE CONSTANT MIND-TOUCH OF LOVED ONES IN THE PALACE --
-- HIS ONLY COMPANION, SAVE FOR SEA SLUGS AND CRABS, THE REPULSIVE ONCE-ELF WHO QUIETLY GIBBERS TO HIMSELF IN A SHADOWED CORNER.

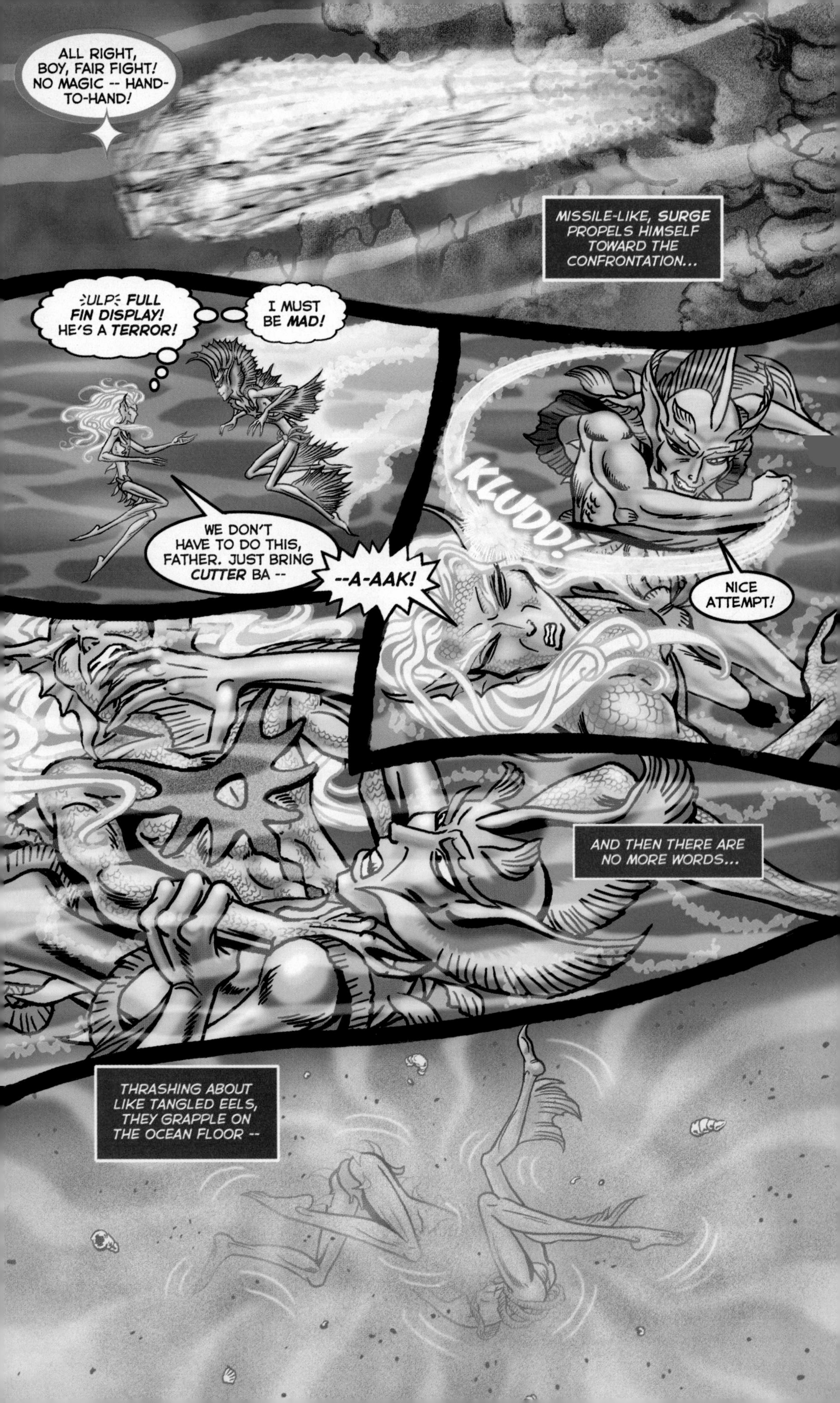
ALL RIGHT, BOY, FAIR FIGHT! NO MAGIC -- HAND-TO-HAND!
MISSILE-LIKE, SURGE PROPELS HIMSELF TOWARD THE CONFRONTATION...
ULP FULL FIN DISPLAY! HE'S A TERROR!
I MUST BE MAD!
WE DON'T HAVE TO DO THIS, FATHER. JUST BRING CUTTER BA --
KLUDD!
--A-AAK!
NICE ATTEMPT!
AND THEN THERE ARE NO MORE WORDS...
THRASHING ABOUT LIKE TANGLED EELS, THEY GRAPPLE ON THE OCEAN FLOOR --

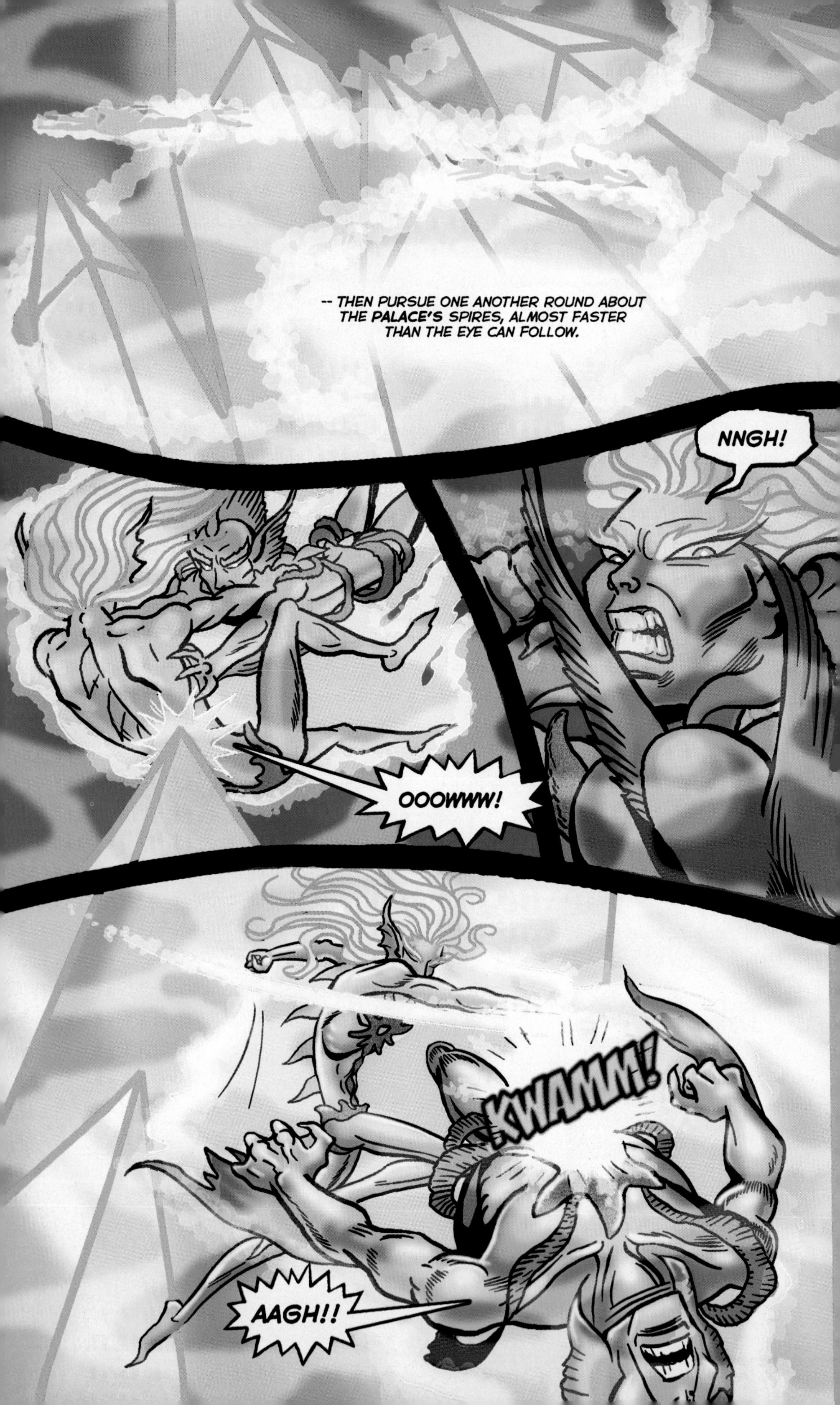
-- THEN PURSUE ONE ANOTHER ROUND ABOUT THE **PALACE'S** SPIRES, ALMOST FASTER THAN THE EYE CAN FOLLOW.
OOOWWW!
NNGH!
KWAMM!
AAGH!!

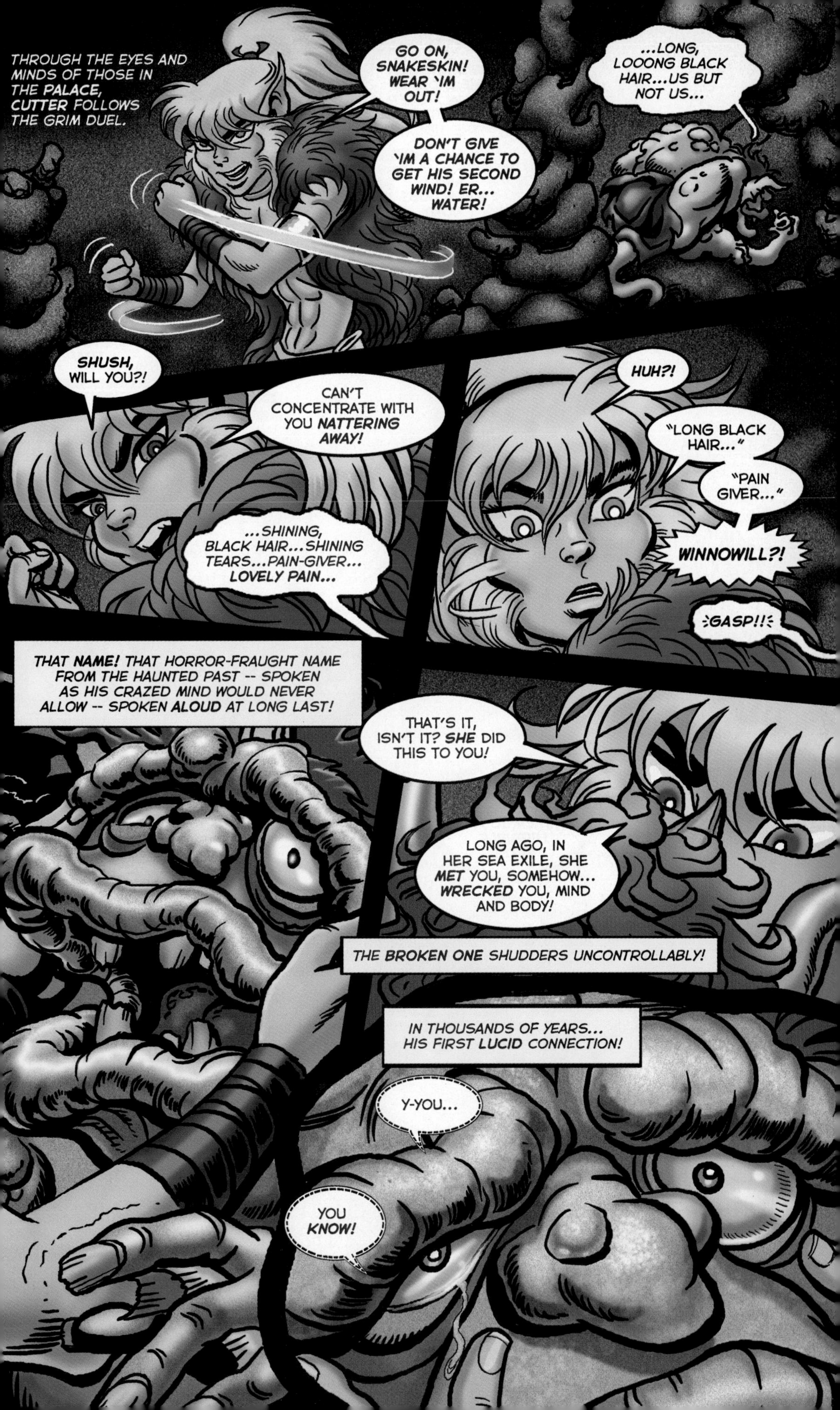
THROUGH THE EYES AND MINDS OF THOSE IN THE PALACE, CUTTER FOLLOWS THE GRIM DUEL.
GO ON, SNAKESKIN! WEAR 'IM OUT!
DON'T GIVE 'IM A CHANCE TO GET HIS SECOND WIND! ER... WATER!
...LONG, LOOONG BLACK HAIR...US BUT NOT US...
SHUSH, WILL YOU?!
CAN'T CONCENTRATE WITH YOU NATTERING AWAY!
...SHINING, BLACK HAIR...SHINING TEARS...PAIN-GIVER... LOVELY PAIN...
HUH?!
"LONG BLACK HAIR..."
"PAIN GIVER..."
WINNOWILL?!
GASP!!
THAT NAME! THAT HORROR-FRAUGHT NAME FROM THE HAUNTED PAST -- SPOKEN AS HIS CRAZED MIND WOULD NEVER ALLOW -- SPOKEN ALOUD AT LONG LAST!
THAT'S IT, ISN'T IT? SHE DID THIS TO YOU!
LONG AGO, IN HER SEA EXILE, SHE MET YOU, SOMEHOW... WRECKED YOU, MIND AND BODY!
THE BROKEN ONE SHUDDERS UNCONTROLLABLY!
IN THOUSANDS OF YEARS... HIS FIRST LUCID CONNECTION!
Y-YOU...
YOU KNOW!

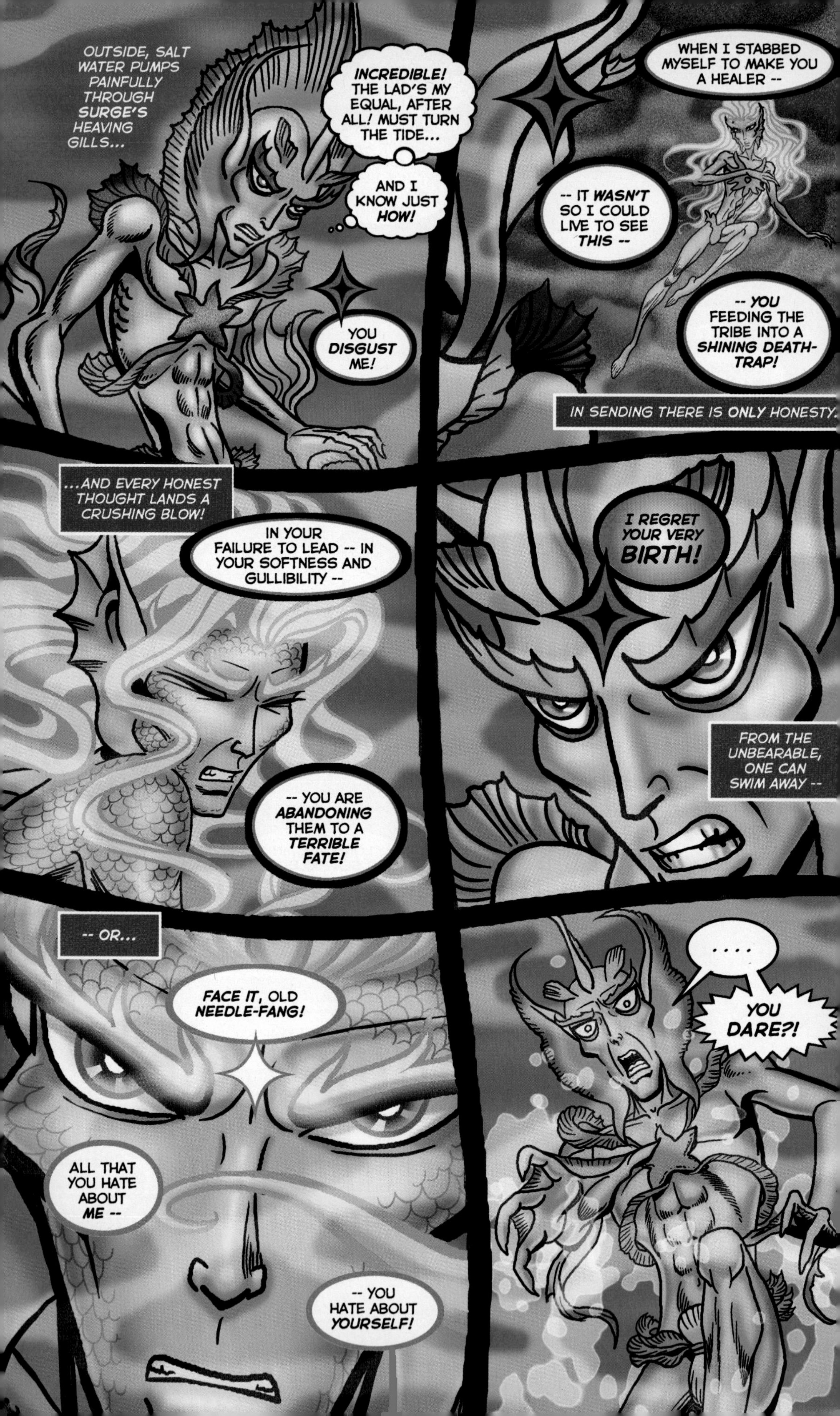
OUTSIDE, SALT WATER PUMPS PAINFULLY THROUGH SURGE'S HEAVING GILLS...
INCREDIBLE! THE LAD'S MY EQUAL, AFTER ALL! MUST TURN THE TIDE...
AND I KNOW JUST HOW!
YOU DISGUST ME!
WHEN I STABBED MYSELF TO MAKE YOU A HEALER --
-- IT WASN'T SO I COULD LIVE TO SEE THIS --
-- YOU FEEDING THE TRIBE INTO A SHINING DEATH-TRAP!
IN SENDING THERE IS ONLY HONESTY.
...AND EVERY HONEST THOUGHT LANDS A CRUSHING BLOW!
IN YOUR FAILURE TO LEAD -- IN YOUR SOFTNESS AND GULLIBILITY --
-- YOU ARE ABANDONING THEM TO A TERRIBLE FATE!
I REGRET YOUR VERY BIRTH!
FROM THE UNBEARABLE, ONE CAN SWIM AWAY --
-- OR...
FACE IT, OLD NEEDLE-FANG!
ALL THAT YOU HATE ABOUT ME --
-- YOU HATE ABOUT YOURSELF!
....
YOU DARE?!

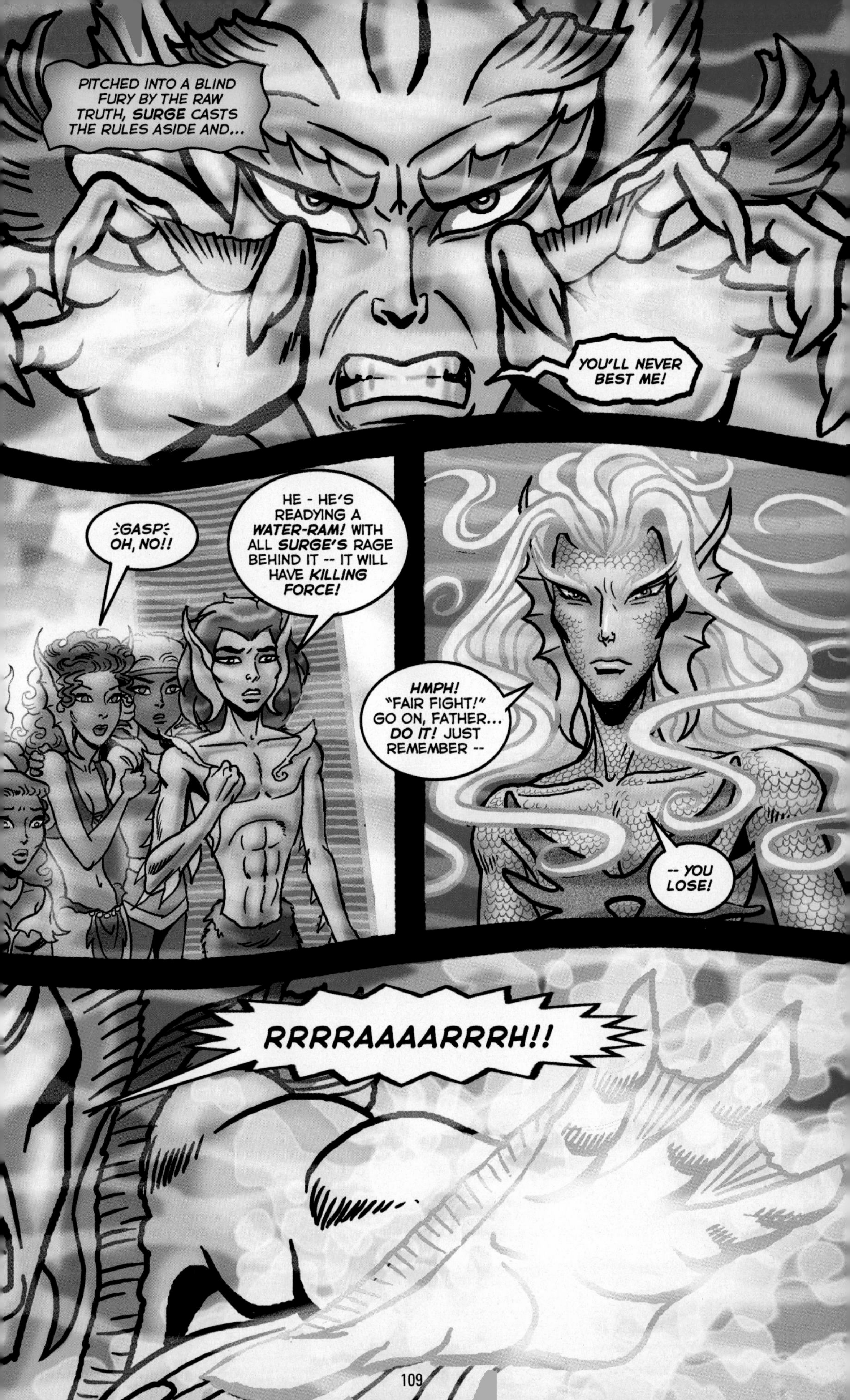
PITCHED INTO A BLIND FURY BY THE RAW TRUTH, SURGE CASTS THE RULES ASIDE AND...
YOU'LL NEVER BEST ME!
:GASP: OH, NO!!
HE - HE'S READYING A WATER-RAM! WITH ALL SURGE'S RAGE BEHIND IT -- IT WILL HAVE KILLING FORCE!
HMPH! "FAIR FIGHT!" GO ON, FATHER... DO IT! JUST REMEMBER --
-- YOU LOSE!
RRRRAAAARRRH!!

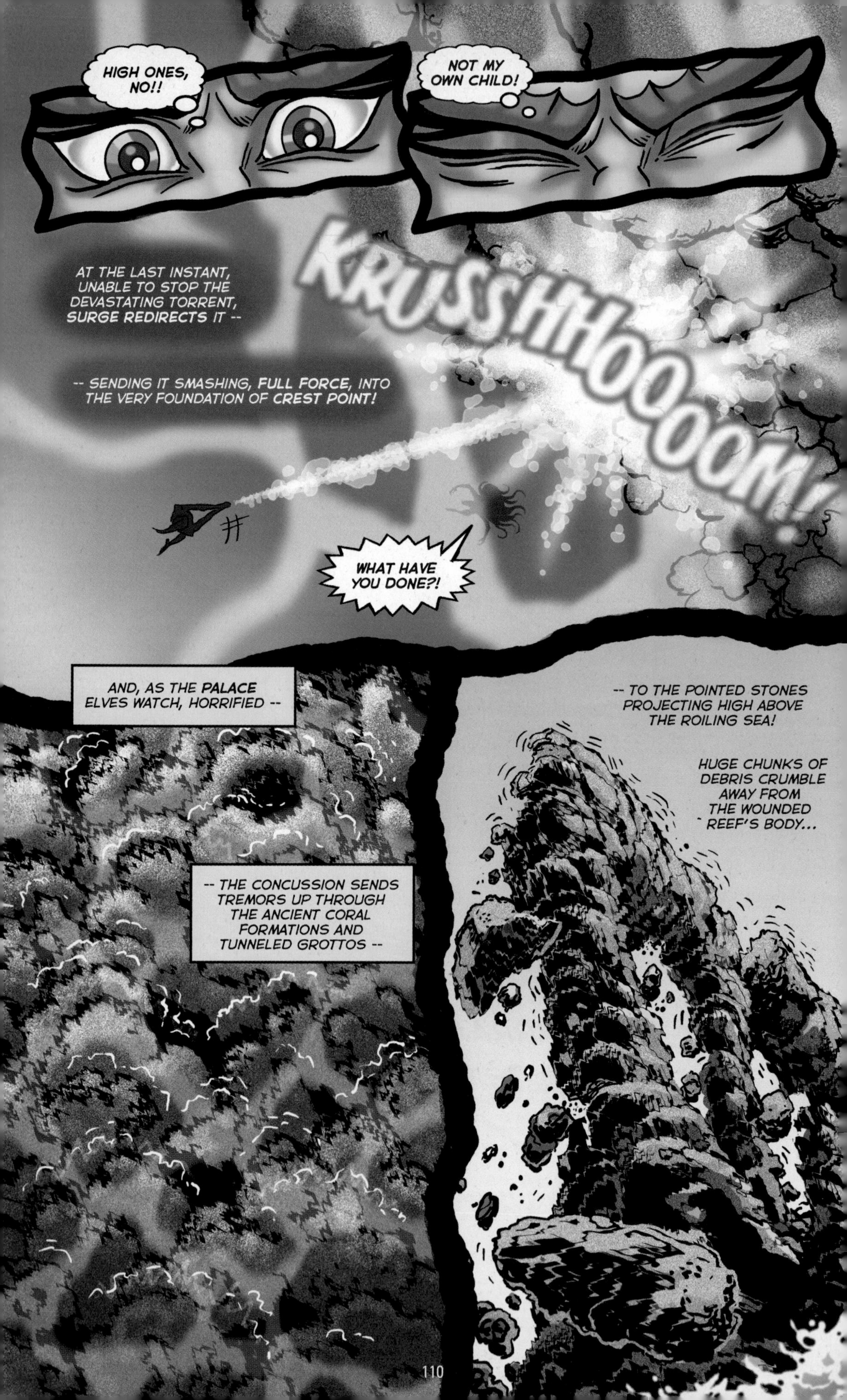

HIGH ONES, NO!!
NOT MY OWN CHILD!
KRUSSHHOOOOOM!!
AT THE LAST INSTANT, UNABLE TO STOP THE DEVASTATING TORRENT, SURGE REDIRECTS IT --
-- SENDING IT SMASHING, FULL FORCE, INTO THE VERY FOUNDATION OF CREST POINT!
WHAT HAVE YOU DONE?!
AND, AS THE PALACE ELVES WATCH, HORRIFIED --
-- THE CONCUSSION SENDS TREMORS UP THROUGH THE ANCIENT CORAL FORMATIONS AND TUNNELED GROTTOS --
-- TO THE POINTED STONES PROJECTING HIGH ABOVE THE ROILING SEA!
HUGE CHUNKS OF DEBRIS CRUMBLE AWAY FROM THE WOUNDED REEF'S BODY...

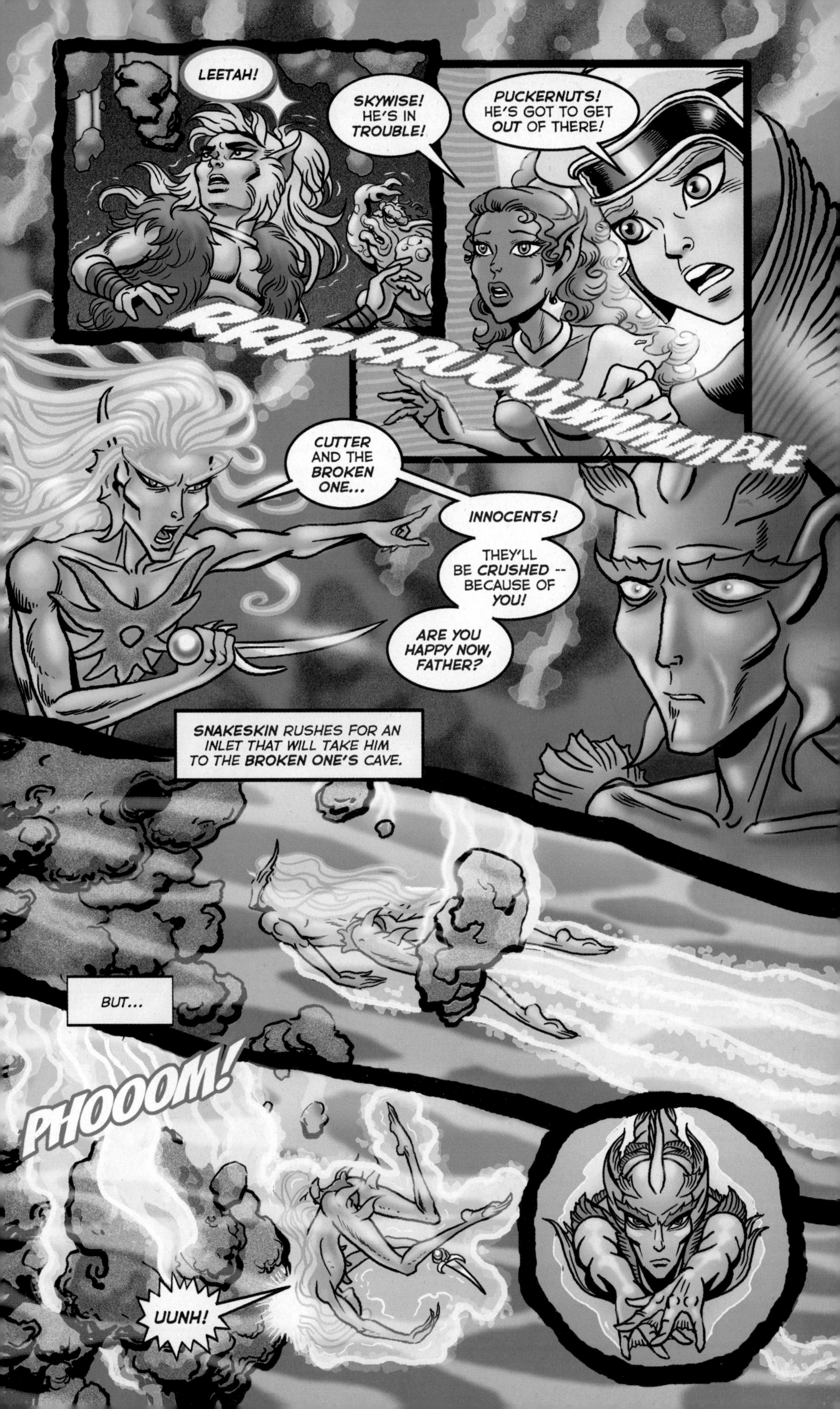
LEETAH!
SKYWISE! HE'S IN TROUBLE!
PUCKERNUTS! HE'S GOT TO GET OUT OF THERE!
RRRRRUMMMMMBLE
CUTTER AND THE BROKEN ONE...
INNOCENTS!
THEY'LL BE CRUSHED -- BECAUSE OF YOU!
ARE YOU HAPPY NOW, FATHER?
SNAKESKIN RUSHES FOR AN INLET THAT WILL TAKE HIM TO THE BROKEN ONE'S CAVE.
BUT...
PHOOOM!
UUNH!

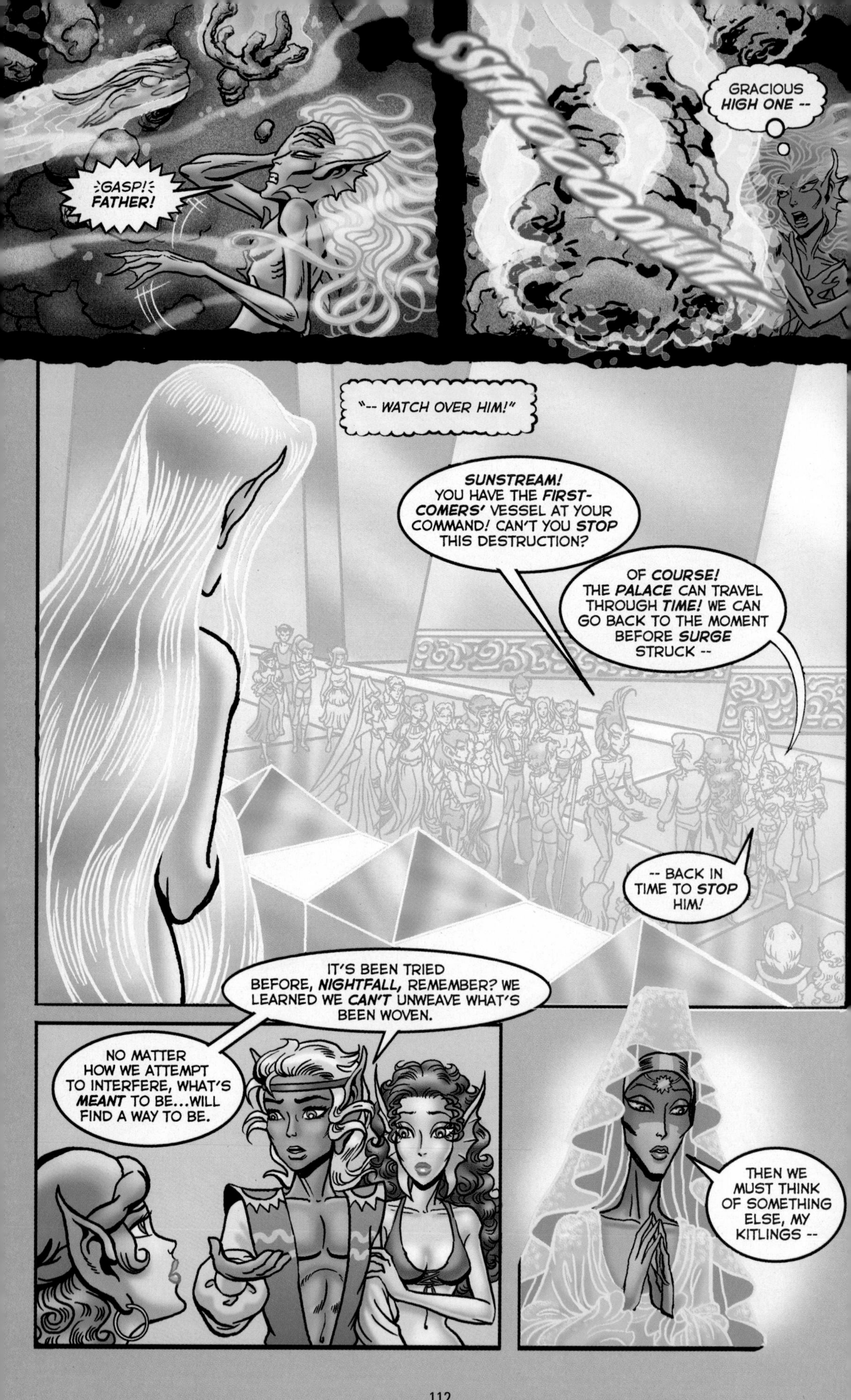

GASP! FATHER!
GRACIOUS HIGH ONE --
"-- WATCH OVER HIM!"
SUNSTREAM! YOU HAVE THE FIRST-COMERS' VESSEL AT YOUR COMMAND! CAN'T YOU STOP THIS DESTRUCTION?
OF COURSE! THE PALACE CAN TRAVEL THROUGH TIME! WE CAN GO BACK TO THE MOMENT BEFORE SURGE STRUCK --
-- BACK IN TIME TO STOP HIM!
IT'S BEEN TRIED BEFORE, NIGHTFALL, REMEMBER? WE LEARNED WE CAN'T UNWEAVE WHAT'S BEEN WOVEN.
NO MATTER HOW WE ATTEMPT TO INTERFERE, WHAT'S MEANT TO BE...WILL FIND A WAY TO BE.
THEN WE MUST THINK OF SOMETHING ELSE, MY KITLINGS --

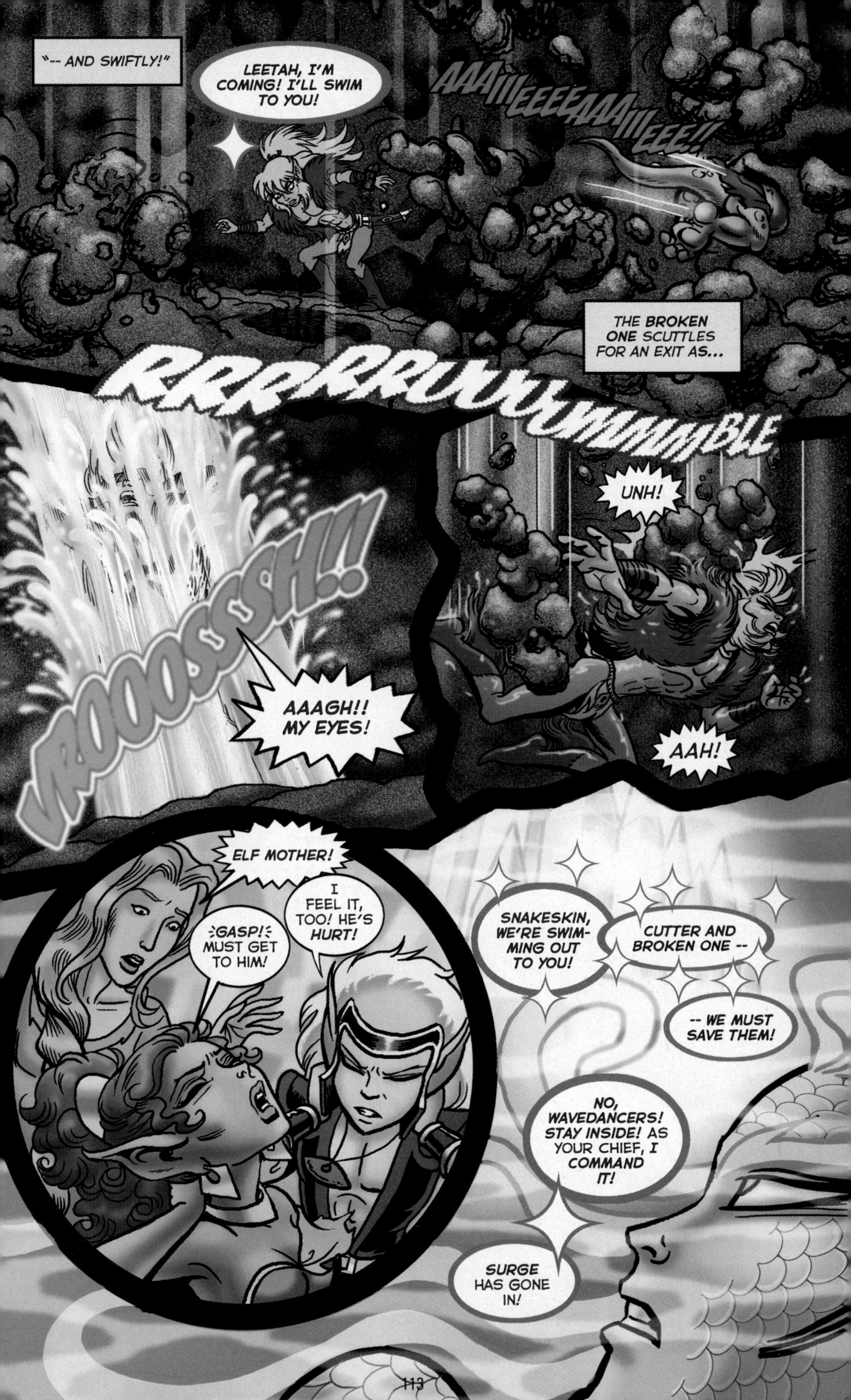
"-- AND SWIFTLY!"
LEETAH, I'M COMING! I'LL SWIM TO YOU!
AAAIIIEEEEAAAIIIEEE!!
THE BROKEN ONE SCUTTLES FOR AN EXIT AS...
RRRRUUUMMMBLE
VROOOSSSH!!
AAAGH!! MY EYES!
UNH!
AAH!
ELF MOTHER!
:GASP!: MUST GET TO HIM!
I FEEL IT, TOO! HE'S HURT!
SNAKESKIN, WE'RE SWIMMING OUT TO YOU!
CUTTER AND BROKEN ONE --
-- WE MUST SAVE THEM!
NO, WAVEDANCERS! STAY INSIDE! AS YOUR CHIEF, I COMMAND IT!
SURGE HAS GONE IN!

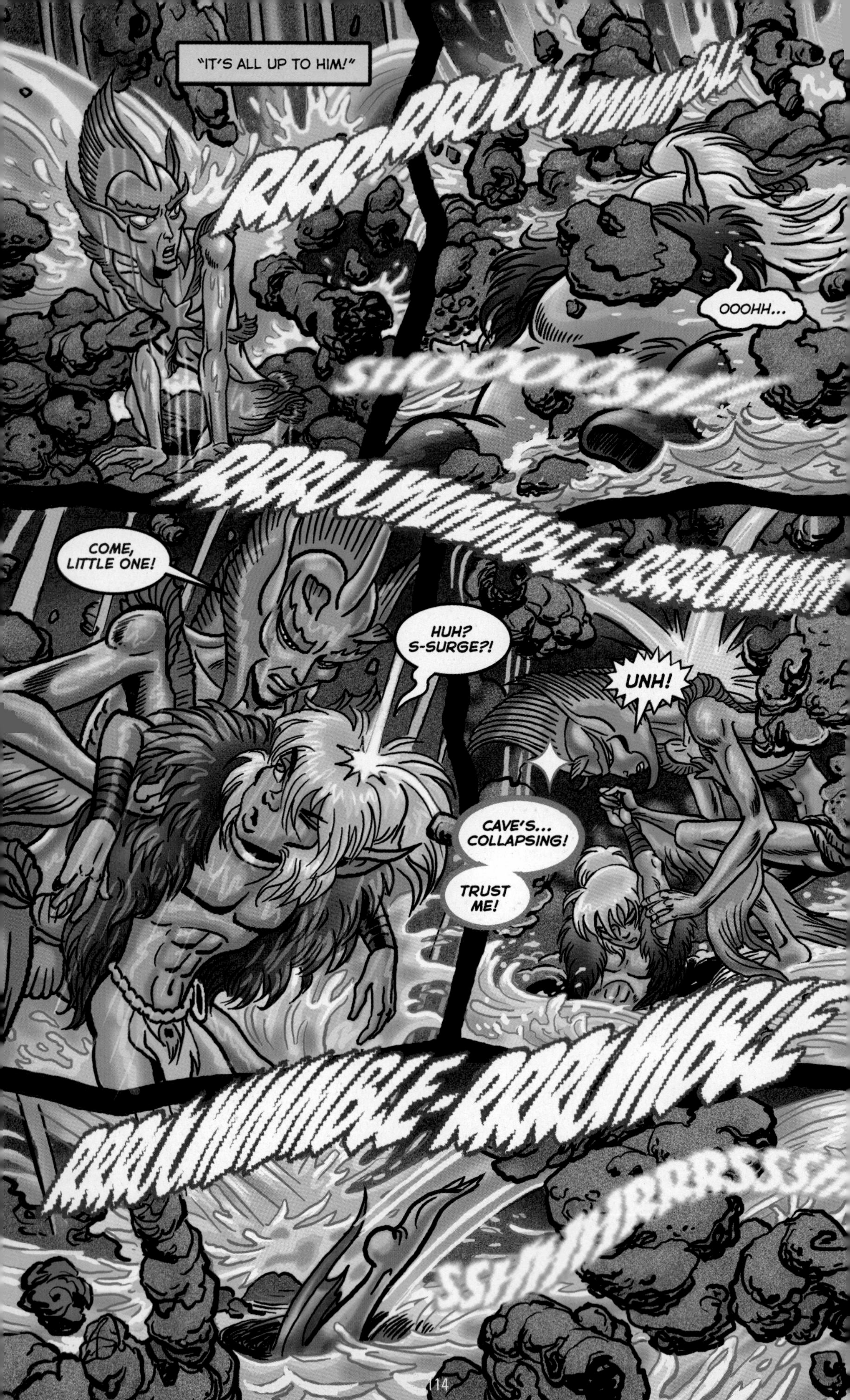
"IT'S ALL UP TO HIM!"
OOOHH...
COME, LITTLE ONE!
HUH? S-SURGE?!
UNH!
CAVE'S... COLLAPSING!
TRUST ME!

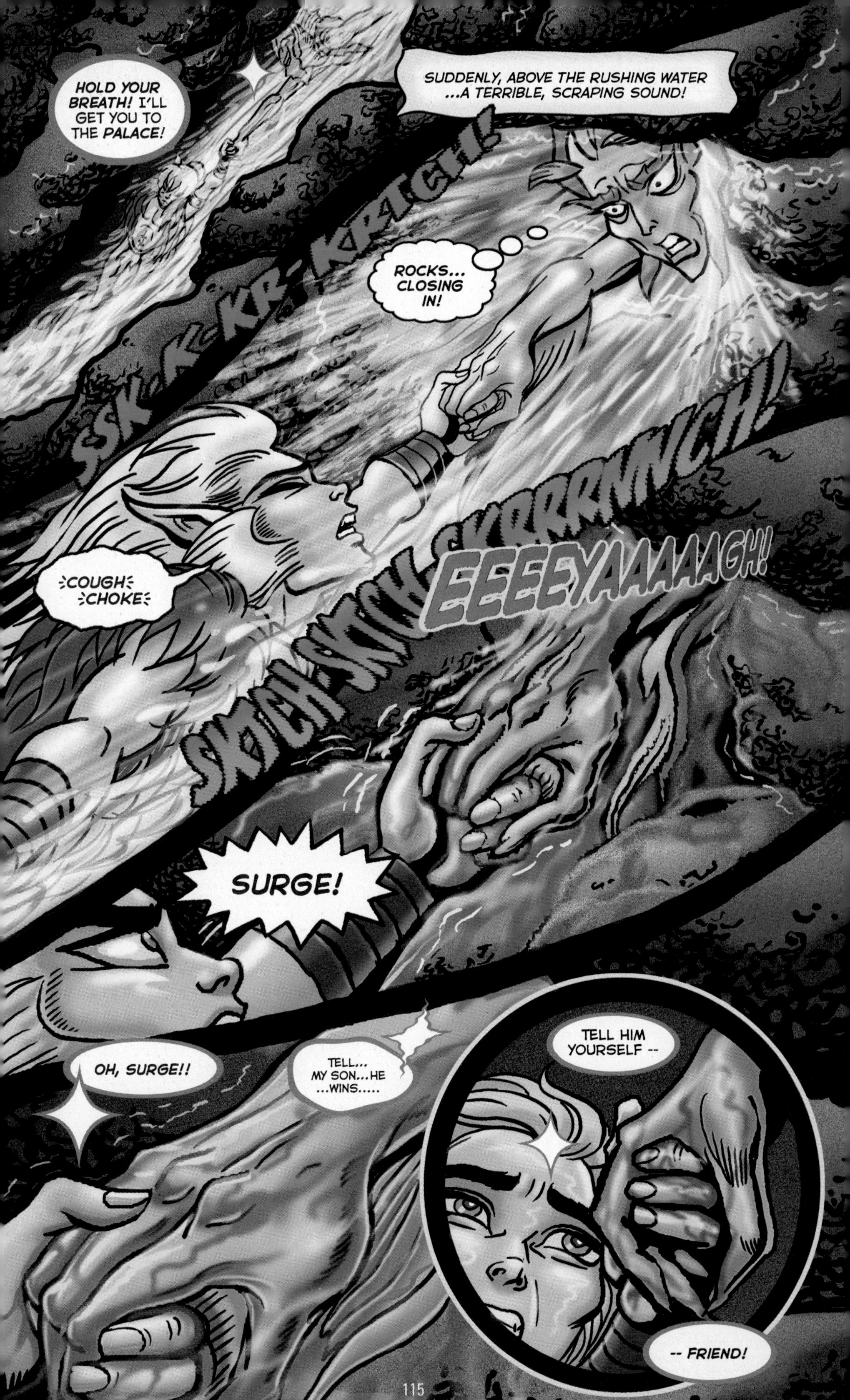
HOLD YOUR BREATH! I'LL GET YOU TO THE PALACE!
SUDDENLY, ABOVE THE RUSHING WATER ...A TERRIBLE, SCRAPING SOUND!
SSK-K-KR-KRTCH!
ROCKS... CLOSING IN!
COUGH CHOKE
EEEEYAAAAAGH!
SKRRRNNCH!
SURGE!
OH, SURGE!!
TELL... MY SON...HE ...WINS.....
TELL HIM YOURSELF --
-- FRIEND!

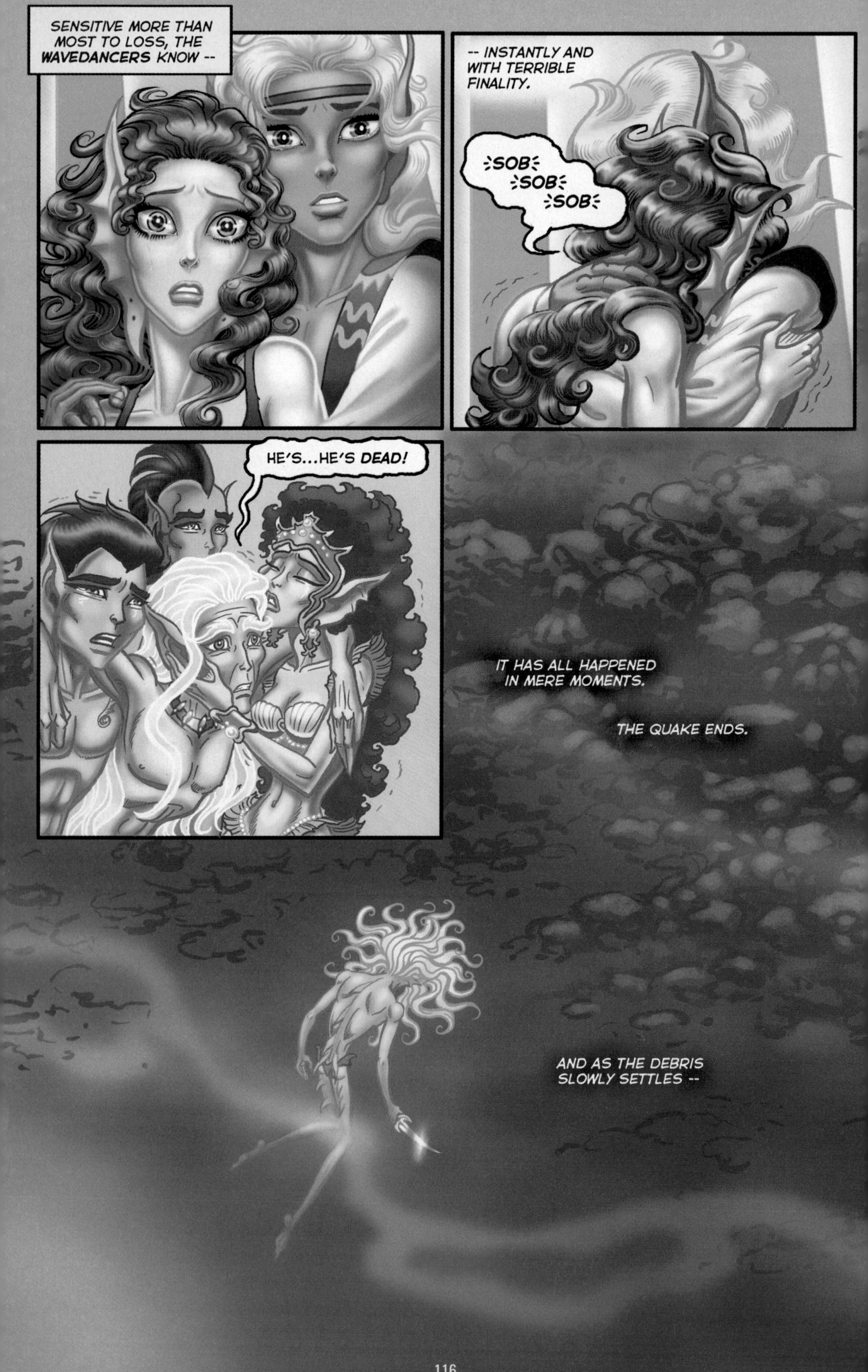
SENSITIVE MORE THAN MOST TO LOSS, THE WAVEDANCERS KNOW --
-- INSTANTLY AND WITH TERRIBLE FINALITY.
SOB SOB SOB
HE'S...HE'S DEAD!
IT HAS ALL HAPPENED IN MERE MOMENTS.
THE QUAKE ENDS.
AND AS THE DEBRIS SLOWLY SETTLES --

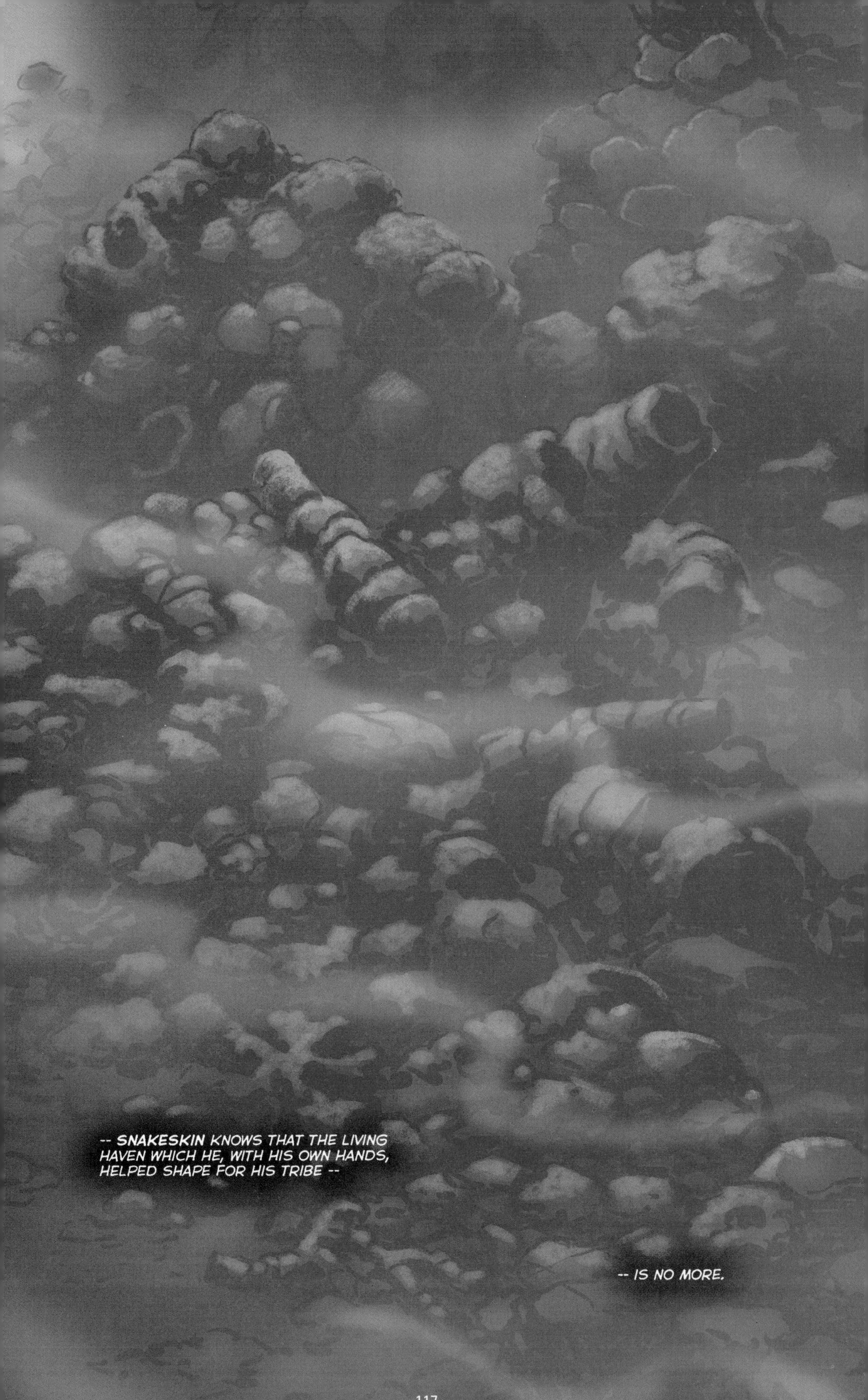
-- SNAKESKIN KNOWS THAT THE LIVING HAVEN WHICH HE, WITH HIS OWN HANDS, HELPED SHAPE FOR HIS TRIBE --
-- IS NO MORE.

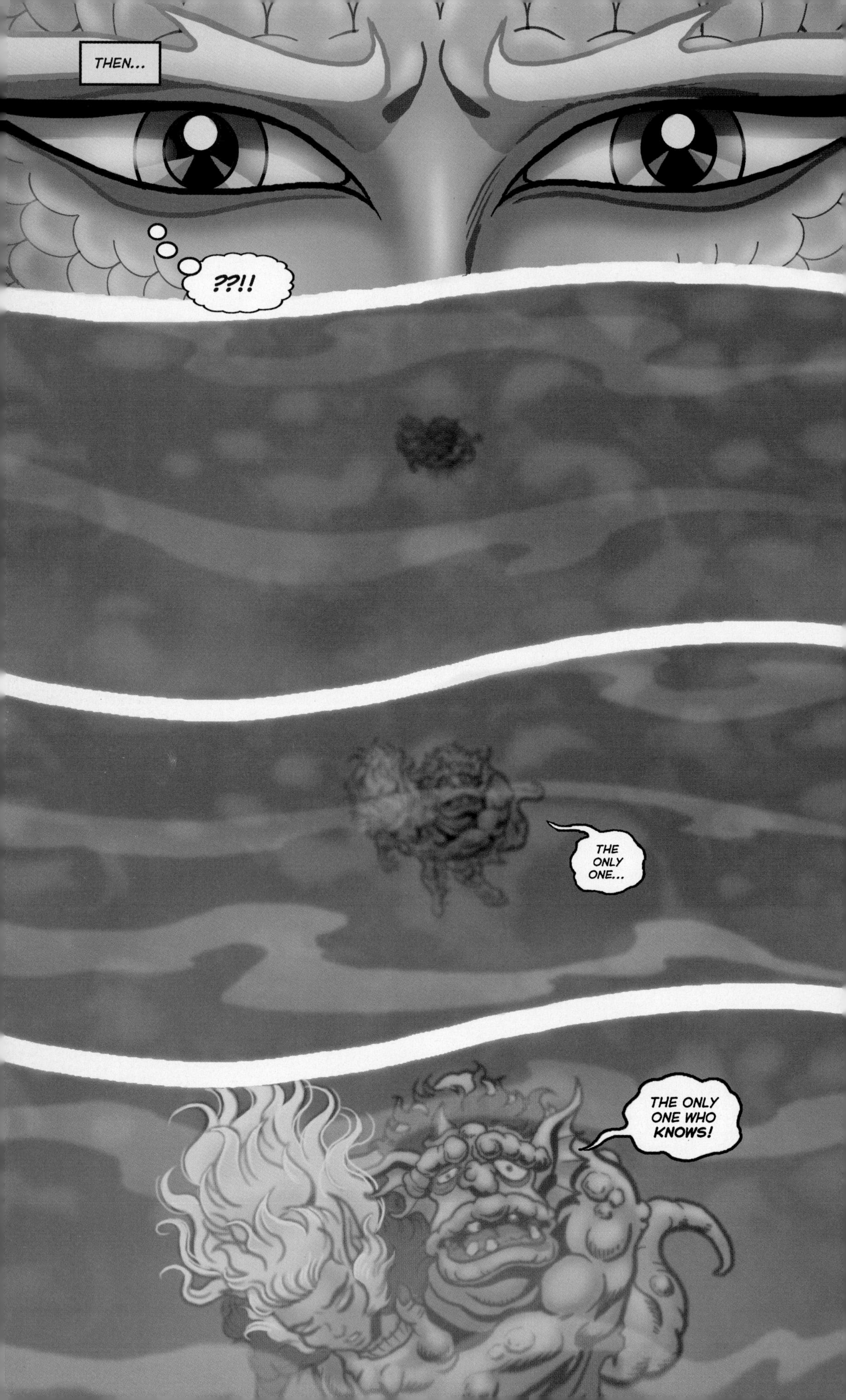
THEN...
??!!
THE ONLY ONE...
THE ONLY ONE WHO KNOWS!

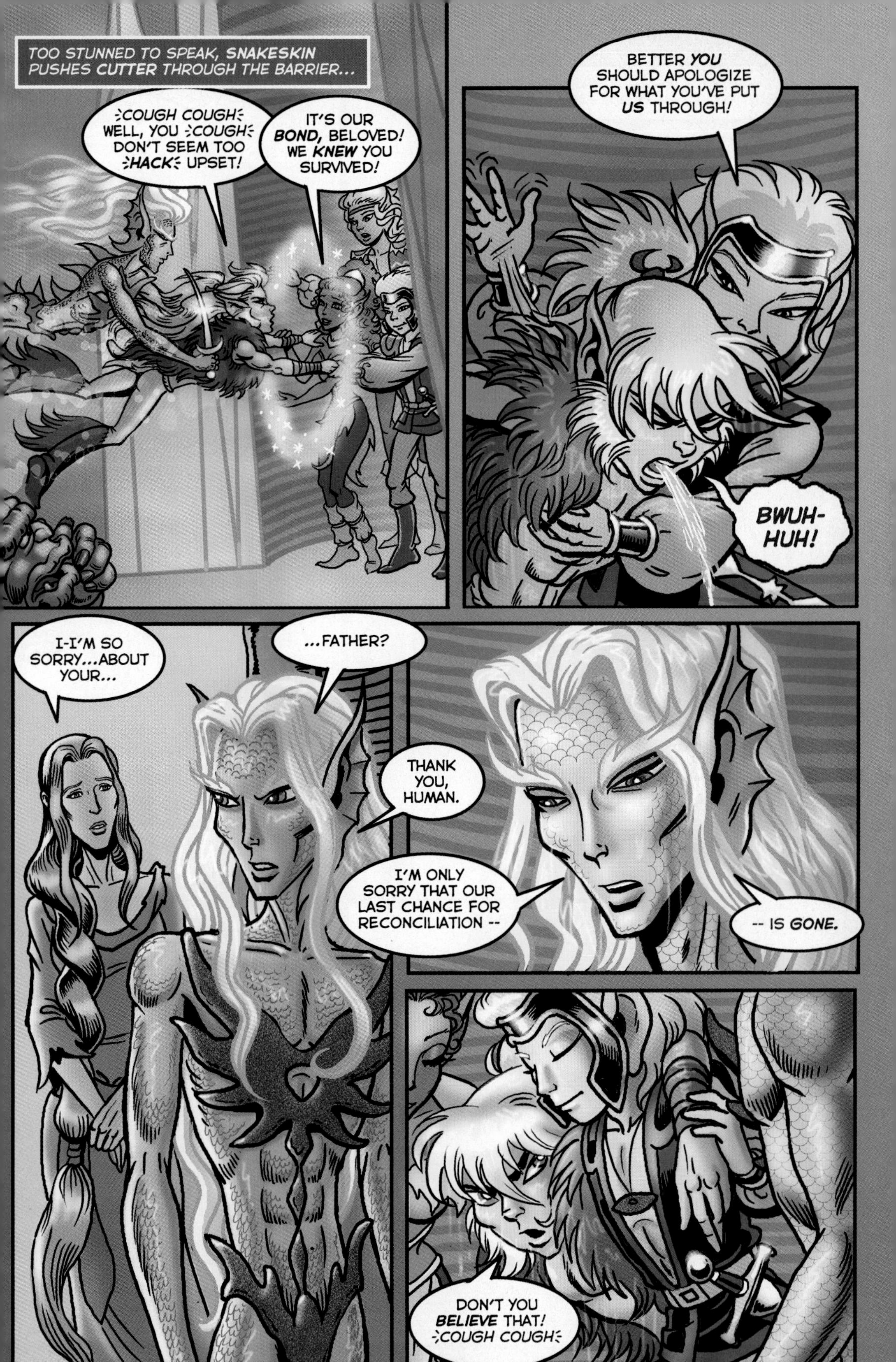

TOO STUNNED TO SPEAK, SNAKESKIN PUSHES CUTTER THROUGH THE BARRIER...
COUGH COUGH WELL, YOU COUGH DON'T SEEM TOO HACK UPSET!
IT'S OUR BOND, BELOVED! WE KNEW YOU SURVIVED!
BETTER YOU SHOULD APOLOGIZE FOR WHAT YOU'VE PUT US THROUGH!
BWUH-HUH!
I-I'M SO SORRY...ABOUT YOUR...
...FATHER?
THANK YOU, HUMAN.
I'M ONLY SORRY THAT OUR LAST CHANCE FOR RECONCILIATION --
-- IS GONE.
DON'T YOU BELIEVE THAT! COUGH COUGH
DON'T EVER BELIEVE THAT!

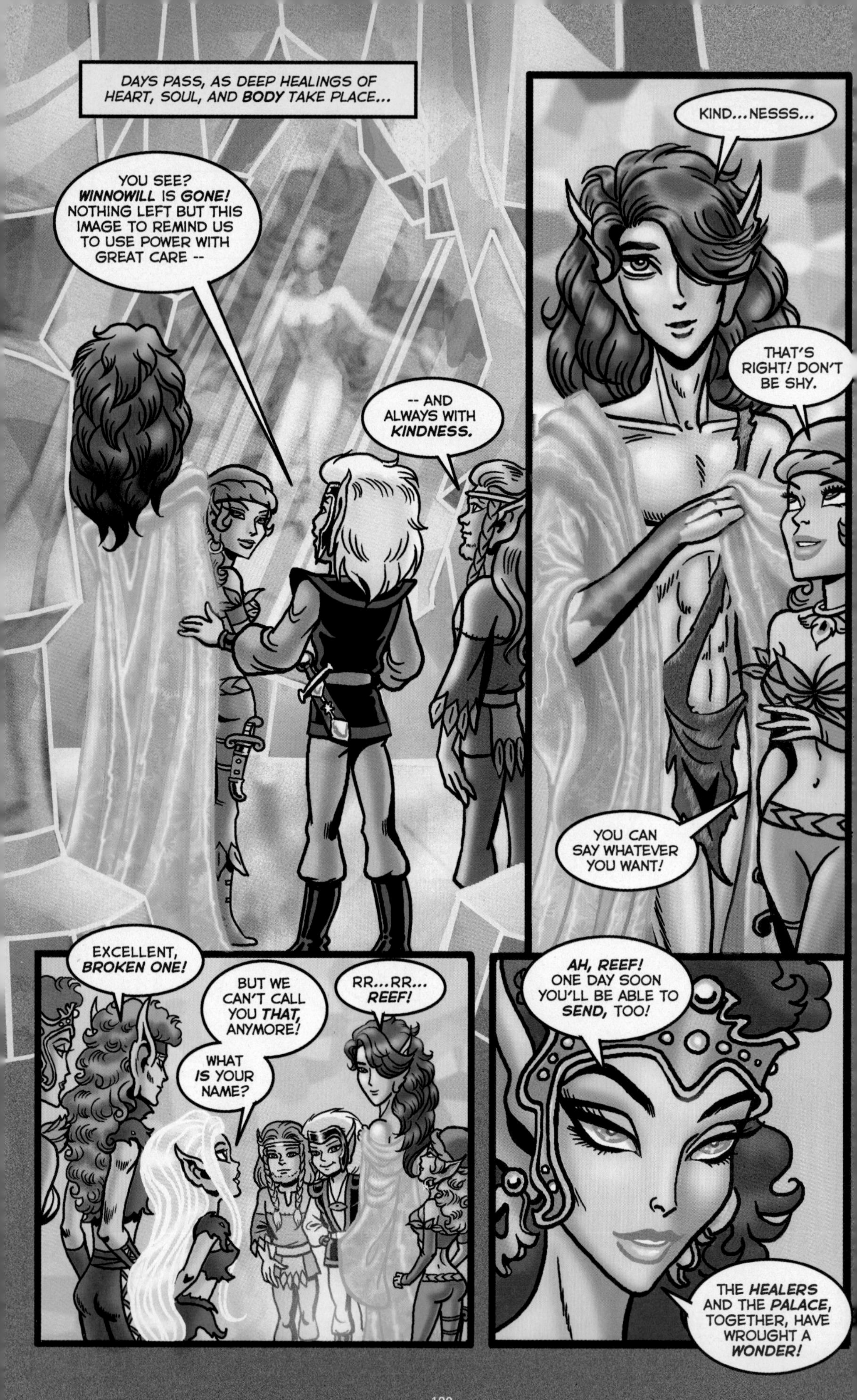

DAYS PASS, AS DEEP HEALINGS OF HEART, SOUL, AND BODY TAKE PLACE...
YOU SEE? WINNOWILL IS GONE! NOTHING LEFT BUT THIS IMAGE TO REMIND US TO USE POWER WITH GREAT CARE --
-- AND ALWAYS WITH KINDNESS.
KIND...NESSS...
THAT'S RIGHT! DON'T BE SHY.
YOU CAN SAY WHATEVER YOU WANT!
EXCELLENT, BROKEN ONE!
BUT WE CAN'T CALL YOU THAT, ANYMORE!
WHAT IS YOUR NAME?
RR...RR... REEF!
AH, REEF! ONE DAY SOON YOU'LL BE ABLE TO SEND, TOO!
THE HEALERS AND THE PALACE, TOGETHER, HAVE WROUGHT A WONDER!

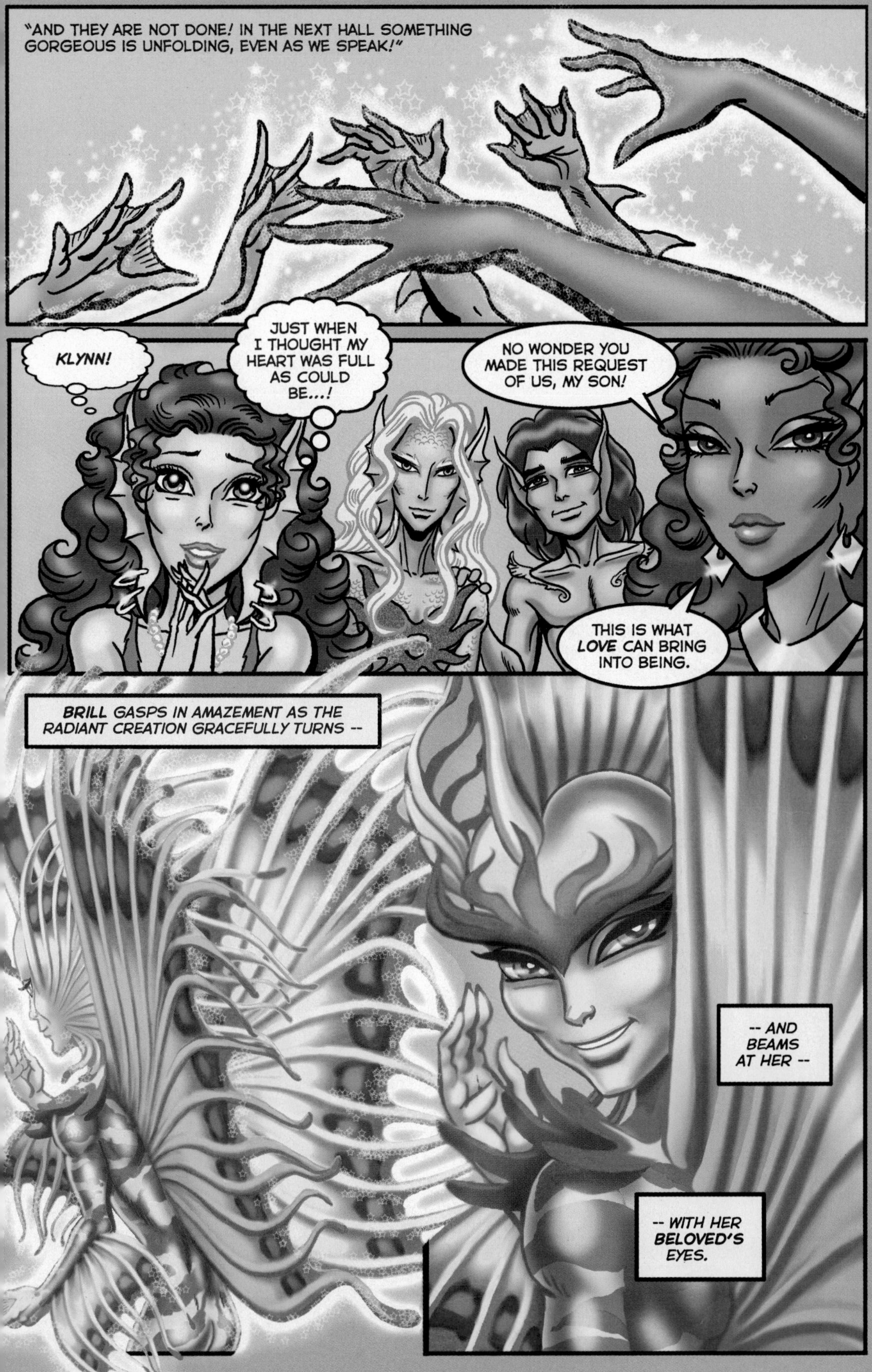
"AND THEY ARE NOT DONE! IN THE NEXT HALL SOMETHING GORGEOUS IS UNFOLDING, EVEN AS WE SPEAK!"
KLYNN!
JUST WHEN I THOUGHT MY HEART WAS FULL AS COULD BE...!
NO WONDER YOU MADE THIS REQUEST OF US, MY SON!
THIS IS WHAT LOVE CAN BRING INTO BEING.
BRILL GASPS IN AMAZEMENT AS THE RADIANT CREATION GRACEFULLY TURNS --
-- AND BEAMS AT HER --
-- WITH HER BELOVED'S EYES.

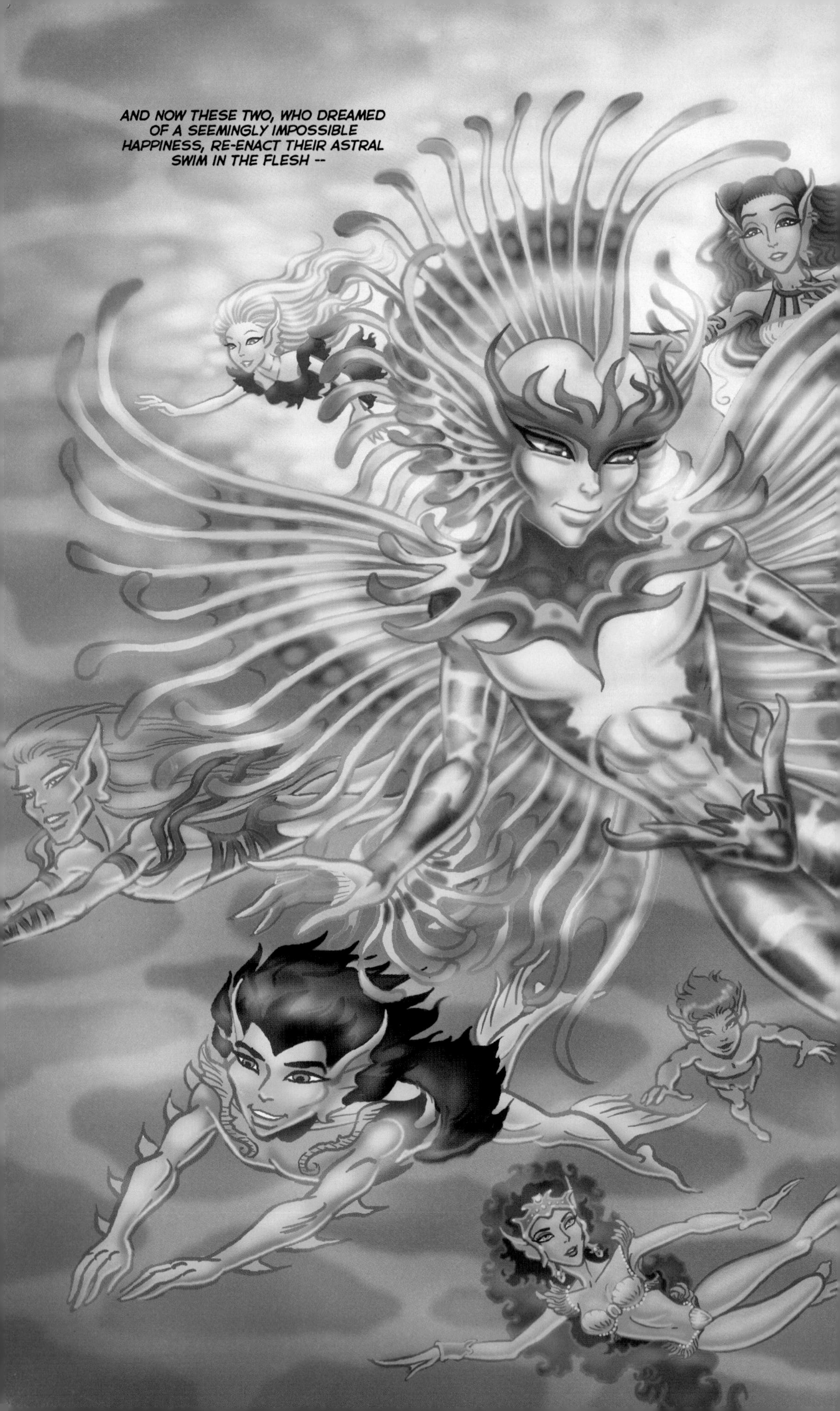
AND NOW THESE TWO, WHO DREAMED OF A SEEMINGLY IMPOSSIBLE HAPPINESS, RE-ENACT THEIR ASTRAL SWIM IN THE FLESH --

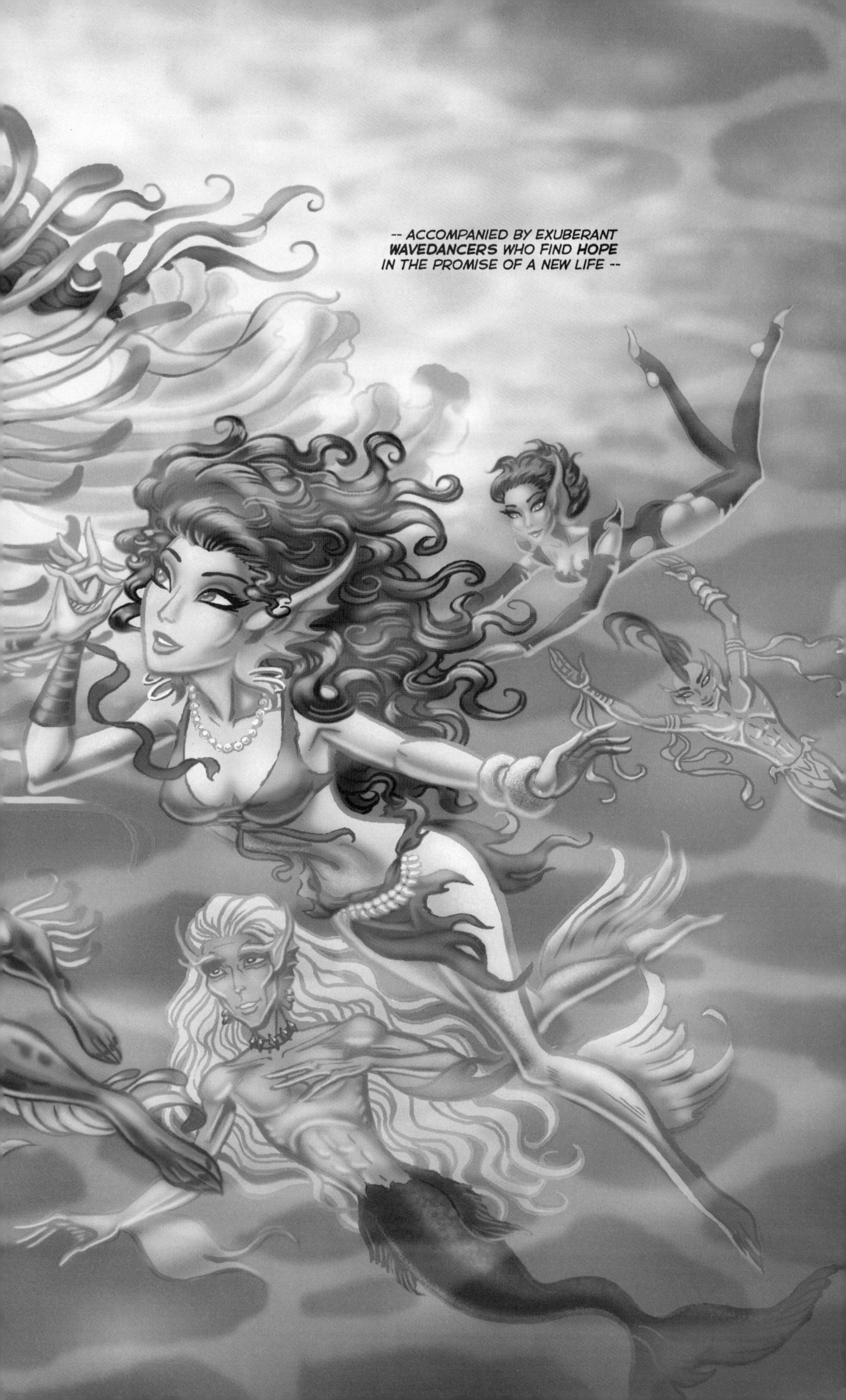
-- ACCOMPANIED BY EXUBERANT WAVEDANCERS WHO FIND HOPE IN THE PROMISE OF A NEW LIFE --

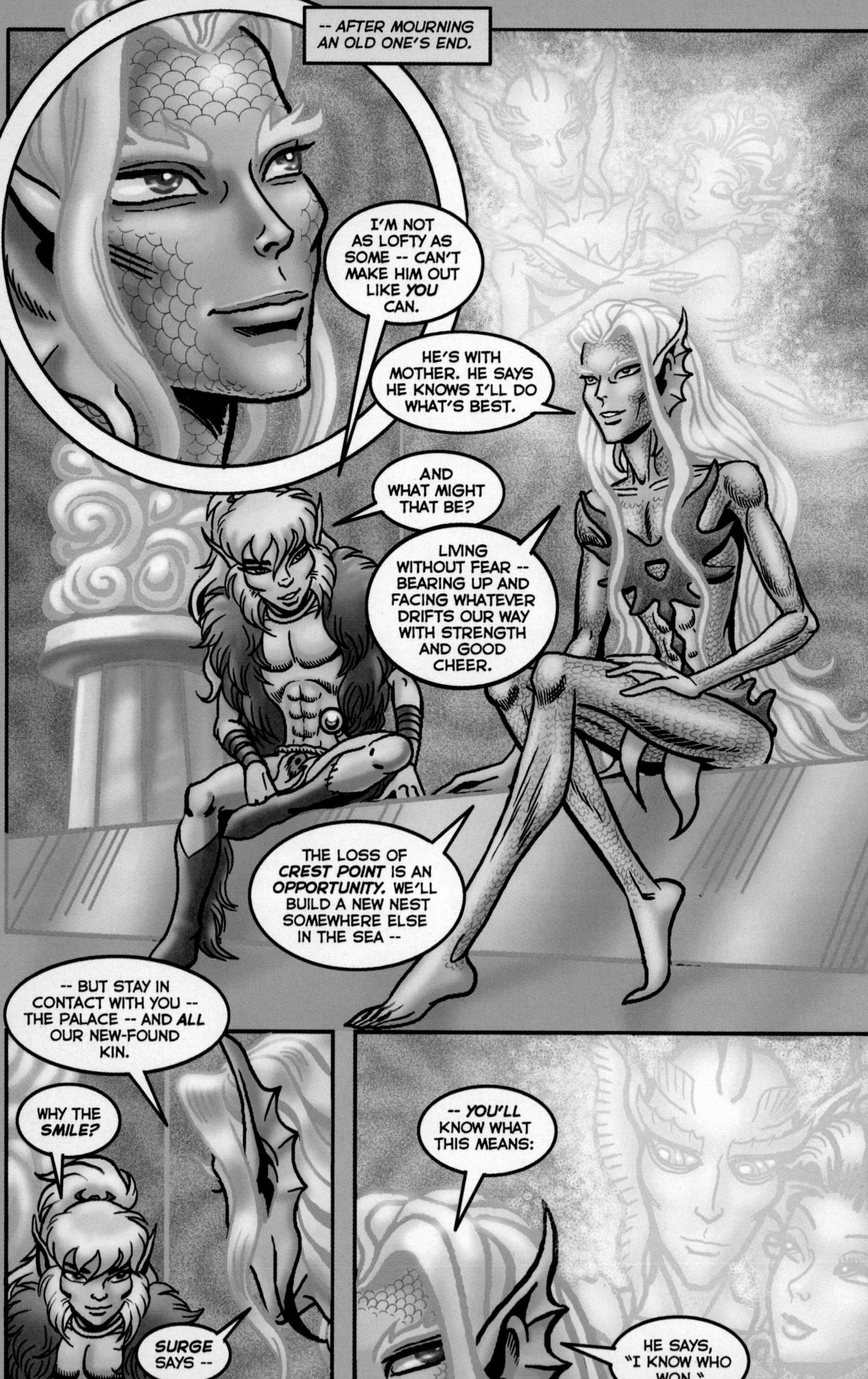
-- AFTER MOURNING AN OLD ONE'S END.
I'M NOT AS LOFTY AS SOME -- CAN'T MAKE HIM OUT LIKE *YOU* CAN.
HE'S WITH MOTHER. HE SAYS HE KNOWS I'LL DO WHAT'S BEST.
AND WHAT MIGHT THAT BE?
LIVING WITHOUT FEAR -- BEARING UP AND FACING WHATEVER DRIFTS OUR WAY WITH STRENGTH AND GOOD CHEER.
THE LOSS OF *CREST POINT* IS AN *OPPORTUNITY.* WE'LL BUILD A NEW NEST SOMEWHERE ELSE IN THE SEA --
-- BUT STAY IN CONTACT WITH YOU -- THE PALACE -- AND *ALL* OUR NEW-FOUND KIN.
WHY THE *SMILE?*
SURGE SAYS --
-- *YOU'LL* KNOW WHAT THIS MEANS:
HE SAYS, "I KNOW WHO WON."

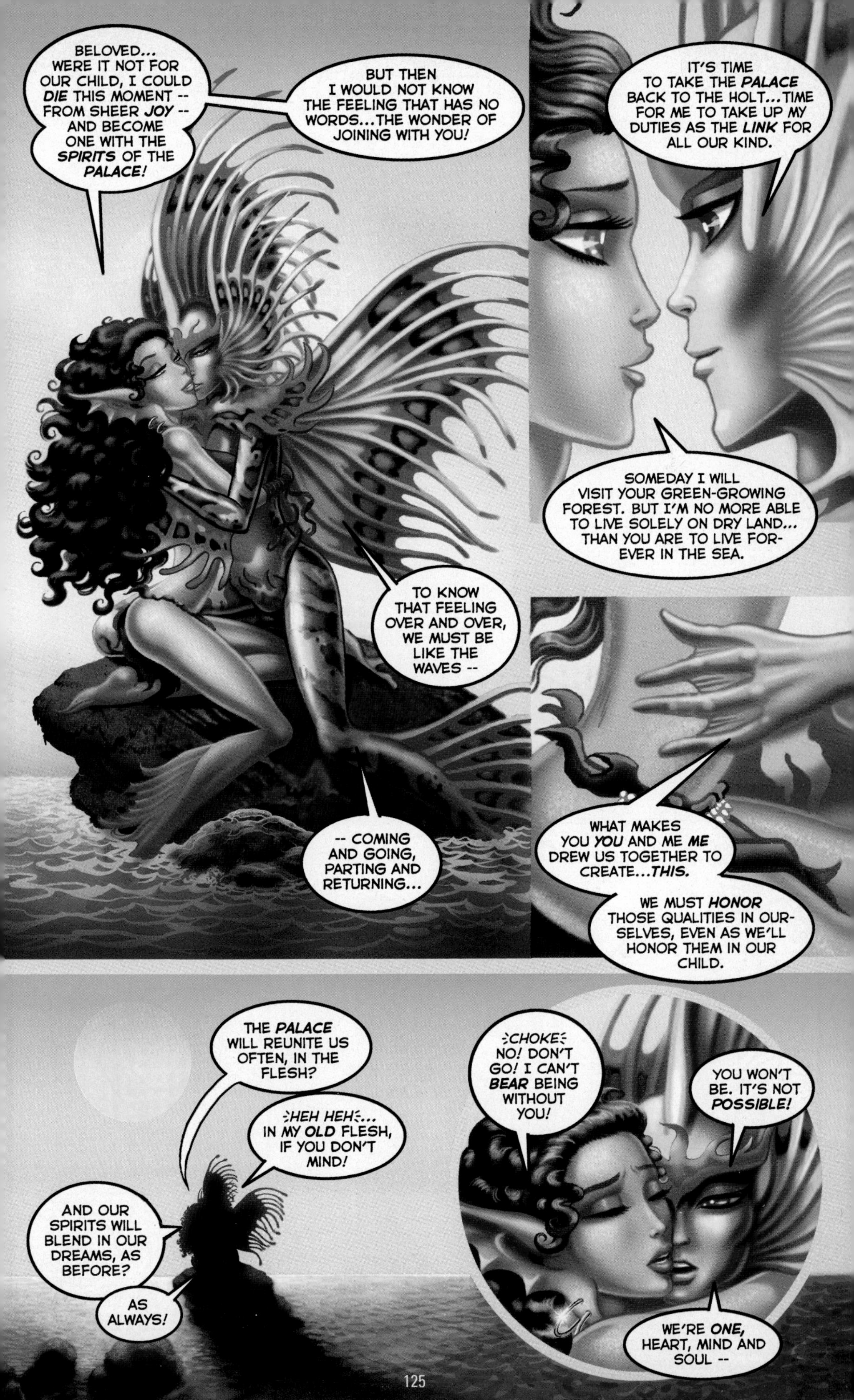

BELOVED... WERE IT NOT FOR OUR CHILD, I COULD DIE THIS MOMENT -- FROM SHEER JOY -- AND BECOME ONE WITH THE SPIRITS OF THE PALACE!
BUT THEN I WOULD NOT KNOW THE FEELING THAT HAS NO WORDS...THE WONDER OF JOINING WITH YOU!
TO KNOW THAT FEELING OVER AND OVER, WE MUST BE LIKE THE WAVES --
-- COMING AND GOING, PARTING AND RETURNING...
IT'S TIME TO TAKE THE PALACE BACK TO THE HOLT...TIME FOR ME TO TAKE UP MY DUTIES AS THE LINK FOR ALL OUR KIND.
SOMEDAY I WILL VISIT YOUR GREEN-GROWING FOREST. BUT I'M NO MORE ABLE TO LIVE SOLELY ON DRY LAND... THAN YOU ARE TO LIVE FOR-EVER IN THE SEA.
WHAT MAKES YOU YOU AND ME ME DREW US TOGETHER TO CREATE...THIS.
WE MUST HONOR THOSE QUALITIES IN OUR-SELVES, EVEN AS WE'LL HONOR THEM IN OUR CHILD.
THE PALACE WILL REUNITE US OFTEN, IN THE FLESH?
HEH HEH... IN MY OLD FLESH, IF YOU DON'T MIND!
AND OUR SPIRITS WILL BLEND IN OUR DREAMS, AS BEFORE?
AS ALWAYS!
CHOKE NO! DON'T GO! I CAN'T BEAR BEING WITHOUT YOU!
YOU WON'T BE. IT'S NOT POSSIBLE!
WE'RE ONE, HEART, MIND AND SOUL --

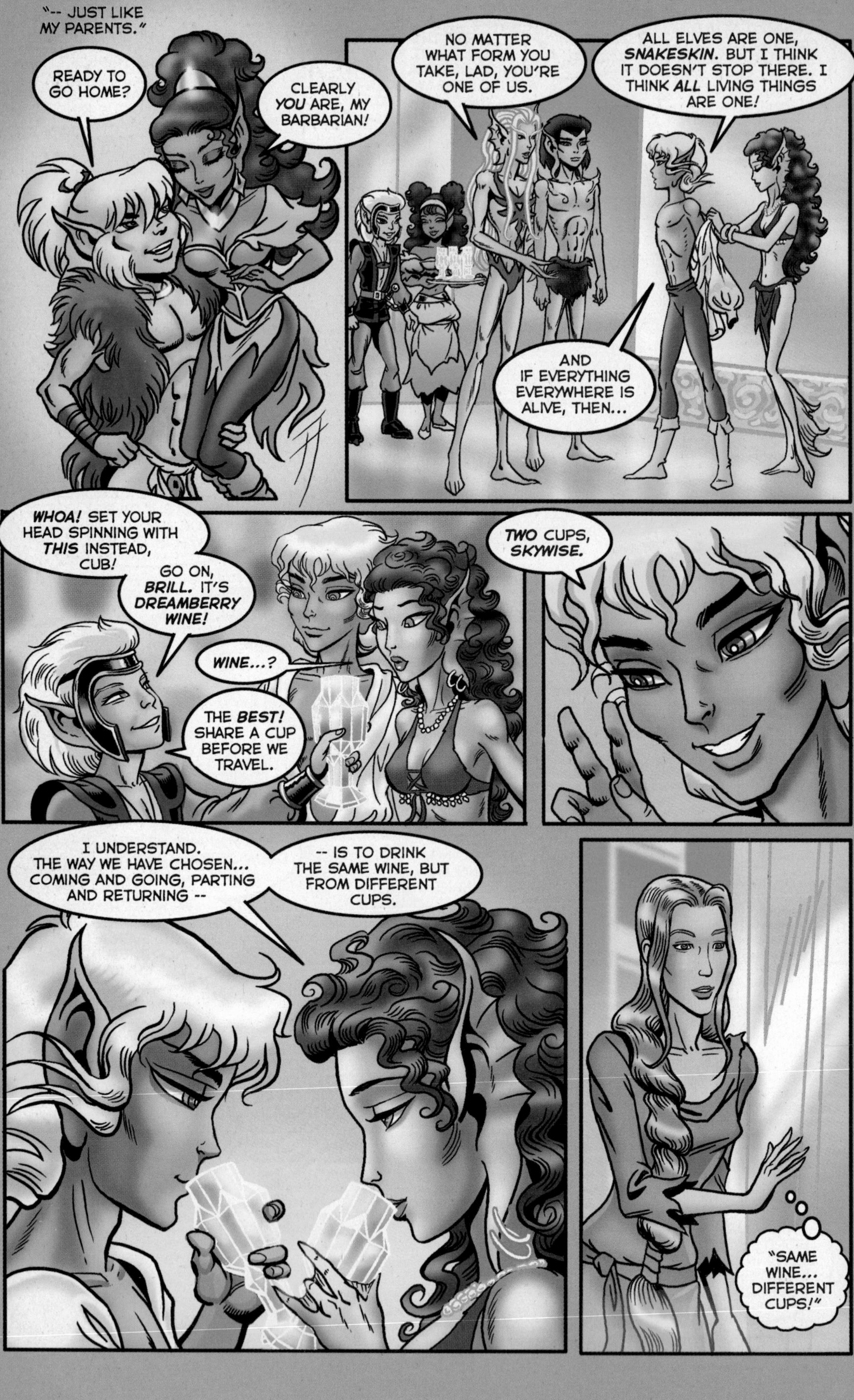
"-- JUST LIKE MY PARENTS."
READY TO GO HOME?
CLEARLY YOU ARE, MY BARBARIAN!
NO MATTER WHAT FORM YOU TAKE, LAD, YOU'RE ONE OF US.
ALL ELVES ARE ONE, SNAKESKIN. BUT I THINK IT DOESN'T STOP THERE. I THINK ALL LIVING THINGS ARE ONE!
AND IF EVERYTHING EVERYWHERE IS ALIVE, THEN...
WHOA! SET YOUR HEAD SPINNING WITH THIS INSTEAD, CUB!
GO ON, BRILL. IT'S DREAMBERRY WINE!
WINE...?
THE BEST! SHARE A CUP BEFORE WE TRAVEL.
TWO CUPS, SKYWISE.
I UNDERSTAND. THE WAY WE HAVE CHOSEN... COMING AND GOING, PARTING AND RETURNING --
-- IS TO DRINK THE SAME WINE, BUT FROM DIFFERENT CUPS.
"SAME WINE... DIFFERENT CUPS!"

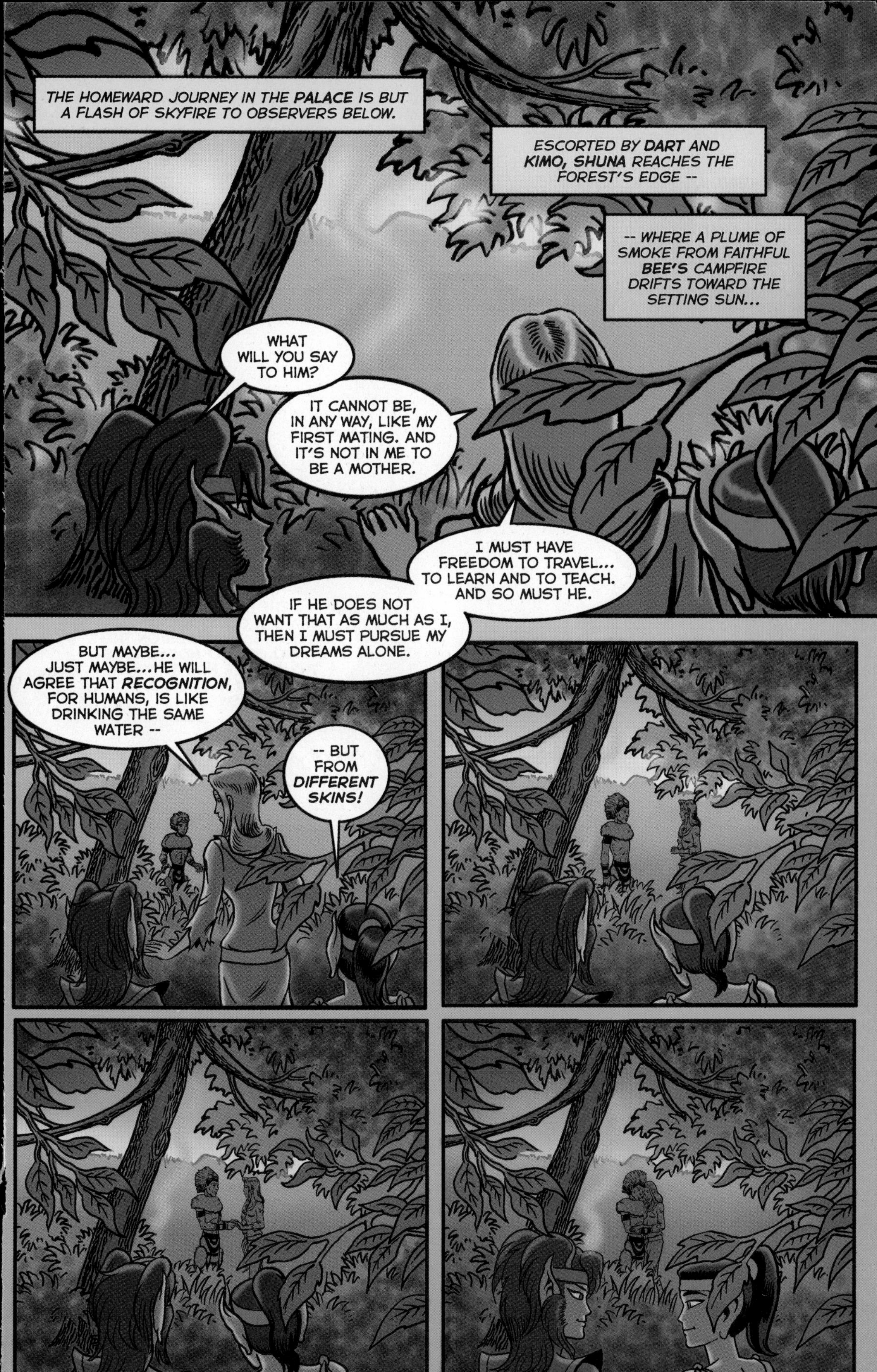
THE HOMEWARD JOURNEY IN THE PALACE IS BUT A FLASH OF SKYFIRE TO OBSERVERS BELOW.
ESCORTED BY DART AND KIMO, SHUNA REACHES THE FOREST'S EDGE --
-- WHERE A PLUME OF SMOKE FROM FAITHFUL BEE'S CAMPFIRE DRIFTS TOWARD THE SETTING SUN...
WHAT WILL YOU SAY TO HIM?
IT CANNOT BE, IN ANY WAY, LIKE MY FIRST MATING. AND IT'S NOT IN ME TO BE A MOTHER.
I MUST HAVE FREEDOM TO TRAVEL... TO LEARN AND TO TEACH. AND SO MUST HE.
IF HE DOES NOT WANT THAT AS MUCH AS I, THEN I MUST PURSUE MY DREAMS ALONE.
BUT MAYBE... JUST MAYBE...HE WILL AGREE THAT RECOGNITION, FOR HUMANS, IS LIKE DRINKING THE SAME WATER --
-- BUT FROM DIFFERENT SKINS!

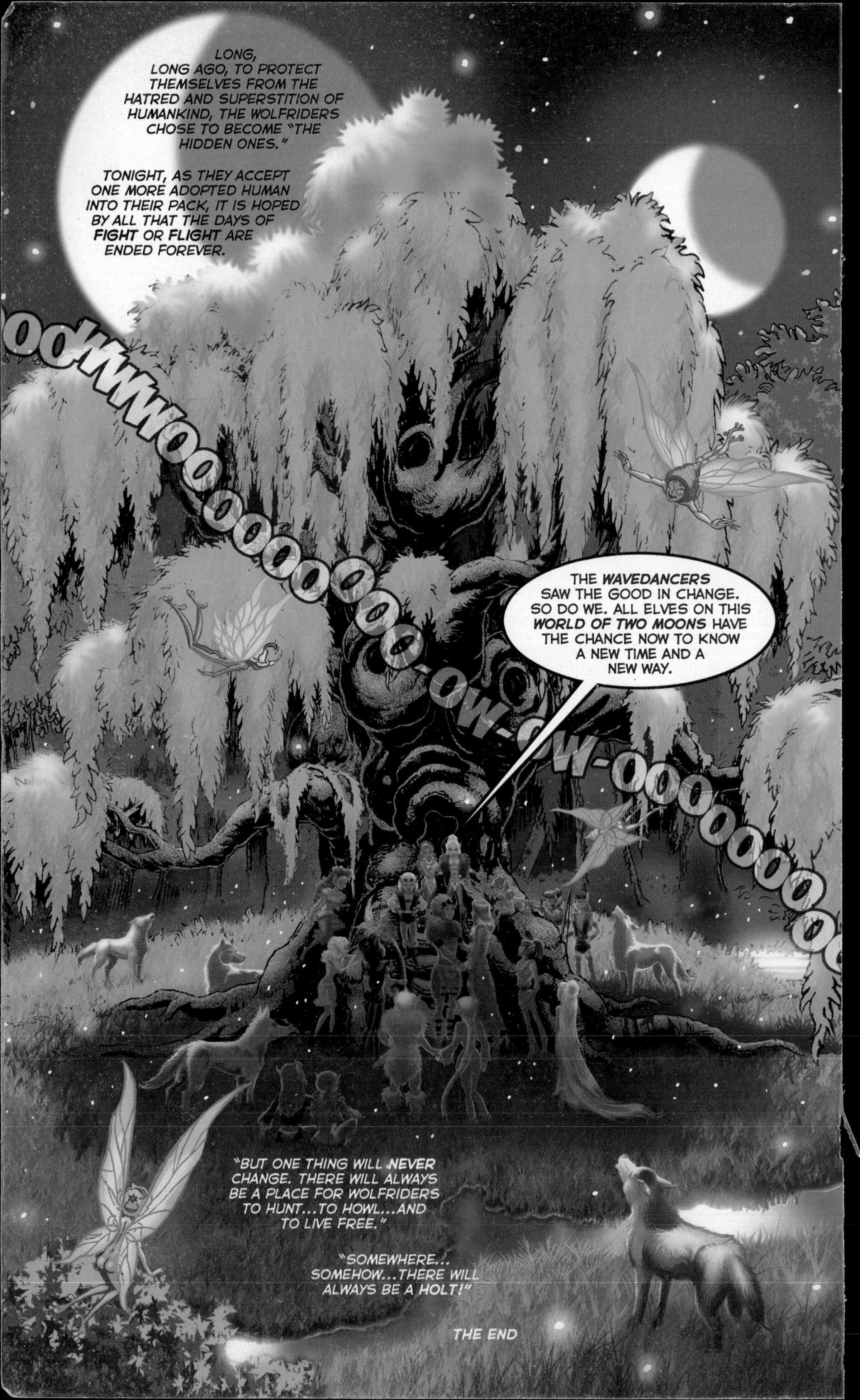
LONG, LONG AGO, TO PROTECT THEMSELVES FROM THE HATRED AND SUPERSTITION OF HUMANKIND, THE WOLFRIDERS CHOSE TO BECOME "THE HIDDEN ONES."
TONIGHT, AS THEY ACCEPT ONE MORE ADOPTED HUMAN INTO THEIR PACK, IT IS HOPED BY ALL THAT THE DAYS OF **FIGHT** OR **FLIGHT** ARE ENDED FOREVER.
THE ***WAVEDANCERS*** SAW THE GOOD IN CHANGE. SO DO WE. ALL ELVES ON THIS ***WORLD OF TWO MOONS*** HAVE THE CHANCE NOW TO KNOW A NEW TIME AND A NEW WAY.
OOWWWOOOOOOOOOOOO-OW-OW-OOOOOOOOOO
"BUT ONE THING WILL **NEVER** CHANGE. THERE WILL ALWAYS BE A PLACE FOR WOLFRIDERS TO HUNT...TO HOWL...AND TO LIVE FREE."
"SOMEWHERE... SOMEHOW...THERE WILL ALWAYS BE A **HOLT!**"
THE END